VISIONARY
AYAHUASCA

"This is the first book that anyone thinking about taking ayahuasca, or taking it again, must own. The manual section is honest, revealing, invaluable, and packed with everything, including how to find a safe and sane teacher, how to sit during ceremony, what kinds of clothes to bring, and why *dietas* are necessary for real healing. Jan's own journal of his progress is unusually candid in disclosing the obstacles and difficulties that arise even as your commitment to this path deepens."

JAMES FADIMAN PH.D., AUTHOR OF
THE PSYCHEDELIC EXPLORER'S GUIDE:
SAFE THERAPEUTIC AND SPIRITUAL JOURNEYS

"This is a great book for anyone who is planning to attend an ayahuasca ceremony. It is packed with useful information, observations, and relevant facts providing a valuable guide to what you can *really* expect from the vine of souls."

ROSS HEAVEN, AUTHOR OF *PLANT SPIRIT SHAMANISM:*
TRADITIONAL TECHNIQUES FOR HEALING THE SOUL

"A rich, honest, informative testimony based on numerous courageous acts, this book is both extremist and full of good sense—outlandish and matter of fact. A filmmaker's guide to the cinematic world of ayahuasca."

JEREMY NARBY, ANTHROPOLOGIST AND AUTHOR OF
THE COSMIC SERPENT AND INTELLIGENCE IN NATURE

"Jan Kounen's descriptions of his experiences with ayahuasca are informed, poetic, and at times authentically visceral. This book provides excellent insights into the discipline and the rigors of the traditional plant diet as well as the underlying relationship between human and plant consciousness. This is definitely a book for both the person considering working with ayahuasca and for those with significant experience with the plant. It was a pleasure to read this book."

HOWARD G. CHARING, COAUTHOR OF
PLANT SPIRIT SHAMANISM AND
THE AYAHUASCA VISIONS OF PABLO AMARINGO

"In *Vistionary Ayahuasca,* 10 years of experience with *ayahuasca medicina* is laid out beautifully. It has lots of information for anyone considering going down the ayahuasca trail. Don't leave home without it!"

ALAN SHOEMAKER, AUTHOR OF *AYAHUASCA MEDICINE*

VISIONARY AYAHUASCA

A MANUAL FOR THERAPEUTIC AND SPIRITUAL JOURNEYS

JAN KOUNEN

TRANSLATED BY JACK CAIN

Park Street Press

Rochester, Vermont • Toronto, Canada

Park Street Press
One Park Street
Rochester, Vermont 05767
www.ParkStPress.com

Text stock is SFI certified

Park Street Press is a division of Inner Traditions International

Copyright © 2011 by Mama Editions
English translation © 2015 by Inner Traditions International

Originally published in French under the title *Carnets de voyages intérieurs: Ayahuasca medicina, un manuel* by Mama Editions, Paris, France
First U.S. edition published in 2015 by Park Street Press

All rights reserved. No part of this book may be reproduced or utilized in any form or by any means, electronic or mechanical, including photocopying, recording, or by any information storage and retrieval system, without permission in writing from the publisher.

Library of Congress Cataloging-in-Publication Data
Kounen, Jan, 1964–
   [Carnets de voyages intérieurs: ayahuasca medicina, un manuel]
   Visionary Ayahuasca : a manual for therapeutic and spiritual journeys / Jan Kounen ; translated by Jack Cain ; foreword by Alejandro Jodorowsky. — First U.S. edition.
       pages cm
   ISBN 978-1-62055-345-9 (paperback) — ISBN 978-1-62055-346-6 (e-book)
   1. Kounen, Jan, 1964– 2. Motion picture producers and directors—France—Biography. 3. Ayahuasca—Psychotropic effects. 4. Shamanism—Amazon River Region. I. Cain, Jack, 1940– translator. II. Title.
   PN1998.3.K679A3 2014
   615.3'2379—dc23
                                                                2014015973

Printed and bound in the United States by Lake Book Manufacturing, Inc.

The text stock is SFI certified. The Sustainable Forestry Initiative® program promotes sustainable forest management.

10 9 8 7 6 5 4 3 2 1

Text design by Virginia Scott Bowman and layout by Priscilla Baker
This book was typeset in Garamond Premier Pro with Myriad Pro and Biondi Sans used as display typefaces

Drawings on pages 84, 123, and 194 from Jan Kounen's comic strip *Doctor Ayahuasca,* Editions du Lombard

*This book is dedicated to
my brother Kestenbetsa,
to the Shipibo people,
and to madre ayahuasca.*

I dream that this book, yellowed with time, might one day be read by an unknown man or woman, having been found perhaps in a bookstore, in a library, or buried under a pile at the bottom of a crate . . .

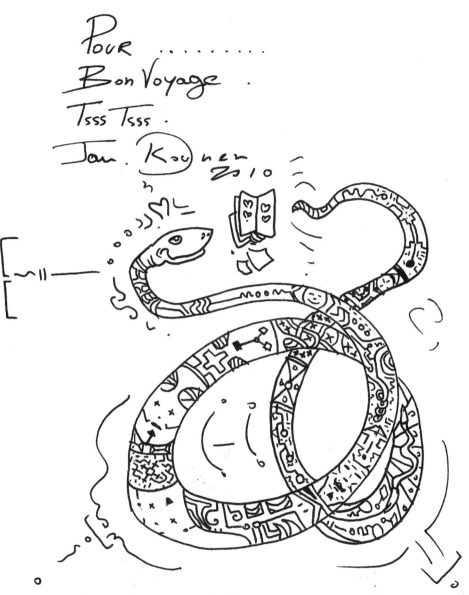

If you write your name in above, you can more readily
lend this book. If you lend this book to ten people,
nothing special is going to happen to you. It's not going
to change your life. But you will be circulating this text,
and that is going to make me really happy.

CONTENTS

Inner Journey Notebooks
August 1999–November 2010

Ayahuasca Medicina, A Manual
Forty Questions and Answers

FOREWORD

Marpa, the especially cruel teacher of the Tibetan Saint Milarepa, taught detachment, affirming that all is illusion. One day his son died. Marpa began to sob uncontrollably. His astonished disciples said to him, "But really master, why are you crying? After all, everything is illusion." The guru replied, "This was the most beautiful of all illusions."

In a universe where nothing is real, anyone with an imagination crashes into dreams that run the gamut from the most atrocious hell to the summits of paradise. There are those who allow themselves to be vanquished by the nightmares, who accept their horror, and who demonize those who boast of being "normal, just like everyone else." And there are others who stroll along the path of sainthood in search of the most attractive illusion. The alchemists sought it in the philosopher's stone; Plato saw it in the world of pure ideas; the Zen Buddhists called it enlightenment; the surrealists venerated unrestrained love; and most human beings are simply looking for happiness. All religions, all political doctrines, all of science—all of these pursue the most beautiful illusion. Of all the arts, the cinema is the one that has tried to show us this illusion—but nothing comes of that, because cinema has turned into a money machine.

What is initiation? It is the spiritual activity that teaches us that when we are confronted by two options we should always choose the one that is most beautiful.

From time to time, in the midst of the circus of the creative directors who've sold their souls, an idealist appears who aspires to film the most magnificent of illusions. Starting right from his first attempts, the forces of darkness attack with their agonizing economic nightmare. He's told to not go too far, to promote harmful products, to dress up what is untrue, to praise exaggerations of all kinds, to wave the national flag, to stroke the public's erogenous zones, or to bury himself in infantile pursuits. He who seeks the most beautiful of illusions feels very much like a fish swimming upstream.

Having chosen the craft of cinema, the director has to make concessions in order to survive. With hypocritically commercial products—and as soon as we speak of commerce you have to forget the most beautiful of illusions—the director has to surreptitiously slip in a few sequences, scenes, or images that act like a subtle perfume in reminding the audience of the ultimate purpose of this life of titillation: coming to know the most beautiful of illusions.

This is what my friend Jan Kounen has tried to do throughout the course of his life in cinema. Because his approach was not frivolous and because in the depths of his heart he felt that the approach toward something is not the thing itself, he made the leap that allowed him to go beyond industrial limitations and to conduct his research with total honesty.

Aware that he couldn't realize his heart's desire on the screen, he embarked on an odyssey in an effort to reach the most profound depths within himself. This is what he describes in such a passionate way in his book. For ten years he turned himself over, heart and soul, to a torrent of images that were initially incisive, unsettling, and destructive. The most beautiful illusion was found in the depths, buried under layers and layers of diabolical illusions spawned by a decadent world.

In mythic tales the hero sets out to find the elixir of eternal life and faces a thousand and one ordeals. When he finds it, he comes back to his point of departure and he has his people partake of this elixir. In whatever he has overcome, nothing must be held back from others—everything must be shared.

In reading his account, which has been as engrossing as the adventure stories of my childhood, it seems to me that, having penetrated the ultimate secret of ayahuasca, Kounen will turn once more to the cinema, that authentic seventh art, and he will provide for us all, using images distilled from the light, the most beautiful of illusions.

Having spent my whole life looking for it, I believe that the most beautiful of illusions is our consciousness.

ALEJANDRO JODOROWSKY

Alejandro Jodorowsky is a playwright, filmmaker, composer, mime, psychotherapist, and author of many books on spirituality and tarot and more than thirty comic books and graphic novels. He has directed several films, including *The Rainbow Thief* and the cult classics *El Topo* and *The Holy Mountain*. He lives in France.

Jan, everything you can see exists.
And another reality,
different from the normal one,
also exists, separately.

KESTENBETSA

AYAHUASCA

Illegal Drug or National Cultural Heritage?

U. S. Law

DMT (dimethyltryptamine), which is present in ayahuasca, was placed under federal control in Schedule I of the Controlled Substances Act in 1971. As such, it can only be legally obtained for research purposes with the approval of both the Drug Enforcement Agency and the Food and Drug Administration. Ingestion of ayahuasca as part of a religious sacrament was the subject of a 2010 agreement between the DEA and União do Vegetal, a federally recognized church, and is strictly monitored.

Canadian Law

Possession of ayahuasca is illegal in Canada pursuant to the Controlled Drug and Substance Act. While requests have been made to Health Canada's Office of Controlled Substances for an exemption to that prohibition to permit importation of ayahuasca for sacramental use, no such exemption has yet been granted.

U. K. Law

DMT is banned as a Class A drug pursuant to the Misuse of Drugs Act of 1971 and as such is illegal to possess.

Australian Law

DMT is listed as a prohibited substance in Schedule 9 of the Poisons Standard issued by the Australian Government Department of Health and Aging. Substances on this list cannot legally be possessed except for medical or scientific research, or for analytical, teaching, or training purposes, which require governmental approval.

French Law

Ingesting ayahuasca is forbidden in France. It is listed in supplement III to Schedules I, II, III, and IV of the 1971 UN Convention on Psychotropic Substances.

Peruvian Law

The traditional knowledge and use of ayahuasca practiced by the native communities of the Amazon have been officially declared part of the national cultural heritage of Peru by the National Institute of Culture. National Directorial Resolution Number 836/INC provides as follows:

> WHEREAS, the ayahuasca plant—*Banisteriopsis caapi*—is a plant species that has had an extraordinary cultural history, due to its psychotropic properties, when used in a drink that combines it with a plant called chacruna—*Psychotria viridis*.
>
> WHEREAS, the above-mentioned plant is known by the indigenous communities of the Amazon as a plant of knowledge and as a teaching plant* that confers to initiates the very foundations of the world and its component elements. The effects of ingesting it constitute an entry into the spiritual world and into its secrets such that traditional Amazonian medicine came to be structured around the ayahuasca ritual. These effects are essential for those who assume the role of a privileged disseminator of these cultures, whether it be those who are in charge of communication with the spiritual world, or those who manifest it in art forms.
>
> WHEREAS, the effects produced by ayahuasca, widely studied for their complexity, are distinct from those usually produced by hallucinogenic substances. One part of this difference is found in the ritual that accompanies its ingestion and leads to various effects, but

*[Also sometimes called "master plant." —*Trans.*]

always within a culturally defined framework and with a purpose that is religious, therapeutic, and culturally affirmative.

WHEREAS, according to the information provided, it follows that the practice of ritual ayahuasca sessions constitutes one of the fundamental pillars of the identity of the Amazonian peoples and that its ancestral usage within traditional rituals assures cultural continuity, linked to the therapeutic qualities of the plant . . .

IT IS THEREFORE DECIDED TO DECLARE AS A NATIONAL CULTURAL HERITAGE the traditional knowledge and usages of ayahuasca practiced by the native Amazonian communities in order to ensure cultural continuity.

JAVIER UGAZ VILLACORTA
MANAGER OF THE NATIONAL DIRECTORATE
NATIONAL INSTITUTE OF CULTURE
LIMA, PERU
JUNE 24, 2008

INTRODUCTION

For ten years now I've been going to the Amazonian part of Peru to meet *curanderos* (healers).

Ten years takes you from exploration to apprenticeship. On this path I quickly found my place—that of ferryman. Then, little by little, I became *ayahuasquero* through the force of circumstances. After you have undergone a few hundred ceremonies, you no longer question it: ayahuasca is part of your life—you have become a practitioner. It's simple. I practice with the Shipibo, an indigenous people living primarily along the Ucayali River in the Amazon rain forest of Peru. I follow their work, I learn, I receive the teaching. Then I write or I film.

Over the years I became a silent practitioner in the *medicina,* perhaps too silent through timidity or simply so as not to position myself as a curandero. Even though it was recently that I entered into the dance, I will come back to it*—I am a filmmaker first and foremost. *Cineasta ayahuasquero,* a filmmaker who embraces ayahuasca.

After ten years of adventure, you arrive at the age of reason, or unreason. Anyway, it's time to assess my apprenticeship in this medicine and to revisit many human encounters.

At the beginning of this adventure, in 1999, I was usually the only white person in the midst of Indians and metis (those of mixed blood). A few Westerners came through, or we heard about them from the ayahuasqueros. There were not many of them, perhaps only a few hundred in the whole world. Today, apprentices are numerous and some have become skillful healers. Thousands take the journey

---

*See "Bonus Track 2," page 243.

to meet ayahuasca. The time of bringing cultures together is now behind us.

Over the past few years I often found myself in the Amazon surrounded by people coming for their first ceremony. When I began myself, I often felt pretty helpless as I faced the experience, so I would naturally offer such people lots of advice. And it was also true that people down there would approach me, because it was often my films that had led them to travel there.

I discovered that some advice could be really useful and other advice less so on the day after the ceremonies. From one year to the next, I was able to refine this work. Also I was often the translator in private conversations between the healer and the patients during treatments, and that gave me a deeper knowledge of the questions asked by patients and a better sense of what they were looking for.

The idea of making a practical manual to prepare someone for an ayahuasca ceremony began forming in me when I realized that, among all the writings that were coming out about it, there was no such manual. In spite of a wealth of information, there was little or no concrete advice on how to prepare yourself for an ayahuasca ceremony or on what to expect, nor was there precise information on how to make your way through the experience. The need was there. I received lots of questions by e-mail or on Facebook. Recently a young woman accosted me on the first night of an art gallery exhibit and asked me if I was who I was. Then, right away, "Hey, you've been shamanized. What's it like to be shamanized?" Yikes!

Besides, I had a series of texts on my hard drive, written between 1999 and the present. In going over them I realized that my own accounts contained a lot of information and that it was time to share it.

I sorted out my notes. The reason I had written them in the first place was so as not to forget, but I was also thinking that later—one day—I would make a book out of them that would follow the course of events chronologically. After rereading them I put together a text made up of bits and pieces, creating a hybrid narrative object, something between an autobiographical novel and a film scenario. It was a text that suited the kaleidoscopic aspect of the adventure.

Certain notes were written the day after a ceremony and others after a few weeks, some even years later. The main core of the voyage consists of chronological notes made every day during my stay in 2009 when I underwent seventeen ceremonies in twenty-five days. It was one of the rare times when I actually wrote something every day. These notes allow you to follow the course of a diet,* and they provide an overview of these past ten years.†

Some of these notes are funny, and I often laughed in rereading them; others, clearly, are less so, but putting them together brings out an intimate view of my adventure.

Accounts and questions—the book had assumed a form: The "Inner Journey Notebooks" relating my experience make up the first part of the book; "*Ayahuasca Medicina,* A Manual," a practical manual, forms the second part.

The notebooks tell the story of what this medicine did for me and how that took place.

So now here's this little guidebook—one I would have liked to have had on my first trip ten years ago. I have also included in the appendices a glossary of plants and a guide to Shipibo lexicon that you may like to refer to as a resource.

This guide will help you, I hope, to prepare yourself in a practical way for participating in an ayahuasca ceremony. It contains simple advice and suggests internal attitudes and external postures to help you make your way through the experience and through the moments following it.

What's interesting to watch is the internal movement: its amplitude, its reach is big. This is the powerful oscillation of the medicina. Ayahuasca offers us the experience of our own reality, lived from our irrational part. In short, there are no previews.

---

*[The word *diet* is used in a special way by ayahuasqueros: it means, as usual, restrictions in what is eaten or drunk, but it also includes a regimen of taking the specially brewed plant mixtures that are part of the ceremonies. Beginning such a regimen is called "opening" the diet. —*Trans.*]

†To learn more about diets, read "A diet? You get put on a diet?" beginning on page 144 of this manual; I also elaborate my personal history with diets there.

I hope that the description of these voyages, feelings, thoughts, joys, and fears—accompanied by their allotments of incoherence, contradiction, perdition, and enlightenment—will set up between the lines an operational mosaic of this mysterious medicina.

This is going to be a personal tune. Its orchestration is that of Guillermo Arévalo Valera, known as Kestenbetsa ("echo of the universe" in the Shipibo language). It was he who opened the doors of this world for me, he who taught me, he who cared for me and treated me. He was at first a maestro; later he became a brother. He had me meet other Shipibo healers, Panshin Beka among them. Kestenbetsa is, of course, the man at the center of this account.

I'm sure some passages will evoke states that you'll be going through if you go there (and memories of them for those who have already been). In any case, movement, climax, and resolution are naturally the mothers of all such accounts.

The readers who are simply curious about this adventure will find here their own accounts, at least that is my wish for you.

In contrast, you will find very little in this book on the history of ayahuasca or its pharmacology, which is a subject dealt with in depth elsewhere.

The form is that of a metaphysical drama, constructed in flashback mode, in which I am the hero.

You're going to laugh . . . at my expense. That's what it's for.

Have a good read and above all a good trip if you voyage far, very far, to encounter a culture and . . . yourself.

FADE TO BLACK

INNER JOURNEY
NOTEBOOKS

August 1999–November 2010

CREDITS

The jungle becomes abstract and turns into fractal images. The title appears:

INNER JOURNEY
NOTEBOOKS

BLACK

The decision not to believe is one more belief, just as is the decision to believe.

TARIQ DEMENS

Shadow and light are the two sides of the coin of my existence; liana, the forest vine, tosses it toward the sky and films it in slow motion, as in one of Saul Bass's credits for Scorsese . . . as a macroscopic jungle. The coin turns, again and again.

Let the film begin.

Ícaro (Song)

Rama kano abano
Now I am opening the visions

ayahuasca kano abano
I am opening the ayahuasca visions

enque quepen youbano
I am going to open them for you

ajon shaman akindra.
I will do this nicely.

Quepen quepen vainquin
Open, open

nete yabi quepenquin
open its world

ayahuasca medicina;
ayahuasca medicine;

ayahuasca kuchi kuchi medico
the very strong medicine of ayahuasca

medicina maquetai
will penetrate your body

maquetai tonmira.
with the echo of my voice.

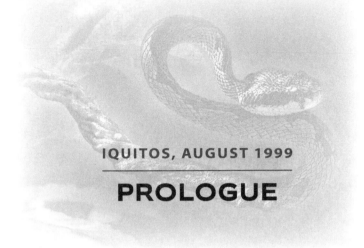

PROLOGUE

I land in the largest city of the Peruvian Amazon, a city of about 400,000 inhabitants. You can get to it only by boat or by plane. It's a very unique place where Indians, drug traffickers, and tourists mingle. Iquitos is also home to an American Army base and casinos. In this astonishing place I meet my contact, Alan Shoemaker, who introduces me to a few métis shamans.

With them I have various experiences, and I take ayahuasca for the first time. It's very different from peyote. I remember being there, in Iquitos, in the middle of the forest, sick, struck down with a terrible nausea, almost regretting having drunk the vine (ayahuasca's nickname). Bent in two over a railing, on the point of throwing up (ayahuasca is also a powerful purgative), I was mightily annoyed: "I've come all this way just to be sick and wanting to be back home!"

Then the first visions, tenuous ones, come. I stalk these visions; I observe them so I can use them in my film. My mind is still the filmmaker's mind on the lookout for documentation.

But, I'm a bit disappointed. So Alan suggests I should meet an aboriginal shaman. "With them, the experience is very strong."

One of them, Guillermo Arévalo (Kestenbetsa), is willing to meet Westerners. He lives in Pucallpa. I fly to this city that is much less touristy than Iquitos.

I have only a few days left before my scheduled return to France.

And I meet Guillermo.

YARINACOCHA QUARTER

The agile and noisy *motocaro* threads its way through the insectlike mass of its brother machines. I'm seated beside Guillermo. We're returning from running a few errands in town. We're going to Soi Pasto, the traditional medicine center he created. No longer are the ceremonies held in a 160-square-foot cabin, or *maloca,* in his garden where the chants mix with the sounds of the neighborhood.

In Yarina we had met an old Shipibo healer who's coming this evening to take the plant with us. Guillermo had said about him, "He knows a lot, and he's been a big help to me."

I've been there a few days, shooting *D'autres mondes* [*Other Worlds*] and being an apprentice. This double role of director and apprentice to Kestenbetsa is difficult, but I'm used to it.

As always, it feels like I've been there for centuries. My thoughts return to memories of the night before. I turn to Guillermo, hit by a revelation.

JAN: *¿Guillermo, somos locos, no?*
(Guillermo, we are lunatics, right?)

KESTENBETSA: *¡Sí, sí, pero locos conscientes!*
(Yes, yes—but conscious lunatics!)

The reflection of his intelligence shines through the dark iris of his eyes.

JAN: *Y tú, es el maestro de los locos.*
(And you, you are the master of lunatics.)

His laugh is swallowed by the thunder of the motocaro, which surges forward up a steep slope on the dirt road. I've only known him for a year, but it feels like a lifetime. Tonight there will be just me; the old healer, Guillermo; and his mother, Maria, taking the drink. On the program: the plant that I took the first time—much stronger than traditional ayahuasca.

SOI PASTO, MALOCA, NIGHT

This evening my assistant Laurence will be filming using night vision for the archives. These images will become the final sequence in *D'autres mondes* [*Other Worlds*].

INNER UNIVERSE, NIGHT

A long vision on the screen of my mind.

I...

In the animal creature's breast feeling is born,
Feeling weaves arabesques as it moves through personality's filters.
Its face changes as it reflects inner landscapes.
It looks hard at itself for a moment.
What is the color of an emotion?
An image?
The shape emerges.
The body reacts.
An organ comes into resonance.
The process speeds up.
Thought arises.

...am

Thought bounces around to find its final envelope, but everything depends on the person it passes through—at this moment, it's me. Thought finds its language of growth through sound, vibration, movement, contraction, the word, and writing. One day? Now?
Time stretches out.
Attention increases.

What's to be done with this thought?

Should it live?

Or disappear into the void?

The animal creature squirms for a moment. A little groan? It no longer knows, it hesitates, it breathes out.

I squirm, I hesitate.

Who are you?

Once again . . .

Who?

WELCOME

A few months ago I sent an e-mail to Guillermo that said, more or less:

Holá hermano,

I'm really prepared, doing all the right things for health, well focused, in shape, and it's the tenth anniversary of our first meeting, so you can gear up. I am ready!

He replied that he was set to go. Cool. All according to plan. Now I'm here. Iquitos is easy. The plane lands, and I jump on a motocaro. Forty minutes later I arrive at Espíritu de Anaconda. I'm happy to be back again at the center. I know everybody, almost everybody; some have been working there since 2002 when it was first set up. *Exit* Pucallpa, Yarinacocha, Soi Pasto. *Welcome* Iquitos and, in comparison, its relative tranquillity.

What joy once again at being with Guillermo, Sonia (his wife), Ricardo (the other healer), María (Guillermo's mother), Vanessa, Bastien, and all the others. The house I'm in every time has become more and more comfortable; I find all my things.

The bike that we're sharing with François Demange, a curandero Frenchman, is in working order. Today's agenda: change the chain assembly and the oil. I have a week to get organized. All is well; being here is perfectly normal. I get my bearings; everything has shown up except my suitcase, which should arrive in a few days.

The high point of presenting my film *Coco Chanel & Igor Stravinsky* a few weeks ago at Cannes is behind me. I have time to slow down my pace. Here it's a bit like coming to a vacation home—at least as I am arriving. Starting this evening, ceremonies are on the agenda. I'm going to chase away my jet lag, as well as the Parisian bustle that cradles my mind.

The new maloca, the traditional round room where the ceremonies unfold, has been enlarged again. I move in my things: my bag with my pipe and tobacco, my bottle of Agua Florida,* and most importantly, a comfortable cushion. My mattress is near the mattresses of Guillermo and Ricardo. I take off to see the boss.

Brief discussion: He asks about my intentions and my projects and I ask him about his. My goals are simple. I feel good; I've kept to my diets. I'm there to make progress in the medicina, to go further, to go deeply, so I can understand more and gain strength. I'm prepared to drink whatever potion he hands me each day. He knows me well—I'm not in the habit of asking him to floor the accelerator. What sauce is he going to cook me in? What's the diet going to be? He smiles. Slowly pointing his finger at himself he says to me, "Your diet is me!"

He's going to connect me up to the light, using the spirits of the plants. Our faces are close; I'm under his gaze.

He continues gently, "Things are simple; there is light and shadow, but sometimes the shadow is disguised as light." I ask him to show me how to tell the true light from the false. He replies that he will.

Beautiful gift: my diet will be the boss! And this way, more discernment will come thanks to the direct transmission from his energy diets. I thank him.

I talk to him about various film projects on the medicina and show him my storyboards about that. Also, I've come with equipment to do an experiment. The concept is always the same: looking for a scientific validation of this medicine and of what takes place in a ceremony. Having said I would keep the protocol confidential, I cannot describe it here. The researchers and Romuald Leterrier, an ethnobotanist and author of *La Danse du serpent* [The Dance of the Serpent], who made the connection for setting up this experiment, stayed behind in France.

As for Guillermo, he has spent a difficult few months—too much work and being exposed to a lot of negative energies. But, today, he is once again in fine form.

---

*A local flower-flavored water used as cologne for cleansing and healing.

He informs me that a new apprentice has prepared a very good bowl of ayahuasca. "You'll see, it's *muy, muy fuerte!*"

Where's the book that he began a few years ago? His computer ate it and he lost the whole thing. He's very busy, and I feel that we're going to wait a long time for this book. Why don't we move ahead as we did for *The Psychotropic Mind** and conduct interviews with Michka and Tigrane, who will look after transcribing them? He likes the idea; something to follow up on.†

He lets me know that there is a group of yogis coming from China next week, then he excuses himself, telling me that he has to go to Lima for a few days. I reply, "So I'll be on vacation." He laughs, then asks me for news of Anne, my companion, and of our daughter, Biri. "When are they going to come and see us?" It's the same question every time. I show him photos. Everyone wants the children to meet each other.

Settling into the kitchen, I get to know the dieters. Some have been there several months; some arrived the day before. In all, there are about thirty people. Benjamin, a Parisian whom I know, an apprentice for two and a half years, is there with a group. There are lots of French for whom my film *D'autres mondes* was a deciding factor in their decision to come to the center. There are also Austrians, Portuguese, Australians, Canadians, and a couple of Americans. I hope that all will go well for them. The day slips by and in an agreeable way. I have it confirmed that in recent weeks Guillermo has participated less in the ceremonies and has rested.

A parabolic antenna has been installed, and we can now connect with Wi-Fi. With my iPhone I can telephone via Skype and send my e-mails. That means I don't have to go into town, twelve miles away, and spend a lot of time and money on communication.

I send a few messages to my sweetie, to my family, and my friends. I take a photo that I put on Facebook for fun, and I let Romuald know that I've arrived safely.

Night falls. Jet lag overtakes me.

The Psychotropic Mind was originally published in French under the title *Plantes et chamanisme* [Plants and Shamanism] and consisted of conversations on shamanism and mind-altering plants. The conversations in the French book were organized and transcribed by publishers Michka Seeliger and Tigrane Hadengue.

†Conversations were subsequently recorded in 2010.

A GOOD DRINK, PEACEFUL

IQUITOS—ESPÍRITU, MALOCA, EVENING INSIDE

There are twenty-eight of us in the maloca, not counting the healers.

A good drink, normal dosage.

The nausea is under control even though the drink is strong. Caught up by the travel fatigue, I doze off sitting up. The intoxication wakes me up, totally "inside." The visions are very strong. The ayahuasca has been apportioned well, the body vibrates. No panic. Just the familiar. I allow the plant to penetrate deeply—peacefully.

Then, very fast, it is not peaceful at all. The intoxication climbs.

I am thrust into the worlds of the various plants, their living visionary temples. The vision becomes that of a sphere around me. Motifs get arranged and move through me.

The nausea is just behind my lips. I feel every organ in my body. A disagreeable and well-known sensation of the intoxication: the impression of being rendered naked. I don't move.

(Intoxication—*mareación*—what is it? For those of you not acquainted with intoxication, browse through the manual where I answer that question beginning on page 162.)

The mareación continues to mount. The boss is really getting into it. I turn toward him to see. He's stretched out; his arms seem to float like a weightless astronaut. His whole body moves slowly; he is smoking his pipe. Wow! I had never seen him like that. Peaceful and distant.

I give myself a quick scan. My thinking part has not engaged nor has it gone down the drain. It has remained amazingly calm. I am totally involved in the perception of the physical body and in navigating the visions.

I smile and think, so far so good.

Suddenly, I open up my perceptions more to allow the intoxication to take me even more deeply. I see how my diet has helped. I'm not afraid. I remember the first years: every time I came back to see Guillermo after an absence of several months I was terrified when the intoxication first began to mount. It's a special phenomenon—remembering the forgetting.

During the ceremonies you enter very specific states of consciousness that are very distant from your natural state. Because of that, when you return to the world you know at the end of the ceremony certain memories disappear as your consciousness returns. When you take ayahuasca again, even a year later, at the moment you reach that specific state once again, the memory comes back too. The memory opens like a book that you thought was lost but had been saved in a hidden spot in your inner library. Certain chapters cause reactions in your mind: "Good God, I had forgotten. No, no, no! I don't want to come back here; I thought I died a thousand times. Why have I come back? I'm a real masochist! I know it's for my own good, but no, I'm not going to have enough strength. I'm not up to it."

I could write a whole chapter on nothing but the thoughts that you mustn't hang on to. In fact, the diets clear out the thinking part, and the practice helps you recognize these thoughts before they take hold of you. You also have to accept the forgetting, or remember that from this forgetting an inner knowledge will arise.

Let's return to the ceremony. The thinking mind can do this: "Oh, boy—strong intoxication! Wow! It's still climbing. Hey, I remember now: before, just there, I was afraid."

At this last thought the body tenses up then immediately relaxes, setting in motion other mechanisms of the mind based on the training in apprenticeship. Using the senses, I bring about the repositioning of my mind, leading it out of dark territory where it was in the midst of wandering around, while directives enter as an inner melodic form, the ícaros.*

---

*Ícaros are discussed later in the manual; see page 154.

Center yourself well.
Descend into your intoxication.
It's for your own good.
All is well.
It's good.
The medicina moves into you.
Stay collected.
Center yourself in your intoxication.
Center yourself in your body.
Center yourself in your senses.
Center yourself in your mind.
Center yourself in your heart.
Align everything—strength, attention, and care.
Do it now.
I do it now.
And there we are . . .

With my body vibrating and relaxed, I set myself down, literally, like a kind of helicopter swaying in the storm of the mareación. The rotor blades are still turning. When Guillermo finally opens the session, a whole hour has gone by.

The serpent breathes out.

Peaceful.

My mind is no longer in the chopper but in a jet speeding through space—through time.

Astral world.

Inner silence.

Pure perception. Total listening.

Thought is gone.

Conscious vegetative mode.

Guillermo's song becomes sharp. Ricardo enters the dance with his powerful voice. I climb up; I feel like I'm getting bigger, extending myself through mysterious space. Everything comes together. I no longer feel where my body touches the ground.

End of song.

Guillermo calls me.

Ouch! Emergency landing procedure.

Open the eyes. Reestablish contact with the place and with space.

GUILLERMO: Jan . . . Jan . . .

JAN: (after a long silence) ¿Sí?

GUILLERMO: (his voice low and soft) *Venga.*

My mind is empty . . . Come? Ah! Right. The song to open the diet! Yikes! Got to get up.

Red alert. First wake up the limbs that will get me going. My poor legs are completely relaxed, send an order, stretch my leg. It trembles a bit. Find your balance. Not too fast. Continue to get up slowly. Whoa! I'm really stoned. Getting up brings back the nausea. Take it slow. Relax, move gently. I manage to move over and sit down facing him. There, I did it. I position myself well, inside myself. Done. Silence.

You need to know that openings and closings of the diet are generally special whether they're luminous or dark. Which type they are is no doubt connected to what you need to sort out in yourself.

Anyway, I fall into dark visions. Much less fun.

Guillermo sings an ícaro—a healing song.

> *Rama kayakayara*
> At this very moment
>
> *mia kepenshonbanon, shinan kepenshonbanon;*
> I will open you, I will open your thoughts;
>
> *kepenshonyontanara*
> in opening them
>
> *mia raromayonai;*
> I will fill you with joy;
>
> *raromakinkayara*
> in filling you with joy

min shinan ponteai, mia ponteshonbanon
I will align your thoughts, in aligning them

jakon shaman akinra.
I do it nicely.

yorayabi ponteai
I will align your body

akon akin shamanra
with marvels

nokon shinan kanonbi;
from my powerful thoughts

shinan koshi kanonbi;
strong and powerful thoughts;

rama mia ashonban (repeat two times)
now, I will heal you

min jointi shamanbo
to the depths of your heart

kepeankebainshonra
in opening it

ramamia ashonban
now I will heal you completely even

min onis kanonbo
your deepest sadness

min masa shinanbo.
your strongest concerns.

I don't move, but I let all my muscles stretch lightly to force my consciousness to focus on their perceptions. Everything takes place automatically. An acquired reflex. I feel my moods—sadness, anger—showing through. I see negative thoughts arising. Fearful visions are cleansing, scouring my mental casseroles that I've been lugging around for a few months.

Keyoakebainshonra
In ending this

raroshinan nichinai
I will give you a huge feeling of joy

raro joi nichinai
and immense joy in words

jakon akin nichinai (repeat three times);
I will do it marvelously;

nichiankebainshonra, mia jiweabanon
in doing this I will give you back your life

yora jiweabanon
I will give life back to your body

shinan jiweayonkin
I will give life back to your thoughts

kaya jiweayonkin (repeat two times);
by giving life back to your being;

jiweayontananra
in giving you back life

min kaya seneman, min yora seneman
I heal your being, I heal your body

jiwi inin kanonra (repeat two times)
with the powerful perfume of the tree

nete sisa ininra.
and with the impeccable perfume of the universe.

I don't move; the song unfolds its final energies.

The diet is particularly open, or rather, it's the cleansing of the pre-opening. I go back and sit down—it's easier. I am peacefully cradled by the ícaros. Mixed into their melodies, there spreads around me the strange musicality of a few pretty vomitings and their cohorts, the long rasping sighs of comfort. General cleansing. I am purging too—precise, deep . . .

I need to say that the dose was big, the intoxication strong. More precisely, I got a little on my mattress and on my pants. Ah, I remember the suitcase I lost in Madrid. After twenty-six hours of travel, the only pants to my name get messed up and I don't have a change. I smile. Welcome home!

Around five o'clock in the morning everything quiets down. I feel very rested, peacefully inhabiting my body. Natural behavioral reflex: a long gurgling and a natural pinching in my sphincters tells me it's time to move toward the closing act of the ceremony. The time has come. Stumbling, I move off to the toilets.

Ayahuasca is a powerful purgative, and I'm going to give you some details about that in this book. Don't be shocked, or if you like, skip over the paragraphs on this subject that follow. In fact, *purga* is the name the métis give to ayahuasca: the purgative. Not very mystical, but you can understand why. "And how about you, are you doing the purge tonight?" It has the ring of a pretty formidable medicine just the same. The ayahuasqueros are called *purgueros*. How do you translate that? The ones who got purged? The ones who purge?

You get it: speaking of what is eliminated through the upper and lower openings of the body is a normal and usual concern of the ayahuasqueros. They encounter it more often than usual and in sometimes surprising ways. That's how it was for me that day: little baby stools, pretty and round. Unusual given the treatment received.

Time now to go and dive into the logical next step: falling asleep like a baby.

ESPÍRITU, DAYTIME

Exit jet lag. Woke up at eight in good shape. Stretch for twenty minutes. It's Saturday; no ceremony on Saturdays. It's a rest day at Espíritu, but Guillermo invites me to go with him this evening to the Luz Kósmika Apprenticeship Center where a ceremony is planned. The place is incredible: it's *The Emerald Forest,* a jungle much wilder than at Espíritu.* We go on motorbike.

---

*The Emerald Forest was a 1985 film set in the Brazilian rain forest.

GUILLERMO: Down there, you'll see, the spirits are numerous and powerful!

JAN: (eyes lighting up) Great!

GUILLERMO: We're going to take a very strong preparation made of eight plants. Besides ayahuasca and chacruna, there will be toé (datura), bobinsana, chay, coca, marosa, and piñon blanco! For me, it's . . .

With his forefinger he points to his head, then to the sky, then, with two closed fists he mimes sitting down and shaking his body gently as if he were imprisoned in a training centrifuge for Russian astronauts, making the face for a big nausea but with a smile on his lips.

GUILLERMO: (with a big smile) *¡Muy muy muuuuuuuy fuerte!*

Yikes and double yikes! A big cocktail of teaching plants. And besides those mentioned, he adds in a few more—Kestenbetsa, the man who is able to fall asleep, whereas for me in the same state, I barely manage to survive.

Okay, I'm used to his humor. But what is his humor exactly? For example, bizarrely, each evening for a week he showed me a bottle of black liquid, telling me that it was so strong that he thought he was going to die taking it. But why did he tell me that? You guessed it. At the end of the week, when I'm feeling really fragile, really freaked by the idea that he'd given me a drop too much, right at that moment he deftly brings out the old black bottle, adding with a smile, "And tonight, I'm taking that. Do you want to join me? Up to you . . ." So then, I could reply, "No, not tonight, my left brain has exchanged with my right brain and vice versa . . ." Actually, I would be kidding: I'm going to drink it anyway. One never refuses this kind of invitation, so just trust it. And until now everything has always ended well.

Guillermo comes by and says, "Last night, we were warming up. Tonight we switch to turbo."

JAN: (unable to suppress a little nervous spasm) Uh . . . Great . . . *ya . . . qué . . . bueno . . .*

He smiles at me; his eyes seem to add, "This is what you asked me for, right?" Right. Exactly. It's all for the best. I wonder when the day will come when I regret the boldness of what I get myself into. Tonight, tomorrow night, some evening next week? He asks if I can take someone behind me on my bike. Cross-country is my thing. That'll be the nice part of the evening. "No problem, the bike is easy; it's the ceremony that's another story!"

He laughs. We're to meet at 5:00 p.m. James, his son, will show up at eight.

The night is black, the rain heavy. Right from the beginning, it's not as nice as I thought it would be. Guillermo gets on behind James; K., my passenger, gets on my bike. This little spin is going to be an ordeal.

In fact, it's a racetrack worthy of the Gilles Lalay Classic,* with local-style rain, which means a downpour. On my little 230cc, equipped with a minuscule headlight that has a hard time lighting six feet ahead of us, I slip around on the sodden ground that has become a field of ruts left by trucks, and the ruts are now filled with water eighteen inches deep. The bridges that are thrown together with tree trunks and slippery sheets of corrugated metal are well supplied with actual holes that could easily swallow a wheel or more. Narrow planks are placed above empty spots so you can get through walls of sand that you discover at the last minute. And we are speeding . . .

Ah yes! We also have to be careful not to get stuck in stretches of sand so drenched in water that they start to move! I cannot stand up to navigate because I have a passenger hanging on to me. Happily, she is not very fierce nor a biker and that saved us. Forty-five minutes later, sweating, drenched, and exhausted we arrive at Luz Kósmika. It's like a rainy remake of *The Wages of Fear*, William Friedkin's† version, with

---

*The Gilles Lalay Classic is a 124-mile endurance motorbike race on rough terrain between Limoge and Peyrat-le-Château that has been called one of the toughest races of all time.

†In 1977 William Friedkin produced and directed *Sorcerer*, a remake of the 1953 film *The Wages of Fear*, in which truckloads of volatile nitroglycerin are being transported over treacherous terrain.

our nitroglycerin still to come—the bottle that Guillermo is lugging around in his bag. We have all the ingredients for a memorable evening.

The construction of the center is now complete. I had come while it was still in progress the previous year. Now, night has engulfed the place. A very long bridge makes its way through the wet forest and leads us to the maloca. In front of us is a stairway. The maloca is perched in the trees. As we make our way up the stairs that are lit dimly by our flashlights, I have the impression of discovering a mysterious temple. The jungle is loud with the sounds of monkeys, toucans, and big insects. The racket reminds us that we are not alone here. I let this moment sink into me so I can taste it and so it imbues me with the feeling of being an adventurer.

HOUSTON, DO YOU READ ME?

LUZ KÓSMIKA, MALOCA, EVENING INSIDE

There are five of us drinking this evening. Guillermo and his son James direct the ceremony. Opposite is K., my passenger, and Virginia, an Austrian woman who has been dieting with toé for several years and seems to be literally merging with the jungle. After a shower, stretched out on a mattress in the maloca, I wait and, battered by the cross-country special, I fall asleep . . .

"Jan? Jan?" Guillermo is calling me. "Yikes! Yes? Where am I?" My arms are aching. The bike. I'd forgotten: I'm supposed to drink. Not fully woken up, I approach Guillermo, who pours me . . . a very big glass. My sleepy eyes become fully awake in step with the measure of his pouring. Whah? The glass is almost full . . . Is he going to stop filling it? My thoughts are more or less as follows:

JAN: (world of thoughts) No . . . Not already! I just got here!

JAN: (dubious) *Sí . . . Gracias . . .*

GUILLERMO: (be tranquil . . .)

Guillermo icarizes the glass—that is, whispers and blows a melody onto its contents to increase its force and imbue an intention. Then I drink the endless glass and go back and sit down with the sensation of having a full stomach, something rare with this drink.

This evening everyone can have a full glass. We're off. Big

intoxication that is very slow. It's an intoxication the size of an ocean liner, a very big ocean liner, and I chase the *Titanic* out of my mind right away. I hear James lean over to Guillermo and speak to him in a low voice.

JAMES: *Estoy un poco mal.*
(I don't feel too good.)

He leaves, goes down the stairs, and vomits, vomits hard—for a long time.

JAN: (world of thoughts) Houston, do you read me? We've got a problem!

Radio silence. This lasts more than an hour. You need to understand what is happening. The intoxication has a tendency to sensitize you physically while weakening you mentally. Fortunately the songs, the ícaros, are there to transform this state into a treatment and to guide the patient or the apprentice. Without a song, a strong intoxication can be compared to the feeling of a driver at the wheel of a vehicle driving through the desert at night with the headlights gradually dying and the accelerator stuck to the floor.

JAN: (world of thoughts) Hmm . . . He has decided not to sing. So don't panic. Yes, I know it's a new intoxication. Normal, given the cocktail! So I center myself well. I center myself in my intoxication. I do it now.

The liner stretches out and twists in a slow heaving motion.

I am penetrated by the worlds of each plant contained in the preparation. Totally immersed in the deployment of abstract visionary material from each of these worlds.

I can no longer perceive the limits of my body; I become the visions. The sensation of my body is new and distinct, it's like a liquid floating in space. I feel a great relaxation at the muscular level and specific movements inside my skull.

In fact, everything is relaxing. I drive out fears that appear with the new sensations. I have to remain calm and alert.

James comes back and sits down.

Time passes.

At the moment Guillermo begins to sing, I realize that I was no longer expecting the songs. I was walking around in each of the worlds offered to me by the plants that I had ingested.

He sings.

I open my eyes.

My body is covered by chestnut-colored serpentine forms, thick, carpeted with motifs, and woven like a suit. It's a sort of high-tech armor, a visionary vegetable material.

The vision is very precise.

With the song, something like extensions arise out of the suit and set themselves up in front of me. Memory awakens. No panic; I'd simply forgotten. These extensions seem to be interfaces that the plants have made available to the healers so they can see information about the patients before undertaking a treatment.

Everything moves into position, but it's hard to give more details: I see the scene, but if I try to describe it today, my mind freezes. A kind of forbidden land.

Exit conceptual thought, giving way to the first part of the upgrade—opening the diet. I have the impression that I'm being realigned with the medicina. What can I say? It's like a piano that you take apart, change certain strings, and then you tune it. I have the impression I'm seeing my body as a shell; inside, the serpents of medicine spread along the energetic meridians—everything gets aligned. It's an adjustment session for the animal creature that I am.

Perceiving myself through archetypal forms, I see the interaction between the medicina and my being. Walls of tangled serpents organize themselves slowly into gigantic mandalas while my body disappears as a boundary in space.

My visions are engulfed in darkness; the alignments are ending. James sings, and I vomit. But I mean *vomit*. It gushes out so strongly that I'm afraid of suffocating; and it's never ending. I mustn't breathe any more, or more accurately, I concentrate so I can breathe briefly between bouts of throwing up. A part of me is happy, because each vomiting is a great liberation, spring cleaning, pruning the trees of my bad thoughts and sad moods. At the same time, I'm uneasy. Highly intoxicated, if I don't maintain a strong concentration, I risk being suffocated—not by going too far, trespassing, but by having a nasty moment. Vomit in the lungs—no thanks. I force myself to stay in a precise position as I hang over the bucket, like a cat held by its neck over emptiness. There I am, a cat, holding himself like that. Subjected to a rapid increase of quick movements in my esophagus, I get through the treatment I've been given pretty well. The bucket is half full.

I have never vomited that much in my life.

Except for Guillermo, everyone got really well purged during the night.

In fact, I am surprised. Since yesterday I've been filling my bucket, although I haven't vomited in sessions for years. I'd have to go back around a hundred ceremonies before I could dig up a memory of this kind of really major vomiting. It's all these new plants no doubt and the strength of the treatment I've received. With that thought, I fall asleep. The sun wakes us up a very short time later.

No time to discuss with the dieters, I promise to return in a week. Guillermo and James left very early. Daytime, the sun! K. wants to go back on foot. I climb on the bike feeling light, strong, and concentrated, even though I only slept a few hours. The return is a breeze. Alone on the machine I'm finally able to maneuver a bit. Fifteen minutes later I am at Espíritu and I have breakfast. It was one of the strongest ceremonies that I'd ever experienced. And, all in all, I'm doing pretty well. I think about it one more time as I'm writing these notes that I'm retranscribing today. In doing so, I notice that I used to write a lot, before. I would theorize, go into detail, draw—then one day it stopped. One morning, after a big ceremony—nothing anymore—a chunk of my metaphysical concerns had gone up in smoke. And that's for the best. I'll come back to this later.

For almost five years, nothing anymore. Just the practice. Very few notes.

How I saw the medicina had been changed. Formerly I spoke of shamanism, of the science of the spirit. For a few years now, I see this knowledge as what it has become for me: traditional medicine—

a quieting down of mysticism, a welcoming of the practical world.

Today I begin over again. The design is using the storyboard launched in 1999 and this text. I don't question myself further, while remembering that before, for days on end, I did nothing but think about all that.

I get out the equipment for the experiment. The batteries are dead so the program has to be reinitialized. I send off an e-mail to announce the bad news and to ask about a recovery procedure. I'll spend the day doing nothing.

Hammock.

Music.

Rest.

I close my notebook.

AYAHUASQUERO FILMMAKER, RUE SAINT-DENIS, PARIS

A Day in 2010, Notes after Rereading

I'm sorting through things. There are things that cannot be spoken about publicly. It's too bad. But that's the way it is. Some facts would definitely pigeonhole me as crazy—someone you would no longer think of as credible or someone you would look at with either fear or pity. I found notes of that kind. With some of them I hesitated for a while, and then I included them.

After all I'm an artist, an entertainer. Artists are a little off-the-wall, right?

If a few people snigger reading this book, that's not going to affect the confidence that my professional colleagues afford me.

A film director has a duty to be a strange bird. When you get to the end of this book, you're going to say that I'm a bit off or a bit wacky for sure, but not all that bad. That's my point. A painter or a musician can really have a screw loose in the act of creation. Not so for a film director—at least not one who wants to keep working. The director is a painter with a heavy palette—each color is very expensive. The paint has to be used fast, because it dries in seconds. Getting your inks requires negotiations that are sometimes rough, and using them expertly is a samurai's art.

Around the director there are hundreds of people working away. Making a film means being part of a team; it means running a small business enterprise. Maintaining a good relationship with the team is important. All artistic decisions have to be vetted by the director—who is expected to be in relation with the filmed result at a level of inspiration that each of those decisions will contribute to. Making a film requires concentration, attention, and management. The profession is closer to that of an architect than that of the artist who paints. It is closer to being a craftsman than an artist. In telling you all this, I'm framing what follows.

During the initial years, I was really in a very unique space. The rumor ran around Paris that I was with a witch doctor in the jungle and that I had lost it. In a way, it was true, and reading this book is going to make you think the same thing. At the same time, I brought to completion a series of films that required an art director who had his head on his shoulders. The films reflect the road that was traveled. They illustrate the choices, the sensitivity, the heavy-handedness, or the lightness of the person who shoots them. They are what shows.

In order to judge the effect that the Amazonian medicine has had on me, you only need to take a look at the film director's journey. It's a good barometer.

A WHIFF OF LOVE DOES YOU GOOD

ESPÍRITU, MALOCA, EVENING INSIDE

I did nothing all day. Peaceful. I had trouble centering myself, and I certainly didn't force the machine. This evening Guillermo is resting. It's clear that the ceremony of the day before tired him; it was his seventh consecutive day of working. He takes his Sunday on Monday. Ricardo is officiating.

I'm returning once again to traditional ayahuasca. The ceremony is difficult. As soon as the spirits show up in the visions, I'm besieged with pain and the visions disappear. I spend the night focused on my emerging stomachache. Ricardo is doing a group healing for a family that comes from Haiti with lots of black magic that needs dumping. During the healing I see big bumblebees—nasty ones—circling around them. Ricardo cleans all that out, then gets rid of it all—straight from his mouth into the bucket. The ceremony ends early, around 3:00 a.m. I have a sweet final vision: the face of my companion, Anne, dressed as an Indian and smiling at me.

A whiff of love does you good.

I don't need to do a washroom stop and I go back to bed, plunged into a feeling of soft and nauseated flesh. I'm joking: certainly purging is a constant factor with the vine—the ceremonies follow one another but are never the same twice.

MORNING

I receive an e-mail that gives me the procedure to restart the program, but the data that appears isn't right. I take screen shots and send them off. We'll see what tomorrow brings. I decide to paint the outside walls of my house, but because I'm tired, I'll buy the paint some other day.

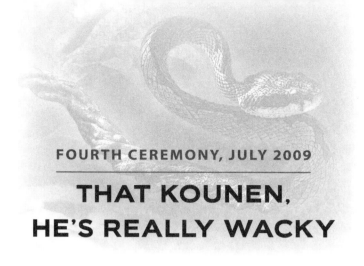

THAT KOUNEN, HE'S REALLY WACKY

ESPÍRITU, MALOCA, EVENING INSIDE

This evening in the maloca, three patients are there for specific healings as well as the apprentices Sita, Bastien, and me.

Things are coming together.

It takes Guillermo about an hour and a half before he begins to sing. Normal. For the apprentices, a part of their work takes place outside the song, and in doing that they really open to their intoxication. Anyway, once again I'm at the sticking point like the day before yesterday. And once again the intoxication is maxed out. I wonder where this story is going to end. But okay, all is well; the warning lights have turned green. I'm just about to throw up. I'm humming like a cricket. I feel the big scanner in action and moving through me. I pull myself together like an animal.

As a tightrope walker, my awareness moves forward, upright, along the fine rope of its emotions, above the abyss of its fears. I think of Coyote just before his endless plunge down into the canyon. Road Runner is watching him. I'm both of them at once—strange metaphor. I blow it a long way out by breathing quietly.

Now I have a good grip on the reins of my thought—a firm and delicate hand.

All is well.

Relax.

Die a bit.

It is a little, symbolic death, a little spasm that makes it into my sense perceptions and calms my mind.

The intoxication is still climbing.

I tense my muscles lightly and then let go so I can stay in touch with my body. Visions are all around me once again. I understand right away what's happening. It follows directly from the previous ceremony with Guillermo.

At Luz Kósmika, I was plunged into the world of each plant that the drink contained and the visions were abstract, solely made up of motifs in movement. The immersion was powerful and complete. In fact, I received the energy of these plants. That energy is in me now and makes it possible for me to have a deep relationship with the spirits of those plants. In silence he guides me.

I'd never seen so many spirits, so many different worlds. They move by in front of me. Today I'm taking advantage of these encounters. The dialogue that is set up is visionary—each spirit lays out its world in detail. The chay presents itself as a big blue bird in an aquatic temple. The other spirits are humanoid and are presenting me with the cities and hospitals they have at their disposal. I had already seen that a few years before with my diets, but never so abundantly. Psychological time is hugely expanded. Guillermo has not yet begun to sing.

Note: if you are reading this without being captured by doubts about the storyteller's sanity you can skip the next part.

As for the rest of you, my apologies for interrupting the reading once again.

INTERLUDE

Anyone who hasn't lived through this kind of experience is smiling. You must be saying, "Oh well, that Kounen is really wacky. His imagination is out of control, and the poor guy is mixing up the imaginary and the real."

I believe that if I hadn't lived through these experiences I would think something like that.

Given that, what's next?

Accept that it's logical to think that way, to think that the guy is swimming around in a full-blown psychotropic delirium? Let's not forget that for four days running he's been taking the most powerful psychotropic substances available on the planet at dosages appropriate for a hardened adult. Our society has taught us to beware of psychotropic substances. They're toxic and dangerous, precisely because . . . they make you lose your reason!

So we have here an interesting artistic experience. Let's take it for what it is, and let's continue to follow the pretty incredible adventure of this tightrope walking.

So be it.

However, as I question my reason and my memory, I come back to myself clearly while I'm rereading this text. At the time of the experience, the day afterward, and today—for me, all of it was coherent.

Note that I didn't say *real*, I said coherent.

During my earlier diets—that is, years earlier—I encountered this same type of experience, and, over ten years, the world of visions seemed, with just a few exceptions, completely coherent. Little by little they fit together and weave a virtual reality of experiences, exploration, and therapeutic tools.

How am I to convince you to embark on this voyage with me, at least in the reading of this book? Imagine that every night you have the same dream. It's not really a dream because you're neither completely asleep nor completely awake—an altered state of consciousness. Each night, sitting in your bed, you are visited by the same kinds of people and, every night, your conversation picks up right where it left off the night before. You would rather that wasn't happening to you. Me too. For sure, it's insanity—which means an experience that can't be fully communicated to others like yourself, an experience that you alone are passing through. And yet it's coherent. You decide to speak about it to those around you and you end up in an asylum.

Nasty business.

Craftily, you don't talk about it; you just live it. A warrior's act in our society.

Now you experience it in a cultural and experimental context that validates your experience. Whew! You're not crazy anymore. You can more easily ascribe a certain credibility to this new meeting ground, not because it's real in the material sense of the term, but in its experiential sense. A reality made up of repeated and coherent experiences—experiences that will transform your behavior later on. You are learning from your encounters.

Change cultures, return home, and the first question is: How do you explain those experiences? Sorry. That's over the top.

It's true. Science, alas, has not yet managed to explain it, even though many have tried. Let's agree that what we're talking about here is not reality but experience.

The story is subtler than that. It isn't just the real on one side and the unreal on the other.

Between the two there are many things.

Refine your relationship with these in-between realities. It's new and it's also, certainly, dangerous for your psychological balance. With ayahuasca the experience that you go through is so real that you risk no longer doubting this new reality. Instead you call it ultrareality.

What reality seems to be overlaying and what is finally being revealed.

What sits next to reality.

The matrix of the real.

The big Russian doll that contains the little Russian doll.

You set about thinking about this world based on the other world and so you mix up and confuse the two of them. The problem is that the mechanics of reflection and analysis in our culture come from outside this metareality. Then, of necessity, most often you mess up.

These other worlds have to continue to be thought about within their own space.

Agreed. I'm wacky again and reassuring you even less! But this is why I'm limiting myself to describing instead of explaining. For now, before continuing to read, accept at least that all this may be the psychological construction of a linguistic bridge (archetypal visions) established between species of the plant kingdom and the human species, allowing these two different intelligences to communicate.

We don't believe in this model of possible interspecies communication. As a culture we deny it. It seems impossible to us, because we deny the possibility of an intelligence in plants. We may have simply lost the interface. Don't forget that it wasn't so long ago that we denied there was intelligence in newborns of our own species.

So let's get back to it. Clearly, you have the right to read the rest of this book as if it were fiction!

Even though it's not.

END OF INTERLUDE
FEBRUARY 2010

DYING OVER THERE

RETURN TO THE MALOCA, ABOUT 11:15 P.M.

So, I'm still in the spirit world. In fact, more accurately, the spirits are not around me in the maloca (as in the vision that I had before, but not since arriving this time)—instead, it's me who is with them where they live.

Guillermo connects me to former diets, mainly the piñon blanco. I recognize these worlds, and I enter into something like operating rooms—light blue. I don't see the spirits, or only see their legs. The immersion is total. I'm aware of a strong vibration filling my body, and I feel the fluid of my blood coursing through my veins. The spirits approach and are now visible. They show me a sort of high-tech table with a number of instruments. The table approaches, or rather I move toward it. Instruments have been placed on it, something like surgical instruments. But nothing very sharp. That's what I think anyway. The designs are futuristic with rounded shapes. Imagine Apple in thirty years, in the style of the suit that I saw myself wearing two nights before.

I slow down my breathing. I center myself to drive away the fears that have been building since I identified the instruments. I know that, quite logically, it's me who is going to "come under the knife"—the one belonging to the spirits.

Fortunately, I've already had this experience, but it was a very long time ago.

I center myself to be as neutral as possible—not rejecting, not asking, just letting it happen.

Maximum neutrality.

Suddenly a surgical object begins floating in front of me; everything else seems to disappear. It turns around itself. Guillermo begins to sing . . . Fusion. I've completely left any awareness of the room and of my body.

At that moment all is well. In fact, I can't be afraid because I have disappeared.

The tool is in my awareness. It changes its form—many motifs that blend together to form a succession of geometric structures in a space without limits. The shapes of the object seem to be letters or signs of an unknown alphabet. They spread out through my mind.

Next, the memories that arise are of a flight over an unknown jungle, then I come back into a plant; I merge with it.

I am far away.

A process is beginning.

I set about feeling death, not my human death, but death in this world. I let it happen, and I suffer an immense sadness, gentle and without any thoughts, followed by a long spasm.

The song has just ended.

I come back.

I don't quite know where I am.

I think, "I let myself die over there."

It was a new kind of symbolic death, one that took place in the spirit world but ended up returning back down here in the human world—a way of coming back.

A language, a technique.

I let this thought circulate.

Guillermo calls Sita, and he sings an incredible song for her.

Nausea unfurls full-blown. I have trouble keeping my awareness steady—a kind of thermal shock from the experience I have just undergone. I can't get my mind centered.

Guillermo calls me, and with difficulty I get up. He literally showers me with a big cloud of tobacco smoke that aligns my intoxication.

Everything settles down.

I find my center again.

One foot in this world, one in the other—general awareness of organs, sensations of my thoughts and of my visions.

Guillermo begins to sing.

I move down into a yellow, golden, luminous world, and immediately I'm aware of an agreeable sensation, but strangely I mistrust it. I concentrate on the words of the song, a song of cleansing.

I remain vigilant. I feel that information is surging out.

I manage to follow the song, every other line. I question what is being presented by asking the plant to give me discernment. Beautiful spirits move forward.

Guillermo stops singing. Concentrating, I think, "Medicina, show me who these spirits are: I am connected to you." I steady my senses in order to not clutch at feelings of well-being that are a little too closely connected to pleasures of the flesh or to a kind of spiritual greed. I position myself in my heart.

The spirit stops moving forward.

I pursue the inner questioning.

A veil is gently lifted, or I could say that the part that is behind the spirit is revealed gently.

I see dark, ugly shapes. I am not afraid. I understand.

Guillermo is guiding me in my request for discernment.

I perceive this beautiful spirit as a marionette of really black energy. I look for what part of my body resonates with it.

An understanding dawns.

Guillermo begins singing again.

And now the intoxication is such that I move in to metaphysical issues arising from my various and varied contacts with different religions and traditions. Here in the jungle there is certainly no quest for fulfillment, no search for satori or enlightenment, just this medicine—ingesting plants for healing oneself, for understanding oneself, for cleansing oneself, and then healing others. If a sound comes out of your mouth or if an intention emerges, they must be connected to the medicina.

This is not a philosophy, not a doctrine, even less is it a religion—it is the practice of medicine.

The end of the song is intuitively an Amazonian Hippocratic oath before moving into this new diet.

End of the song.

I go back and sit down.

Guillermo and Ricardo begin singing at the same time.

Scarcely am I seated when I take off again.

How shall I say it? My awareness climbs, climbs in a dizzying way. I move through the world of spirits, and I continue climbing. A strident whistling comes into my mind, driving out all thought (to my great surprise this whistling was from the *Millennium Falcon* of *Star Wars* passing into hyperspace; I was like that old ramshackle ship hurled into a somewhere else).

Pure light, the old carcass of the *Millennium Falcon* shudders but holds together. Beams of light in slats within strident howls pierce my mind. The opening of the diet ends. (Oscar for the best special effects: Kestenbetsa.)

Then, uncoupling, and I head for the darkness. The light is in me, but the darkness invades me for the rest of the night. Cleanse, leave behind, reject, run through, Lord (hey, it's appropriate)! And I who thought he was a good guy, here I am plunged into my deaf impulses, my spiritual charnel, professional egoism, my lack of generosity, my anger, my doubt. The smell of sulfur invades me, smell of the Last Judgment. I am at one and the same time the accused, the judge, and . . . the executioner.

Great pain throughout the body. The *Falcon* plummets in flames toward the Death Star, but my mind remains cold and concentrated.

A big night.

I remember having heard Guillermo and Ricardo at that point speaking in Shipibo and laughing. I heard my name and understood a few words. They were having a good laugh because they had sent me very far.

I laughed all alone. In my turn it was a good big jugful, as they would say there.

Then Ricardo came to sing *Sua sua vainquin* (Clean, clean) to me for twenty minutes.

The visions were dark.

After this flash of light, I think of God, "Who are you?"

Ricardo sings for me, strongly.

All of a sudden I am struck by a powerful and terrible fact. And instead of being shaken, I have the impression of suddenly being seated in a meadowlike clearing. I am staggered by my revelation. Ricardo's singing seems far away, and yet he is only a few inches from my head, very loudly singing the song *Mawa yoshins* (Chase away the spirits of the dead). His words are sulfurous again and again. And there I am sitting in my field of green grass, my heart in sweetness, observing my revelation.

I lack faith.

That's my problem.

Faith.

I lack faith.

I have faith in the universe, but the universe is too vast. There is no focal point or direction on which to concentrate.

The song ends.

I'm still reeling from what I've just discovered. I have faith in this medicine, I have faith in the universe, but this is not *faith itself.*

Faith is turned toward the Creator of the universe, *Ibo Riosqui,* in Shipibo. Faith connects you to a certain quality of love that I have not yet explored. Faith is not a concept.

Guillermo has never spoken to me about this. I have been connected to spirits of the medicina, I've visited a good many spiritual worlds—human, nonhuman, terrestrial, extraterrestrial, infernal, celestial . . .

Everything falls into place as I remember his words, "Each one has his own path." He never spoke to me about it because it was up to me to discover it.

Today he establishes the connection.

The night goes on. Guillermo sings his last song. Soothed, I fall asleep.

I awaken in the soft dawn light. Most of the participants are still sleeping. Time for the toilet ritual. Swaying, it takes me ten minutes to make it to the *baños.*

Seated on the toilet bowl, I relax my guts and my anus pours out a fluid, regular stream. I have no pain whatsoever and the act relieves me, but I think it's lasting a bit too long.

I interrupt it to take a look. The bowl is full. Lord, I've produced at least two quarts of diarrhea. I flush and start over. Away we go—major cleansing in complete ease.

I almost regret not having a book it lasts so long. I drive out that thought, because I would be unable to read—I'm still intoxicated. A good *Fluide glacial** perhaps? I laugh to myself. Watch out! The intoxication is still there . . . Let's keep it together.

Off we go, it's time to slip this block of thinking meat between the sheets. Nauseous, I go off to bed.

I LACK FAITH

Fifth Day, or Sixth . . . Who Can Tell?

I wake up in full intoxication and full visions around eight o'clock.

The visions are new and incredible—fields of light, cities of light such as I'd never seen before. White light. I think, "Ibo Riosqui," as if I was afraid to say God.

Then a short sleep of about half an hour, and finally I get up feeling fine. I take off to see Guillermo for our daily conversation.

I say, *"Ayer, tu me has connectado con la luz de Ibo Riosqui."* (Yesterday, you connected me to the light of Ibo Riosqui.)

He replies, *"Sí."*

I say, *"Yo falta de fé."* (I lack faith.)

He replies, *"Sí."*

Someone calls him; he moves away.

In Shipibo, *faith* comes out as *Akon kushi shinan*, literally, the good and great force of the senses.

I like this definition: that which maintains us; the great force of the senses; to remain connected to a feeling that is far-reaching, vibrant, emanating from the interior—the feeling of love.

This is difficult when the intoxication is very strong. This goal allows the being to be supported in the most difficult moments, to

---

Fluide glacial is a monthly French comics magazine.

reestablish feeling, to channel it through the five senses and move it through the heart—perhaps the famous sixth sense?

Magnetic north for the ayahuasqueros.

The great and good force of the five senses. Faith in love as a higher force.

I'm a little shaken. Five nights in a row now and not short ones! The cool me and the freaked me will decide later if we're going to drink tonight. Then I say to myself, no, in the end I've seen worse, I'm not trembling. I lack faith. It makes sense—I believe only in what I encounter and, even then, it has to happen twice or more. I'm hardheaded.

For a change, I'm going to do nothing today. I am questioning my lack of faith and taking notes on the day before.

Pulling me out of my thoughts, Guillermo comes toward me and announces, "This evening, we're going to drink outdoors." The cool me takes the upper hand, "Outside, in the jungle under the starry sky. Great! Is it a special preparation?" "No, no, normal," he replies. I think, "Hey, we're on vacation!"

It's sunny. I jump on my bike and go to see Bastien, who lives a few miles from there. He was one of the "victims" of *D'autres mondes,* a young Belgian who saw the movie on TV and said it was for him. Once at the center, he underwent detox from his minor addictions, then the diets, great encounters in the invisible world, and shortly after, apprenticeship. It was hard for him.

He didn't speak Spanish, and I acted as translator. Guillermo was uneasy. He was thinking about Bastien, his life in Belgium living with his parents. Bastien was twenty-two. Indirectly, I tried to tell him he should go home and that he could always come back. Clearly, I felt somewhat responsible. Even though my film has sent many people to the jungle, they all came back. Return home Bastien finally did, except that it was brief; he worked flat out, earned money, and came back as quickly as he could. I found him at that time to be a bit confused, not unlike how I was myself a few years before. In short, everyone really liked him, but nobody thought he'd be able to make his life here, or even that that would be good for him. Ayahuasca is a difficult school; living with the Shipibo people requires its own apprenticeship. The poor fellow continued the teaching, built his house (I must confess that at that point I was bowled over), made his botanical garden, constructed a store to sell handicrafts from the communities, and got engaged to Vanessa, Guillermo's daughter. He married her; a son was born. Bastien's parents came from Belgium for the marriage. It's certainly not easy for Bastien some days. But he's found his place here, and he's a happy man. So it's a real pleasure to go and see them.

The store and the house are still in the process of being enlarged. Bastien works hard. We take time to talk about the life here, projects, and of course the medicina and the center.

He doesn't look at things the same way. Today he is settled, clear, and peaceful. He's really landed. When I see him as a carpenter building his house, it's more than a metaphor.

Now it's my turn to see *his* film—the film of his marriage.

"Bastien, do you remember the first time you saw Vanessa? It was in another film!" (In *D'autres mondes* she is the young fourteen-year-old daughter whose birthday they are celebrating.) There is laughter and giddiness. "Do you remember who you were before? And the encounter with the vine? What madness! What a trip!"

Memories, memories.

BLUEBERRY MADNESS (PART ONE)

I returned from my first trip to Peru and left again for Mexico to reconnoiter for my film *Blueberry*. We were going to travel around the north of the country searching for shooting locations.

Two years before, I had been in Mexico to shoot an ad. I found film crews locally—experienced and very pleasant people. The beauty of the countryside captivated me to such an extent that I thought that this would be the perfect place to film *Blueberry*, a feature film project. Together with Tetsuo Nagata, my operations director, we set off to search for locations in the state of Durango.

This second trip to Mexico was one of the most mind-boggling ever experienced by the totally irrational creature that I was then. If today I am just as full of irrationality, it's an irrationality that is based on my rationality (of course, this is just my own point of view) and with an equilibrium that simply allows me to live more peacefully. At that time peaceful I certainly was not. I was enlightened—with Guillermo and with the *madre* ayahuasca, of which I had drunk jugsful. I had become a *hijo* of the vine, a child of the stars. In short, I was blasted.

So here we were back in Mexico. The scenario wasn't quite finished, but it was far enough along to justify the first serious searches for sites and to establish a preliminary budget. We had two weeks available. The plan was to begin with the states of Torréon, Chihuahua, Coahila, and Zacatécas, ending up with Durango, with which I was already familiar.

There were five of us—Matéo, my childhood friend who was living in Mexico and who had looked for locations before; Michel Barthélémy, my chief set designer; Ariel Zeitoun, my producer; and Philippe, the production director.

Ariel and I go back a long way. When I was coming back from my first search for film locations with the Huichols* a few months before, I had hit him with a tasteless joke. I met him at the door wearing an Indian jacket and two necklaces around my neck. I threw open my arms saying, "Brother, I have seen the light."

ARIEL: (tense laugh) Ha ha ha?

He looks crestfallen. A brief silence. I take off my jacket and necklaces.

JAN: Sorry Ariel, I was just fooling around.

I tell him then that the trip had been fascinating and that I had to return to the Amazon. The goal of my research would be meetings with the shamans; there will be meetings with shamans in *Blueberry*.

He had just been beginning to relax but now tenses up again a little.

Ariel is an intuitive, and his intuition is pretty accurate. From the beginning he felt that all these adventures were going to knock me for a loop at some point, and he was worried about me.

I came back from my trip to Peru two months later. My head was messed up, or finally right where it should be.

Once again Ariel came back to see me, and this time I didn't greet him with necklaces of flowers. I took him in my arms, and, breaking into an expansive smile, I announced that I had come into contact with the mystery and that my adventure had greatly surpassed anything I could ever have imagined. While I was expounding, carried away, eyes damp, on the fraternity of all humanity, I explained that I had gone beyond the mirror of reality and that cinema had become anecdotal in the face of phenomena of such breadth.

---

*The Huichols are an indigenous people of Mexico who live throughout the Sierra Madre mountain area.

The only response I got was his little nervous, repetitive laugh.

I think that he was wondering whether I was putting him on once again or if his worst nightmare was becoming a reality. Joyfully, I shared with him my decision to take a sabbatical year off to travel around the world. I explained that cinema had been my life for ten years and that now it was time to devote myself to something else. We would do a film with the Shipibo, but it would be after a few years. Then he saw that I wasn't joking. I clinched it by saying, "Don't worry about it at all, Ariel, you'll come with me and you'll see for yourself."

Afterward he had the difficult task of announcing this news to his associate Thomas Langmann. A memorable dinner with him was organized. It confirmed what the two of them already suspected: after a costly year of development, their director blithely tells them that he has decided, for a time, to leave the world of cinema.

I learned afterward that they had spent a few sleepless nights. And the news very quickly got transformed into rumors inside the small world of Parisian cinema:

"Kounen has gone to live with the Indians; he no longer wants to make movies!"

"Really?"

"Yes, really. He's even made himself a home there . . . with several women!" (Hard-core gossip.)

"Really?"

"Yeeeeeeees! And he's drugging himself with them in their ritual magic!" (That's one way of looking at it.)

"Oooooh my! Now isn't that really something!"

One night a few weeks later, a new quantum realization springs up: because it was *Blueberry* that had sent me down there, this would be the film, in turn, that would be the vehicle for this encounter.

Don't let this business drop.

I take off to see Moebius* and tell him in detail of my experiences

---

*Moebius is a pseudonym used by Jean Giraud, a French comics artist known for, among other things, creation of a comic series set in the American Old West titled *Blueberry*.

with the Indians. His eyes shine. I tell him it has to be *Blueberry* that brings in this dimension—the heart of the film will be visionary. He validates that with a laugh that is both airy and cavernous at the same time. An aboriginal laugh whose full significance would be revealed only some years later.* All of a sudden I remember Ariel and the adventure begins again. Ayahuasca isn't going to be the end of this filmmaker yet.

Before hunting for locations, I shoot down once again to the Amazon for a couple of weeks to see Guillermo. I take a camera. Once back, all is going well for the producers—I mean the film is going ahead. Without knowing it, by going there I had launched a new film in parallel: *D'autres mondes*. The producers didn't know that they had begun its production either.

So that's how the project started up.

I'm taking advantage of this moment here to offer my apologies to my colleagues and friends for the trouble I put them to.

---

*At the time *Blueberry* came out in theaters, we were on a promotional tour with Jean Giraud and a journalist asked him details on a script project relating to *Blueberry* that he had written some years before. The final scene placed the character Mike Blueberry at the center of a shamanic battle between a priest and the soul of a shaman who was inhabiting Blueberry's body. I was really surprised as I listened to Jean describing it—it was very close to the final scene of the film, and this was the first time he had spoken about it. A thought came to me: "I must have picked up his dream." Then I understood his enigmatic laugh . . . Each culture has its shamans!

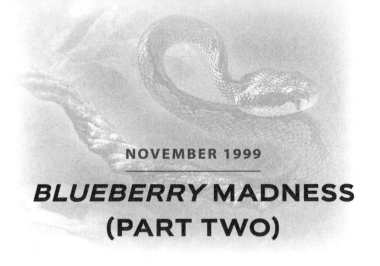

BLUEBERRY MADNESS
(PART TWO)

So, we're traveling through the north of Mexico. The series of great plains in the state of Chihuahua is broken up by rectilinear lines of asphalt where the utility poles are sometimes bent for a few hundred yards, a sign of the recent landing of a small plane belonging to drug traffickers. We study the landscape.

A shout from me or an interested expression on the face of Michel Bartélémy, the head set designer, brings the vehicle to an immediate stop. Photos are taken that might lead to a possible filming location. But on that particular occasion the stop was the starting point of the first serious incident.

A small voice, not connected in any way to the film director, told me to go looking. Looking . . . but for what?

While the team was taking photos, I began charging around on the pampas. No one was bothered by that—my enthusiasm often produced this kind of behavior. I let my instinct take over, and without questioning it I began walking around. I felt like a puppet being controlled by invisible threads. After climbing up a little hill, I stopped in front of a little cactus stuck in the ground. Looking at it hard, I heard a little voice say to me, "Take me."

I comply.

Back in the jalopy, I get in the front and place the cactus on the dashboard.

The car continues on, and my eyes are once again riveted on the cactus. "Eat me," is what the voice of the little cactus seems to be saying inside my mind. I'm not taken in; this cactus is not peyote. I took peyote when I was with the Huichols a few months before. This new friend has plenty of spines; he looks nice, but what if he's poisonous? I chase away these crazy thoughts so I can talk about the film with my colleagues. Then, when I come back to him, having forgotten about him for a while, the little voice picks up again, "Eat me, eat me, *eat me!*"

So, I have to eat him, but not without first having checked with an Indian that this cactus is edible.

A few hours later, following a road along a river, we slowly drive through a pueblo. It is a place stripped bare, out of the way, poor, made up of little hovels of brick or wood. I catch sight of an Indian grandmother who, using a big spoon, is stirring a pot boiling outside her house. She has a look that is deep and cold—like a colorful woodblock print: the witch and her cauldron. The villagers are watching us. We must look a little disturbing, passing through slowly in our big Dodge with its dark tinted windows.

I was used to Indian pueblos, and I knew there was no danger. But I must admit that for my companions the place was a little like something out of a B movie and would not be a good place to stop. As for me, I saw it only as an opportunity to meet someone who could tell me if the cactus was edible.

JAN: (pointing at the cauldron) We're stopping. I need to go and talk to her.

Complete silence. He's crazy?

JAN: Come on, I'm sure she can also give us some grub. She looks nice.

With that I went perhaps a bit too far, but we were hungry. Michel Barthélémy stifled a laugh.

ARIEL: No, we're not stopping!

JAN: Wait. I have to go and see her . . .

Ariel orders Matéo to keep going. The car moves off quietly, suggesting to me a slow tracking shot of this woman of knowledge. I grumble quietly that I'll come back and see her.

"Okay, okay . . ." We leave the pueblo.

At the end of the afternoon we arrive at the closest town and have a briefing in the hotel lobby. Ariel proposes to push ahead with the traveling on this our last day in the state and to make it to the next town before we sleep. We still had a few canyons to see. I had already seen enough canyons on my first trip to the state of Durango, which was going to be our base camp for the filming. They are magnificent.

JAN: Let's skip the canyons. There are more beautiful ones in Durango! We'll be there tomorrow night, and besides I have to go and see that old Indian woman. I told you a little while ago we had to stop. Now I have to go at night!

Of course, I don't mention that it's because I want to ask if my companion, this mysterious cactus, is edible. This was the last straw. Generally, when Ariel gets upset there is a warning in his nervous laughter. Up to then I had always looked for the signs and acted accordingly. But this time it was over the top. I must say I didn't handle the beginning very well. In the hotel lobby, the whole team turned and looked at us as Ariel grabbed me by the collar of my jacket.

ARIEL: Jan! You're stopping this right now! It's impossible! You hear me? The answer is no!

We were all surprised.

(Note: I'm taking advantage of this occasion today to offer him my apologies. Ariel really supported me all through this adventure. We still share projects and have a real friendship to this day. I hope, Ariel, that you're going to laugh reading these lines. Making the film was an even crazier adventure. Perhaps I'll write a second book!)

JAN: (softly) Calm down, Ariel. I'm sorry, but I really think it's the best solution! You'll see, all the canyons we're looking for are there in Durango. Trust me, I've been there. It'll be easier logistically.

I drag Matéo toward the car. In fact, I just walk out and leave them standing in the hotel lobby. Bartélémy's eyes are squished up; he's laughing to himself.*

Ariel's look takes me on a big flashback to the time he saw me welcoming him with my Huichol necklaces; "The nightmare isn't over." Philippe, the production director, looks alarmed. He's saying to himself that perhaps this film project (or its producer) is too strange for him. In fact, he does back out.

Matéo then drives me to see the old Indian woman in the pueblo. During the drive, he tells me that I had gone a bit too far, and he tries to persuade me to go back—it's a waste of time. We arrive at the pueblo. Night has fallen. There are no streetlights. The countryside looks completely different, but we do manage to find the house. The high-beam lights of the Dodge illuminate it. I go and knock on the door, and the *mamita* finally opens the door.

My Spanish is really bad.

JAN: (showing her the cactus) *Holá. ¿Qué tal? ¿Disculpe, sabes que es eso?* (Do you know what this is?)

She looks at the cactus.

JAN: *¿Puedes comer eso? ¿Planta sacrada? ¿Este es como el peyote?* (Can you eat this? Is it a sacred plant? Like peyote?)

She examines me closely for a second and then replies:

INDIAN WOMAN: *Sí, este es el peyote de los Tarahumaras.* (Yes, it's the peyote of the Tarahumaras.)

Done! I thank her and tell her that I'm going to go and eat it on the riverbank. In fact, at the end of the road we found a magic spot, enclosed by two gigantic canyons. A little beach surrounded by shrubs had seemed to me to be the perfect place to call down the sacred.

---

*When a messy situation shows up, Michel always seems to be laughing to himself. His device works pretty well—something I've often been able to observe in the course of various films that we were able to make together.

Cautiously, the old lady responds that it's a good place for that. On the spot I invite her to come and eat the cactus with me. She says she'll think about it for a minute but goes back in her house and closes the shutters. I conclude that she doesn't want to join me. Just another *gringo loco*!

So we'll go alone.

Half an hour later we arrive at the end of the bumpy road. In the car lights, at the center of the little beach, I see that a fire has been laid.

Naturally, I think of an invitation. A mystical breeze whispers to me that this fire has been laid just for me. So I light it and prepare to eat the little cactus.

I lay out in front of me various objects that I had collected in the first week of location hunting, spread out my Shipibo fabric, cut up the cactus, and eat one-third of it.

(Note: In rereading this, I tell myself I was a bit wacko to have lit this fire. I didn't know who had laid it, and the area was full of drug traffickers. It could have turned out badly for me and my buddy cactus if they had showed up.)

Matéo is not far away.

The mescaline in the cactus has a bit of an effect. I plunge into meditation—no visions, just thoughts about the film, feeling the river, a moment of peace.

Two hours later, Matéo comes to see me saying that it is perhaps time to go back—the others are going to be worried about us.

We leave. Alas, very quickly the old Dodge gets stuck, very badly stuck. It must be about 11:00 p.m. We are a half-hour drive from the closest dwelling. Matéo is stunned. He thinks of "Ariel the thunderbolt." I reassure him: what can you do? It's not serious; we'll go and look for a tow truck when it gets light. It's not a big deal. Matéo sees that he's not going to get any help from me. Besides, I quickly leave him and climb up to a little desert plateau where I stretch out and look at the sky. In the desert silence I hear the distant rustling of water. The vault of the heavens is sublime, the air warm and soft.

My friendly cactus is with me.

I breathe softly.

I have the impression I'm floating on the star Earth.

A vessel moving through the cosmos.

I feel the hill, its soft, warm energy that I'm stretched out on. I have the impression that the stars are contemplating themselves through my eyes as mirrors. A fairly long vertigo of well-being, everything is living, everything is unified—the stars, the wind, the earth, the animals, like a speck of fact in total chaos. A few tears later, slowly, gently, I fall asleep. Oscar for the most beautiful falling asleep of my life.

EARLY MORNING

Matéo leaves to look for a tow truck and the team. I'm thirsty. A car shows up followed by a tow truck. They came looking for me. I climb into the vehicle and offer brief excuses. No one talks about our misadventure. Silence in the car as it heads to the airport. Except for me, everybody is a bit tense, and Ariel has dark circles under his eyes. We take the plane to Durango. The other piece of the cactus is rolled up in a tissue and is sleeping peacefully at the bottom of my suitcase.

THE RETURN OF THE SIERRA CACTUS

LOCATION HUNTING MISSION

During the first days—work, work, work. We left to see the locations I had found two years before with Chicho, our local location hunter who raised horses, loved the area, and knew it well. Together as a team we investigate the locations. Most of them are in the film. Within two days we saw the core of what we were missing: canyons, deserts, sierra. Ariel is in heaven. Finally things are going well!

We drive; nightfall is near. We enter a last canyon. We have to hurry—the sun will soon be down. The first incident is not slow in happening, and this time it's no accident I find myself here. We are driving through a strange place—a stretch of hard sand, very flat and covered with a multitude of tiny little pebbles. It could be one of Moebius's drawings for his album *Arzack,* another of his famous comics. In the middle is the road, and on each side about 100 yards away are the walls of a canyon that is not very deep.

Once in a while there is a tree.

Very strange, but it is not for our film. Time to turn around. We stop for a few moments to go and see a grotto, the last hope for a possible shooting location.

In fact, to our disappointment, we find that the grotto is used to house a rough chapel. After a brief prayer, we turn back. The car won't start. I take advantage of it to return to the chapel. It's dark now. I place myself in front of the Virgin, the Mother. I meditate—not to ask her to get the car going but because I've always had a good connection with her. I focus my heart on the mystery. The energy is strong. Deep dive. A half hour later I emerge. I hear the motor, which has just begun to turn over. I return to the others; we leave.

At the hotel, I have a restorative night's sleep. After a good breakfast I go back to my room. I stretch out on the bed and let myself float. Since the grotto, I have slowed down—in a soft torpor. On the bed I stretch my arms straight out to each side, focus my eyes on the ceiling, then close them gently.

Christ.

The word comes, with sweetness.

Christ.

Brrring!

The phone rings.

"Hello?" It's not Christ, it's Ariel. They're waiting for me downstairs; I'm late. And I was in imaginal Judea. I gather my things. At the bottom of my suitcase I fish out the cactus that was half nibbled away at the river and I put it in my backpack. Note: contrary to appearances, I hadn't touched it since the river almost a week earlier.

They're all waiting for me at the car; we take off. The day goes by without any major discoveries; the search for locations will soon be over.

At the end of the afternoon we are in the last canyon for today. Boxed in, wild in the middle, is a small stream. We're walking. I see a black snake that moves quickly on the pebbles a few yards away from me. I watch him and instinctively I begin to breathe out a serpent melody. Ssss sss sss . . .

I stop in my tracks. The snake turns and heads straight for me.

Suddenly a shower of rocks falls on him. I shout to stop, don't kill him. "That's a deadly snake," replies Chicho, who must have thought: "He's crazy, this *gringo director*."

I make my decision. I'm going to sleep in the canyon tonight. I don't quite know why, but the impulse is strong and clear. The hardest part will be telling Ariel. It turns out that it isn't hard. "You're sure?" "Yes." He turns to Chicho. Jan's a cowboy. The idea seems ridiculous to him but not dangerous. No storms in sight. Chicho lends me a blanket. We agree to rendezvous the next morning at 8:00 a.m. They leave. I am alone.

The sun goes down.

Why am I staying behind?

In fact, it's simple. At thirty-five, I've never spent a night alone in nature. I'm not talking about sleeping in the tent with buddies on the GR20.*

I'm talking about being *alone.*

Can I spend the night in the land I sprang from? Can the little mouse spend a night outside its golden cage, in the field? I have a box of matches, a bottle of water, a blanket, my cock, and my cactus. I gather some wood, climb on a big rock in the river, and build a fire. Then I begin my evening meal. Sour and floury. I thank the cactus and swallow the last mouthful.

I open my senses.

I feel nature all around me.

Instinctively, I stare at the fire.

I close my eyes. After more than half an hour, the rush of a long vision rises up in me.

The cactus is at the center of my vision. I connect with him. All his needles leave him like missiles.

He is naked.

I feel pinpricks on my body. As if, from outside, his little spines were being inserted into me.

I open my eyes.

Shit, he's poisonous!

I center myself. I feel the intoxication of the mescaline, which is rather soft.

Don't panic! Yes, I know you're alone and far away from everything. But you've eaten this cactus before; this time the dose is double. It has to be a bit toxic, that's all—nothing serious.

The pinpricks continue.

---

*[The GR20 is a 112-mile footpath that crosses the Mediterranean island of Corsica, described by the outdoor writer Paddy Dillon in his book *GR20: Corsica—The High-Level Route* as "one of the top trails of the world." —*Trans.*]

I center myself. I dissolve into the pinpricks, watch my body, relax it. It's up to me to get through this.

If there's a bit of poison, it will pass; I remain connected to the cactus and to the place I'm in.

I meditate. I get through it. The pinpricks are not as strong and more spaced out. I regain my footing. I don't sleep. I'm sitting with the blanket wrapped around me. A coyote begins to howl, followed by another, and then another. I hear about ten of them from each side of the canyon. They're far away, and the echo tells me that some are high up and others lower down.

It goes on and on.

I don't think, "They're greeting me."

I think, "Do they like nice tender gringo meat à la mescaline?"

I tell myself all I need to do is to put more wood on the fire.

I begin to listen to them. I place my attention on the intonation of their voices. A huge experience.

I feel I'm wolf.

No, rest assured, I didn't take my turn at howling. Well, I confess I almost did, but the memory of the episode with the snake calmed me down right away. "Hey bro, what if you did howl and if they all came toward you with their shiny eyes and their sharp teeth?"

Listening to them even at a distance was a strong experience. Not in the style of, "You see, Marie-Chantal, how beautiful it is—the cries of all these wild beasts in the canyon!" No, more in another style, "My heart was beating like a Navajo drum—slow and powerful. I was savoring the why of my being there. Their cries set the animal part of me vibrating."

I savored every minute of that night right up to sunrise.

Yesterday I was with the Virgin, this morning with Christ, and tonight with the wolves.

I folded up my things and walked for half an hour. I left the canyon a little ahead of time. The plain stretched away in front of me. In the middle of it, a trail of dust signaled the approach of Chicho's Dodge. Perfect sync.

■ ■ ■

We pick up the others at the hotel. All is well. The last location visit is an old abandoned mining town, a possible set for our town of Palomito. We arrive at the place. The setting is superb. I was familiar with the place, and I was delighted that Michel liked it. I'm in the middle of talking with Ariel when the cactus makes a comeback.

JAN: Ai!

ARIEL: What?

JAN: No, no, it's nothing. I didn't say anything.

Ouch! The cactus has returned—in spades. It really hurts.

What do I do? Confess everything and run to the emergency room? An extreme measure that would definitely have me lose all credibility. My creative side quickly fabricates a scene that would go something like this:

"Ariel, I have to tell you . . . You remember the cactus that I picked up? Good. I went to see the old Indian woman and she told me I could eat it. So I did last evening, but now I think I've been poisoned because I hurt all over—here and here and here.

"Please, Ariel, can you take me to the nearest hospital?"

Undoubtedly he begins to laugh nervously.

Then two possible scenarios unfold.

The first: he strangles me (not likely).

The second: concerned and caring, he takes me to a hospital (more likely), then he stuffs me on a plane and good-bye film (extremely likely—I'd do the same in his place).

So, I tighten my ass, I remain aware of the needles, reconnect myself to the little cactus, tell him that he needs to leave me alone now and that this film is something I'm doing for the good of plants and I'm not going to get a second chance at it.

The cactus is nice. He leaves me alone ten minutes later.

We return to Paris with all the locations set, the film has been launched, it will be shot . . . three years later.

End of the adventures of the sierra cactus.

Stay tuned for the collapse of the Manhattan towers.

NAUSEA UNDER THE STARS

OUTSIDE UNDER THE STARS, SIXTH NIGHT

The anticipated "holiday paradise" night under the stars. I'll be blunt; it was a difficult night. Holidays? That'll be for some other time.

Return to the world of ayahuasca. The strolling around with spirits is gone and done with. Instead there is pain in the body; fear comes back. Cleansing. Very dark visions. I align my intoxication by singing inside; afterward the healers help me. I feel dirty, fragmented. My thoughts begin looping a little, my faith having wandered off somewhere in the cosmos. I am a bit sad to find myself here. I catch myself up with the thought, "What did you think, my big fellow—that this state would never come back? Come on, come on. Remember, you're working—that's all. Get to work! Let this state move through you; don't hold on to it."

In the body, the pain is strong—it tears me out of the world of visions. I don't get upset, and I have my mind repeat the refrain— "Medicina, penetrate my body." I come back and quiet down.

All that lasted a few hours.

Now I relax, smoke tobacco, then turn my gaze upward.

The Milky Way has risen. The town is far away; there are no lights. The spectacle is unbroken. I close my eyes a little to allow the visions to appear with the stars as a background.

Through the visions I see the sky, the universe.

Metaphysical vertigo.

The universe of my emotions is projected on the infinity of space. I savor this touching moment and the vision changes. My inner world is illuminated and happy for an instant to reflect on the infinity of the cosmos—a single image for a double vertigo. Then, too much emotion and thought crowds in. I relinquish this beautiful state.

I'm doing better but still a bit out of sorts. My head hurts. Hmm. Am I finally reaching the limits of my fatigue? I fall asleep heavily. And I'm awakened by the dew. I drag my carcass to bed.

THE NEXT DAY

Waking up in full intoxication, I feel that my body has calmed down; something became unblocked during sleep. Maybe it's just that I rested well. It's late—my first sleep in.

Let the day begin. I'm hungry. I have to get moving. After a big breakfast I head for Luz Kósmika. It's time to go and chat with the long-term dieters.

There are not many apprentices: two Russians, two Norwegians, Virginia (the "merged with the jungle" woman with whom I had done the ceremony), and three Frenchmen—Teddy, Yann, and Benoît, all young, in their twenty and thirties. I had seen Teddy at the center a few years before; this time he's here for a year. Benoît is also staying for a year and Yann for six months. I spend most of my time with the three of them.

The diets are very strong. As soon as I come near them, I feel the energy of their diet—a great wave—powerful, a great, sensitive wave.

I move my body gently. Instinctively I lower my voice. I shift to their rhythm. I open my perceptions—it's a question of listening and sensing. I have admiration for all of them. Benoît, for example, whom I met in Paris after a brief trip, decided to come here. We had run into each other at Amma's, during her annual visit near Paris.* He had driven me home. At three in the morning, in the car and outside my front door we had a long talk. As I watched him leave I was a little worried about him.

---

*Amma is widely regarded as one of India's foremost spiritual leaders. Her full name is Mata Amritanandamayi.

Today, after eight months of diet in the jungle, he's not the same. He is much more collected, supersensitive. They all tell me about their lives as dieters. Spirits are close to them all the time; sometimes it's terrifying and always exhausting. There is also the solitude and isolation in their individual cabins in the heart of the jungle.

At night, when the candle goes out, the boundary disappears. The reflection of the moonlight on the trees is a new boundary, and that's where they are, alone in their silence and their visions.

I see them as a band of explorers of consciousness.

I see them pursuing their journey. I think going home is going to be difficult. They tell me that themselves. Teddy says, "I can't imagine how I could sleep without the noise of the jungle, without this life . . ."

They do one ceremony a week, but Guillermo doesn't often come and sing for them and they feel a little abandoned. I try to reassure them. That's how it is with apprenticeship. The teaching is difficult. "Meaning" has to come from the depths of oneself. The maestro leaves us to simmer. We have to find certain doorways on our own. He is there to guide us at critical moments. When the door is too heavy and when we have been knocking on it all night long, finally he comes to show the way. We have to find out how to align ourselves without him. I tell them about my own falls along the way.

I dive into my memories.

MYSTIC TERROR

MAY, CEREMONY

This evening I don't feel like drinking. I'm dragging my feet as I enter the maloca. I arrived at Pucallpa a few ceremonies earlier, less than ten of them ago. It's always the same thing. I look forward to each of my trips there. I look forward to this specific moment, the greatest adventure I've ever been able to experience, and yet, as soon as this adventure happens, fear enters into the dance. Fear mounts from night to night, in step with new invisible encounters. It turns into terror the last few days, and on the last night I end up making my way through it. This is my fourth trip in less than a year. I know the process—I've learned to work with it. I just have to follow it right to the end; so each evening I drink the dose that is offered me even if it's big. I need to keep this objective in my line of sight and in doing so implant in myself confidence in Guillermo's work. Drinking the whole glass means overcoming the shadow of fear that is trying to get hold of me every day.

This evening it's hard. The ceremony is getting closer and my belly is as tense as a block of wood; I can't manage to relax it and I'm shaking. I'm having a lot of trouble keeping the fear at a distance . . . I'm afraid.

I'm intoxicated as I walk into the maloca. I sit down. Guillermo is not there. His mother, Maria, and the other healer are waiting. Suddenly, I calm down; I let myself be grabbed by the vertigo. You need to understand that for me the ceremonies extend into the day. The process is going through an accelerating phase. Now the filling and emptying of my lungs is slowing down. Sometimes the quiet waves of the breathing create undulations in the body. The effect of the intoxication increases slowly. In spite of the well-being, a little anxiety springs up: "I haven't drunk yet and I'm already *mareado* (dizzy) . . ."

I relax even more, letting that thought hit the road along with its anguished little sisters. Now, each time that I'm about to take the vine, my body readies itself a few hours before. I'm used to that, but this time it's stronger.

The relaxation tapers off all of a sudden. Guillermo enters the maloca. He sits down to chat, laughing with the others. This evening he's laid back. His eyes are lively. He yawns as he is pouring a glass of ayahuasca, then in silence he bows his head toward the glass and remains motionless.

My intoxication comes back immediately.

A thought emerges: "If I felt the intoxication that strongly, it's because he's been working on me at a distance. He's showing me that now." This isn't a demonstration of power, but just a sign of our well-established connection. He was controlling the situation, and the trip began well ahead of the ceremony. He tells me that in the course of the ceremony we're going to take another teaching plant, renaco (*Ficus schultesii*), which he'll show me the next day.

I drink and then sit down, surprised and a little nervous about this new plan. He turns out the light—an old circular neon bulb that the insects constantly crash into. A metaphor comes to me: "I too want to go toward the light, but watch out—approach gently my little ayahuasquero mosquito. Otherwise, zap!"

BLACK

I feel my intoxication mount without visions.

My body begins to vibrate more and more. I secretly hope that he will begin to sing. A half hour passes this way in silence, then he calls me. It's the moment. I am very intoxicated, trembling. The visions come and it's necessary to drink again?

The preparation is translucent, and there's at least a half a pint of it. The curanderos each drink in their turn, as well as the others who are present.

Then everything happens very fast.

In a flash, reality is totally changed. Different spirits that I have never seen before surround me. Cries and moans of terror assail my psyche, but they are stillborn, assassinated by my mind, which has been vitrified by what is in the process of taking place.

The most eloquent image would be the "mystical science fiction" of a Tex Avery.* I am as if suspended in a space between two thoughts.

I am aware of the spirits in their own space. They are entirely covered with designs that are moving. They remind me of the patterns of powwow dancers or of certain costumes of shamans from the Urals. Unbelievably beautiful and dazzling, the designs move animatedly on their eyeless faces. They seem like sophisticated puppets, marionettes assembled by a genius of celestial mechanics.

They are seated in a room. One of them approaches me. He leans over my head in absolute silence. I open my eyes—he is there. Sounds gather together and a cone of designs descends from his mouth toward the top of my head. Slowly, it moves into me. On this luminous cone a new and strange vision is drawn and comes toward me. Crocodiles in lively colors. Volume has disappeared—these are living prints redrawn in two dimensions. Incredibly chiseled, they interlay over each other.

I think for a moment of Escher's impossible drawings.

The word *death* tries to emerge in my inner space, but a series of little spasms push it away.

The crocodiles descend into me. I let them. I return to an awareness of my body.

Slowly, a melody comes in. The designs come bouncing back onto the background of my guts and from their slow movement a melody springs up, an ícaro.

I clench my teeth so as not to sing.

Then, all of a sudden, I am brought back to the perception of the upper part of my body by the liquid that is rising at top speed from my stomach toward my mouth.

---

*Frederick "Tex" Avery was an American cartoonist famous for producing animated cartoons beginning in the 1930s and creating such well-known characters as Bugs Bunny and Daffy Duck.

A thunderstruck return.

I have just time to open my mouth, and I vomit.

Later, Michel, one of my "companions of the bucket" told me I had vomited just a few minutes after having drunk, whereas I had the feeling that my encounter had lasted a lifetime.

Thought inscribes us in time.

With thought gone, time expands infinitely.

Then, freed from the liquid, I no longer control anything. Still in silence, as if freed, I fly off into the spirit world.

An anaconda slithers through a series of gelatinous cavities—the setting is my brain, and the feeling is ecstatic. He starts rattling while a strong feeling of power grows in me.

I seize it with the two hemispheres of my encephalon, and I emit a dull growl. The anaconda takes off, but he has the voice of a predator wolf.

At this precise moment two of the curanderos vomit.

My body flash freezes in profound terror.

It's my fault. My lack of concentration, forgetting myself—we are all in the same vehicle, and I made a bad move. My thoughts began looping.

I grab this blinking thought as soon as it rises up in me.

I go straight into my hell.

The strange conviction grows in me of having torn away all the security barriers.

I open my eyes and center myself so as to stay in the maloca. I'm crouched down like a wild cat with eyes wide open, looking at all my human brothers, trying to keep my thoughts in this world. The uneasiness mounts—I jump on the high-speed train of my guilt. Concentration gone, fear invades me.

Tears rise up. I feel sadness for having acted badly through inattention.

This terrifying loop inexorably unrolls its mastery over my mind. The visions become chaotic.

"My God, what have I done?"

My body trembles; tears flow.

"Center yourself!

"Center yourself!

"Now!

"Fuck! Shit!

"Drop all this mental bullshit!

"Get out of this apocalypse!

"Arrrrrghhhhh."

(That's a summary, of course.)

Guillermo gets up. He positions himself in front of me like the spirit I'd seen earlier. He bends his knees a bit. He seems enormous—an indigenous sumo wrestler. He sings, an inch or so away from my forehead.

Meanwhile in the maloca, the others begin shouting for help. "Jan? Jan?" Er . . . I have to say that before the ceremony I was reassuring them. "Look guys, if there's a problem, call me, I'll help you go and see Guillermo." I confess that I didn't expect to be in this state. In response to their calls, my little finger moved a fraction of an inch toward them. That's all I'm doing this evening to help my friends. One after the other, they call out, "Guillermo? Help!"

He is on me and is singing loudly. A song that is muted, quick, warrior-like. It's a voice that I had never known to come from him. I'm trembling like a chick that has fallen from the nest into icy snow. The song penetrates me deeply. It gives rise to brief, terrifying visions, but mostly it creates shocks in my organs. It unfolds from the meaning. The energy of the song activates new thoughts. My head moves in time with the rhythm of the song. With each movement an inner sweep of control takes place, like a mental armoring. Following the rhythm of his songs, my thoughts go something like this:

"Don't let these negative thoughts take control of your mind!

"The feeling of guilt—look at it with your serpent eyes.

"Don't let yourself be taken.

"Look at it for what it is: negativity.

"It's part of the past.

"You can't change anything.

"You'll only make yourself sick.

"See the mental mechanics of it.

"True or false.

"The only thing you can do is, with your inner eye, watch this feeling, recognize it when it emerges once again. True or false doesn't matter. Recognize it quickly, don't let it start moving.

"Recognize it quickly before it gets too big.

"Kill it in embryo.

"May this journey leave you with this teaching.

"A teaching of vigilance."

My head begins to jerk. It's too strong. I groan.

The song ends. I am even more intoxicated.

Everyone begins moving around in the maloca. The boat is sinking. The other healers begin singing, and Guillermo takes care of each person.

It lasts the whole night through, right until sunrise.

An eight-hour-long storm. Eight hours of madness.

I remained crouched like a cat, driving out thoughts. The visions were unbearable, impulses, fear. Every time, it's the same thing: the higher the trip goes, the more difficult the landing, as if one couldn't take place without the other.

The two sides of man's nature—light and shadow. Knowledge needs to happen in both directions. The medicina. The whole night through I was confronted again and again with the fear of myself. In this sensitive state where we were all connected, it was difficult to find relaxation in the vigilance, especially given the strength of this new preparation.

In the end we all got home safely. Back to the state we all share, to the world we know. Guillermo comes up to me and asks me how it went. The crestfallen survivor's face that I show him makes him burst out laughing, a disarming laugh.

He says to me, "*Bastante fuerte para mí.* (Strong enough for me.) I traveled across the universe." He points at the ceiling of the maloca, then says to me, "In my belly, things were moving around. My guts were wriggling." I smile as I think to myself, "Hell, for me it wasn't just my guts that were wriggling around, it was my whole body and my brain along with it." He looked at me, then mimed a little wriggling, a gently mocking parody of my movements during the night. "I heard you all night long in my head. You were saying (imitating a small child's voice), 'Daddy, Daddy, help me, *ayúdame*.'"

He bursts into a warrior's laugh, which has an immediate thera-peutic effect on me. I laugh; relaxation comes in all at once. I laugh at myself. It's so true and at the same time so good. I needed to relativize what I had just gone through.

Then he goes to lie down.

At dawn, calmed down, I fall asleep. As I wake up, I imagine the curanderos as surfers; the effect stimulated by the teaching plant is their wave, it opens the door to other worlds, it is their support. Last evening was a tsunami, but I was with the Silver Surfer.

I crawl out of my sleeping bag. I drink some tea and nibble a cookie, carefully.

Later I meet up with Guillermo. We're sitting in the garden of his little house in the Yarinacocha quarter, a haphazardly cleared jungle in front of the maloca. He is nonchalantly caressing a shrub with twisted roots. "This is who you met last night." His fingers slide over the plant while his gaze remains on me. Without me having asked him anything, he intones this sentence: "My grandfather always told me, 'Don't grab the energy.'" Then he withdraws and moves away leaving me with my thoughts. I'm surprised. In general our verbal communications—I don't dare say conversations, my Spanish is too rough—are limited to purely material questions. Now his words take on a whole other meaning related to the night I have just experienced.

I remain thoughtful. Bits of the night come back to me; the memories of certain moments mix with what he has just said—with a look, a smile, the tone of voice. The intention in his words, a memory, and the fact that he gives me a message indirectly by using someone else's words to illus-trate an attitude of mine make things move into place in my mind. The whole thing amounts to a richer message, between sensation and words, between attitude and memory, which makes it into something like this:

"Let your thoughts go.

"They are like a stream; if you stop its flow, it's like you're creating a dam. You flood your consciousness.

"Let your thoughts flow with a good feeling.

"The stream expands and becomes a peaceful river."

I set aside my notebook for a moment because while writing I'm getting flashes! I'm not watching my thoughts—I'm possessed by them.

Vertigo.

Practical work.

I spend the day trying to meditate, then I reflect, and in the end I elaborate a bit.

In the world of visions, you will observe the birth of a thought. You will identify the feeling it comes out of, the emotion of which it is an echo, so you can choose—not through thinking, but by listening to your feelings. You will choose to allow or not allow this space to form in you and around you.

Your thoughts must be kept under surveillance, for they are your active link with the invisible world.

If you are peaceful in a quiet joy—it is an expression of simple but deep well-being.

The mind in the heart.

I admit that this is largely on the level of personal interpretation. But don't think that, under the guise of psychomagic, I'm being tricky and that I'm distilling what I think by crediting Guillermo. This is not what he said to me, and it isn't something that emerges from my own reflection alone either.

It's very difficult to explain and to share.

This text is being written with my eyes wide open as to my own subjectivity, and yet it seems to be whispered in my ear by the man and the spirits that are around me.

Over the course of the years, the concordance between Guillermo's attitude and my felt sense leads me to see his work as an education of the sleeping consciousness. He has the keys, coming out of his knowledge. He seems to be aware of my state in a very subtle way. I believe he can recognize not what I'm thinking but the forms, the faces of the thoughts that run through me, the energies and the spirits that swirl around me.

In a less esoteric way, he knows the psychological movements of the human being; he observes them in another light, in an archetypal world, and through an energetic perception of the other person.

Shipibo healers don't talk a lot.

The songs transmit the healing and the teaching.

Rarely have I extracted oral information from Guillermo. If I shared my problems and my reflections with him, he would often reply, *"Gracias para tu información, las respuestas a la noche."* (Thanks for your info; replies during the nighttime.) The responses come in the form of visions.

Every time he conveys a message to me, it's in an indirect form. "Such and such a thing happened to me. Certain curanderos say that . . ." He recounted an experience from when he was young, during his first shamanic journeys, telling me what that experience meant, just when he had me undergo a similar experience the night before without ever making a direct reference to that experience. And this was done simply to reassure me or to enlighten me on the nature of what I had experienced, because I was going down a wrong path in my analysis of it.

He would also use the presence of a group to get a message to me.

I think the crocodiles are making me think today about a ceremony that took place six months ago.

TONIGHT, SOME PEOPLE WILL ENCOUNTER FEAR

The day after the ceremony I'm in bad shape. Usually I'm happy and contented in the early hours of the morning, but this time I'm really not good at all. If I close my eyes, I see my spiderlike shapes getting expelled during the night and getting swallowed back down in the morning. Deep impulses awakened in the night stare straight into my soul. I feel orgiastic desires for raw meat and bestial sex rise up in me—*I* being the same person who the day before was so sensitive I could scarcely get down a few grains of rice and saw myself as a human hummingbird.

Fuck! What's happening? Is this Vibroboy* waking up? What the hell is this mess—I'm a nice boy . . . Aren't I?

No.

In the mind a dull force is resonating.

Upset and a little psychotic, I go to see Guillermo. I let him know what I'm going through so he can understand that I'm really not doing well and that I'm beginning to seriously freak out. "Tonight you need to be a little gentle with me." His reply, full of good-naturedness, is the usual nonchalance that I was telling you about earlier: *"Gracias para la información, vamos a ver a la noche."* (Thanks for the information; we'll see about it tonight.)

Reassured, I tell myself that the info has been passed on. I trust

---

*[*Vibroboy* is a 1994 short film of Kounen's in which a strange statuette starts exerting demonic power over some poor tough guy. —*Trans.*]

him—everything will get resolved during the night. I just have to relax and pay attention to what's happening to me.

The day has allowed me to see another face of the rather terrifying little animal that is also me: a predator, full of impulses. Really deep down in the being, unconditional love undoubtedly exists, but before you get to it you have to dig around in the mud. Anyway, unconditional love has left me; I'm in the gutter of who I am.

In the jungle, during the time of the diets, when night falls it really falls. It literally falls on your shoulders. The energy changes and your body turns to lead. Next, with the ceremony approaching, fear makes its entry. It's only a light discomfort that makes you think, "Um, er, this evening I don't think I should take the vine because I'm not feeling very good." This thought comes up often, and you get used to not stopping there. But this particular night, it turns into terror.

No relaxation is possible, and I am accompanied by the thought, "There's nothing to do except just go ahead and trust; it's just a bad moment you have to get through." Trust in the maestro's knowledge plays an important part. And I had that from the first day on. It had been sorely tested, but it is a refuge.

I sit down to prepare myself. Several Westerners are present—fellow adventurers who wanted to accompany me into the jungle so that they too could have this experience.

My problem this evening has to do with my own survival.

In general, the curandero doesn't make a speech to the group, only short personal conversations during the day. But tonight, surprise! Guillermo addresses himself to everyone, "This evening, some among you are going to encounter *miedo* (fear)." He said, *"Mi-eee-dooo."* Each syllable of the Spanish word for fear stands out very clearly. He pronounces it like the surname of an enemy that you're going to coolly assassinate in the coming hour. As if you are a commando leaving for the assassination of Master Fear.

A great silence floats through the group. Er . . . What is this? An invitation for a bad trip?

A big spasm takes me.

Brrrrrrrr.

The whole body.

The bastard! This announcement is for me! The one who is going to encounter fear is me, and like a good student I've already dived into it. He continues, "Fear must be mastered."

End of the big lecture in two sentences.

I smile a tense smile. My head must look like a street theater actor. The cliché of the uptight guy who wants to look relaxed. I have a raging desire to run far away, really, really far away from all that. "Shit! Why didn't I keep my mouth shut this afternoon?" In fact, the devil kept me simmering and now I'm cooked to perfection.

It's my turn to drink the vine. I'm last. He serves me the normal dose, half a glass, and holds it out to me slowly. My hand reaches out quickly to take it. He stops the movement of his arm and makes eye contact with me gently. No emotion, no tension. He reflects my own confusion back to me. He brings the bottle to the glass and about to pour he says, "¿Un poco más?" (A little more?)

Alert, I instantly review my day: the mounting fear, his attitude leading up to this offer. Immediately, all is crystal clear. "A little more?" already contains the possibility of refusing. But more than that, it's the possibility of going further. It's an invitation—to trust, once again. I master my terror sufficiently: "I trust you, do what seems right." This is my way of saying, "Okay! I'm going along with you, but don't abandon me my friend; I'm in bad shape this evening." He fills the glass with a triple dose. "Jesus, Mary, Joseph . . ." It came out by itself, a saying that my grandmother used in Corsica when, as a child, I would come back at night with my body covered with scrapes and scratches after getting lost in the bramble-infested highlands.

I drink.

The drink is never ending.

Glug, glug, and glug some more.

The bitterness is so strong that my body feels a long spasm starting at my toes and dying out at my cheekbones.

After this artistic spasm, Guillermo looks at me and asks, "You okay?" The bastard, now he's making out that he's worried! Anyway, it's too late, I've drunk it. Grimacing, I hand the glass back to him and murmur a "Yes, yes." Then he addresses the group: "This evening Jan is going to sing for you."

Magical effect.

My fear disappears.

Not only am I going to take the journey with him but now I'm going to set it in motion for the others as well! Suddenly buoyed by this unexpected mission, I am recharged. I settle in, center myself, and prepare to give voice to the song of the serpent. The fear has not left me, but I have a new strength. Before the slightest sound can leave my mouth, Guillermo begins to intone an unusually quick lament that has the effect of immediately launching me into the journey. Ecstasy and fear—the visions are like a stretched canvas that you move across endlessly. Ecstasy? The jeweled crocodiles, barely perceived by the mind, come back and turn into a vile swarm of spiders.

Surrender to the fear. Don't grasp it. Let yourself be traversed by it; in a shiver, reconnect body and mind, making magnificent visions arise, the two sides of the coin. I have never really succeeded yet in translating onto film this passage from one universe to another, so I still have films I need to make. The first part of the voyage from this night is modeled in *D'autres mondes*.

Regardless, I don't budge all night long, not even a little finger. I don't tremble, curled up like an Incan mummy. Dark beings dance around me.

Deep descent into fear.

Icy terror.

The winds of madness.

The mind like a knife blade.

The songs are warriors.

Implacable.

No way out.

Clip precisely the slightest thought that arises.

Move forward.

Stay in touch with the body.

Right in front of me are the faces of my most secret, violent sexual impulses.

Further away are the terrors of childhood.

Very quickly, the two people beside me start vomiting. Guillermo doesn't stop singing. And we gradually begin the return toward the light.

In the early morning I return. My jaws hurt. I didn't unclench my teeth the whole night long. I finally breathe and stretch my legs. I'm good now—relaxed, the mind light and empty, filled with pure cool air. I'm finally okay! A hummingbird covered with the skin of a multicolored serpent. One of my friends comes up to me, "Weren't you supposed to sing for us this evening?" Guillermo leans toward me, and, laughing, I translate the question for him. I already know what he's going to say. And he replies with a big smile, "It's aboriginal humor." I laugh.

The word dances in my mind.

My mind dances in the word.

I've never encountered this simple, ultrasophisticated sense of humor anywhere else—the humor of the curanderos. They kindly made fun of me. But I deserved it. You arrive dying, and all of a sudden you find yourself at the top of the ladder! Human mechanisms! I laugh at his aboriginal humor that shows me what a little animal I am, capable of a sudden, complete turnaround. And it throws back in my face the question: Why do I want to learn?

A panoramic shot of my metaphysical concerns goes up in smoke. It's for the best; I'll come back to it. The mistake was holding on to what I was given to experience by swapping one world for the other. Imagine that I was an aboriginal invited by astronauts to circle around the Earth and who, once back home in his community, thinks to himself, "Because I went around the Earth, that makes me an astronaut."

This evening, I am a poor, trembling little animal; in the morning, the survivor puffs out his chest and thinks that he's a curandero. Interesting. Disturbing.

THE WAGES OF FEAR

My lively beginnings with Guillermo relaxed the dieters. I saw in their eyes that they too had each had their own allotted journey, and we laughed about it. Memories, ayahuasquero anecdotes, intimate moments—they're deep, and I said to myself that I needed to find that again in Paris. They make me think of a jungle version of *Harry Potter and the Sorcerer's Stone*. I tell them I'm going to come and drink with them. Panshin Copé (the curandero name of James Arévalo, one of Guillermo's sons) suggested I do that.

I return to Espíritu before nightfall. I run into Panshin Copé, who bought parts for my bike and wants me to give him a hand with the repairs. We'll do that tomorrow. We decide to meet at 9:00 a.m.

An American has just arrived. He wants to know if he's likely to be robbed at the center. I tell him that he shouldn't leave too much cash lying around on the bedside table, and, as for the rest, it's pretty quiet—more secure than a hotel in town. He's there for only one night and has no lodging. I joke with him: "You can just take your bag into the maloca." Either he's going to have some big thing happen to him, which he has no idea about, or nothing . . . I'm always intrigued by these people who drift through for one or two days. Then I remember that it was like that for me at the beginning.

I run to the kitchen to have an herbal tea and find that everyone is there eating. Surprise: it's 7:30 p.m. They tell me, with a joy tinged with relief, that there's no ceremony tonight. So I eat—a chance for a break. I think that the American is going to have to change his plans.

How good it is to eat in the evening! While I'm savoring the well-being of my satisfied body, I see Ricardo, another healer, who is setting up in the maloca.

Ceremony? Hey . . . I enter. The American has moved in. I go to see Ricardo.

JAN: *¿Ricardo, hay ceremonia?*
(Ricardo, there's a ceremony?)

RICARDO: *Sí.*

JAN: *¿Con Guillermo también?*
(With Guillermo too?)

RICARDO: *Sí.*

JAN: *Yo como, no sé si yo puedo.*
(I've eaten. I don't know if I can.)

RICARDO: *Puedes, yo comí también.*
(Yes, you can. I've eaten too.)

Hell! I'm not going to miss this—a good chance to work with a full stomach, to scrape the bottom; a little training session. I put away my things and come back in an hour. When I come back, there is no sign of Guillermo. Ricardo tells me he's not coming. Immediately I prepare to leave the maloca, then I reconsider. In the end, out of respect for Ricardo, I stay. He passes me the bottle and I pour a small glass for myself and drink it. He comments that it's not very much. I reply that it was only an hour and a half ago that I ate and so my body is still digesting. "Oh. I see. In my case, I ate at five."

The ceremony is good work—the intoxication not too strong, small visions and nausea just behind the lips. I post an ad to the invisible world: Has anyone seen my faith?

"Looking for a faith gone astray, probably in childhood, early on."

A memory comes back. As a child I spoke to God, sometimes to ask him for a moped, but before that to thank him for having me born. Really? Now there's a more serious direction.

Faith gone astray? That's where I'm at when Ricardo does a protection song for me for more than twenty minutes. I hurt, really hurt all through the body. I also see my mental blockages. His song weaves the five senses together—and the sixth (the awareness of the five others in the moment) stabilizes. There are a lot of parasitical thoughts. After the song I tell him what I have seen and felt. He confirms it. He will continue the treatment tomorrow. The American said he didn't have any visions. Ricardo laughs and says to me in a low voice, "But he did; he had them. I saw them, but his mind was not focused and he immediately forgot them!" It happens that way with ayahuasca. Oh yeah, that's rich. Malicious laugh between the two of us. It's early; I'm going to be in bed and asleep before 2:00 a.m.

THE EIGHTH DAY

Spent the day with Marlene, Vincent, and Claude, three terrific people from France who are passing through for a couple of weeks. We go out on the Amazon—a touristy excursion that does us good. They are fine, the beginnings were difficult, but the benefit is beginning to come through; just a few more days and they're going home. Don't want to write more. Rest.

EVENING

After this beautiful excursion on the river, the relaxation brings back the tiredness of the diet. New ceremony. The patients begin vomiting. Every time someone vomits, my intoxication opens a little more. It's always kind of magical, this sense of the collective state when a patient is purging. It's as if the heavy dirigible ship that we are all traveling in and that is having trouble getting off the ground has just dropped a sack of ballast.

Ricardo begins to hum, then strings together two long songs. The visions open, and I descend into the depths of the worlds of the medicina. Visions of crawling insects, cathedrals of millipedes, or other beetles.

Before I had been terrified; I thought I was traveling through hell. Now I recognize one of the therapeutic dimensions: negative energies leaving. As long as the visions are not aggressive, meaning that the archetypes don't throw themselves on you, but instead, slowly, weave an organized form (for example, a carpet of insects moving gently on the organic walls), it means a cleansing or, in my case, a scouring. Pockets of colorful insects open and spill onto the carpet of my visions while my stomach gurgles a not very melodic ícaro.

Still no news about my faith; no one has responded to my ad. My visions have expanded a lot; I'm aware of the visionary space in the room. Ricardo has stopped singing. In the silence I see in front of me a crocodile swimming in the space. He does a loop, comes toward me, and enters (in the world of visions) my sacrum. I feel a big energetic push in the bottom of my back that moves up all along the spinal column, something really strong. The croc moves through me. My spine seems to be trembling, the whole body vibrates, my thoughts fade away, my energy centers light up. My head straightens up and the crocodile exits through the top of the skull, leaving me in an ecstatic state. Invigorated by this inner shower, I head off to bed.

NEXT MORNING

Guillermo sends someone to find me. I have to be the translator for a series of meetings with individuals. My Spanish is rough, but all in all, with the passage of time the boss and I have come to understand each other pretty well. The patients speak about their goals and their physical and psychological problems—it's intimate and intense. I pay close attention so as not to mess up the translation, the topic is delicate. A new patient arrives, a Russian, between forty and fifty years old, dry. He's nervous and agitated, speaking quickly. He had to flee from his country; he's in danger. I pick up that it has to do with the world of business, a victim of the stock exchange, that he perhaps lost money that wasn't his. We won't find out much more than that. He came to gather strength and to return to struggle in his country. I begin to get nervous—I think that he wants to find black magic tools. In that case, he needs to know he's in the wrong place. I begin talking to him about this in English. Result: I hadn't understood well. He wants to gain physical and mental strength in order to be able to face his problems in Russia. Relief. The man is feverish. I translate for Guillermo.

GUILLERMO: Ask him how long he can stay.

THE MAN: A maximum of one week.

I think it's too little, but I continue to translate.

GUILLERMO: What are you willing to do to attain your goal?

THE MAN: Anything. I'm living on borrowed time.

I look at him closely. He's nervous but determined. During a long silence, Guillermo scans him and reflects about what to do. A memory from *The Wages of Fear* comes back to me. Will he find a hidden packet of nitroglycerin?

GUILLERMO: I'm not going to give you ayahuasca. You're going to seclude yourself in a *tumbo** in the forest. I will come to see you to give you a plant that you will take only once. It is very strong and will shake you up. You will need to stay there and not eat for a whole week. Someone will bring you water. This plant will give you the strength that you are seeking. If you're only staying one week, this is the treatment I am suggesting.

The Russian agrees. End of conversation. Next person. Once the meetings are finished, Guillermo asks me how I'm doing with my diet. I tell him that it's going very well; I'm up and down, but in a good way with clear thinking during full intoxication. My previous diets with piñon blanco have really cleaned up my thinking. I thank him for his generosity in sharing his knowledge. Curious, I ask him what he's going to give the Russian. It's a very strong plant that will work away in his flesh right down to the bone and will reinforce his thinking. The only problem is the very fact that it is so strong, and he's never given it to a foreigner before. But he feels that the Russian is desperate, he's strong, and he hasn't much time left.

During the day I hear cries of pain coming from the jungle, howls. A little while later Guillermo tells me that the Russian has reacted to

---

*A *tumbo* is a rudimentary shelter consisting of a roof, mosquito netting, and a mattress.

the plant really well. I'm dubious given the howls I'd been hearing. With a satisfied smile he mimics that the man has very quickly vomited and evacuated below. Someone is going to take him clean clothes.

I do a test of the software program that I managed to get running again, but once running it won't stop. I'll have to wait until the batteries run down completely, which will make my job more complicated, because there is only electricity four hours a day.

EVENING

This evening Guillermo sings me a long ícaro, full of visions, cradled from a distance by the sporadic, weaker and weaker groans and cries of the Russian.

I go and sit down, saying to myself, "I know why I've dropped grand metaphysical theories for a few years now."

I'll do a drawing; I think about it a bit. Before going to bed I make a draft and now here it is, cleaned up (page 84).

The visions that I had make me think of Olivia, also known as Panshin Beka. She is an incredible woman, a healer from the Peruvian community of Juventus San Rafael, on the upper Ucayali River. After the ceremony, I fall asleep thinking about her.

I had first met her during the shooting of *D'autres mondes*. In the film she's the person who, while singing, is painting the face of the young woman for the ceremony. She sings for Kestenbetsa and makes him cry. While I was doing the Shipibo casting for *Blueberry*, I wanted to see her again to have her take the role that was finally taken by Maria (Panshin Biri, Guillermo's mother). Panshin Beka came to Pucallpa. After our reunion, Guillermo suggested that I do a ceremony with her. She's an adorable elderly lady with the joy and the soul of a young girl. I accepted with pleasure. However, I quickly understood that this ceremony was not going to be the quiet walk in the park I had hoped for. When she learned that we were going to do a ceremony, Olivia changed completely. Her childlike look disappeared, giving way to a pair of serpent's eyes. She jammed her pipe in her mouth and smoked *mapacho*, a brown tobacco, all day long. When evening came there were five of us: Maria, Guillermo, myself, and Olivia, along with my assistant Lawrence.

I had suggested that he participate instead of filming because a woman was going to direct. Guillermo wore his *kouchma,* his traditional ritual costume, something he rarely did.

That evening I really got clobbered. Only Olivia sang. The nice old lady was transformed into a warrior of implacable love. All night long I inwardly begged her to stop sending me so much love. It was too much. Water flowed without a break from my eyes, which were open to the visionary world. I closed *D'autres mondes* with her face and her song, filmed the day after the ceremony. But this sequence was not enough for me. I wanted to film her more, which finally happened some years later. She is one of the heroines in *Pashin Beka winoni* [The Story of Pashin Beka], my part of the film *8.* * I was finally able to get her energy moving and capture her face and her emotions. There are people who you see for only a few hours who stay with you for the rest of your life. Pashin Beka is one of those people.

---

*This is a short film I produced in 2008 as part of the collective film *8,* made with seven other directors. We each presented in our own way the eight goals of the United Nations on the challenges that the planet has to face. *Pashin Beka winoni* has a theme of improving the health of mothers. (Available in French on YouTube; type in "Pashin Beka" in the YouTube search box or go directly to the site: www.letempspresse.org.)

FACED WITH A BREAST

ONE MORNING, METAPHYSICAL
QUESTIONS DISAPPEARED

I realize that I've spoken about it several times, but on finishing the compilation, I found no trace of the notes on this subject and the experience connected to it. And for good reason: it's gone right out of my head.

I leave behind an enigmatic drawing . . .

I owe it to myself to come back to it.

When someone asks me today whether I believe in reincarnation, or where does man come from, or what is the meaning of life (to paraphrase *Monty Python*), I draw a blank for a moment; my head seems empty of any reply. This kind of question has disappeared . . .

I must have become someone poor in spirit.

As has been said by someone who was a great curandero—and much more—from a long ago time, "Blessed are the poor in spirit."

Of course.

But what happened?

First let's go back to the source.

From a tender age, as the saying goes, I was entranced by the big questions. I admit—this doesn't show in my first films. I wanted to know the secrets of the universe; I dove into notions of the infinitely great or infinitely small, into a *Godspell,* not from the religious point of view but from a quest for meaning. At the root there were several questions, reading from right to left, that, as an adolescent, I liked to spin around in my head, like most humans at that stage of their existence.

What's beyond the infinite?

What's before the beginning?

Why is there something instead of nothing?

To amuse myself, I would look at the stars with my little telescope and watch the satellites of Jupiter appear and disappear. I wavered between becoming an astronomer, an astrophysicist, or a cartoonist. In the end, my talent for drawing set me on a course, not toward the cosmos but toward imaginary worlds.

The big questions quietly went to sleep.

Nevertheless there would on occasion be talk of metaphysics, but it was during wine-soaked evenings with friends. Intoxication would bring the questioning back.

At eighteen, somewhat late, I smoked my first joint of grass with some buddies. We had gone into the mountains in the South of France where I stretched out below the Milky Way. This is how I encountered my first psychotropic plant, and when I go back to it now, I think it was my first escapade toward shamanism, done in an intuitive way, with the crazy hope of feeling the universe.

This experience was not conclusive, and I vomited (fancy that!). It wasn't because of the grass but because of the rice and sausage salad we brought that sat in the sun all day in the trunk of a Volkswagen beetle. (We all got food poisoning.)

I had not intuitively sensed the concept of the diets!

Later on I became obsessed by cinema and the questions resurfaced after my first feature-length film—a climb out of the depths.

I immersed myself in the writings of Eastern and Christian mystics.

When I reread my jottings on mystic thought, I see that they came out of that encounter. Ayahuasca—the jungle version of learning about the nature of the self? Anyway, that's how I made my way through these experiences for a few years. At the end of each ceremony I would set about elaborating diverse and varied theories on the relation between the visible and the invisible and on the architecture of that relation. I remember making a ton of drawings that I showed Guillermo in the first months—graphics that in fact represented the various worlds and their interconnections. I remember that once, after I rolled out my explanations of the invisible for him, he looked to the right, to the left, then straight in front of him.

I immediately got nervous and asked him, "Is something happening?"

He said, "No, no. Nothing."

Today I think that he wanted to show me that instead of constructing theories I needed to sense and observe where these kinds of thoughts were taking me.

But nothing, or no one, was able to slow me down. The process slowed down naturally by itself, because each new year my theories were blasted into smithereens while others replaced them (that's why you will only find one fragment, the thought that follows this paragraph—the others are in the wastebasket).

The teaching was astonishing; I compared it to a puzzle. Each ceremony is one piece, but you don't know it at the time. You study the piece as if it's unique and definitive, one that seems to open up an exploratory panoramic view that is different from the one before. At the end of a year, there is a key ceremony, and not only do you discover that it's a puzzle but what's more is it's made up of the songs. Integration is when all the pieces come together in overlays.

Of course, a few days later a new theory emerges, a lighter one, finally simpler—and so on it goes.

The theory then gives way to simple operational concepts connected to the medicina.

And then suddenly a few years have gone by, I'm midway through, perhaps five years after the beginning, and one morning the questions had disappeared.

And it was not that I had received responses the night before or mystical revelations on "the big questions." Or perhaps I did? And, if I had, a too strong intoxication made me forget them! So what really happened? You notice that from the beginning I've been pushing away a direct response to that question. I'm pushing it away because I don't have a precise answer, since I don't remember at all. It was too strong.

■ ■ ■

The day before, I met the spirits and I was then carried, guided by them in an astral world. I had the impression I was moving through layers that were more and more vibrant and that I was climbing continually higher toward the light. It was very difficult for me not to go into a tailspin, even though the ícaros of Guillermo were guiding me precisely. It felt like I was dying, or dissolving into the light.

A blank.

Then I regained consciousness and came back down. My body began to tense up, and I was flying over endless charnel fields of tangled bodies—the world of the dead. I was overcome by an immense sadness, tears flowed. My mind was once again a sword that allowed me not to lose myself in this ocean of suffering. My teeth were clenched, tears were flowing, no groans, my thoughts had stopped. I had the impression of being in the presence of my suffering and the suffering of my ancestors and the suffering of humanity. I was implicated. I got through that, but then I remembered nothing more.

In the morning I was fine, as if freed. I swept the area in front of my door.

We are linked to the unknowable, and we are able to perceive it. What are the energies that thinking of the unknowable connect us to? Doesn't thinking about the unknowable move us away from being able to feel it?

Up to each one of us to see.
Reality is a private affair.
When faced with a breast,
The suckling child will see the next meal,
The adolescent, an unfathomable mystery,
The man, the object of his desire,
The painter, a pure form,
The mosquito, a restaurant,
And the bra, the reason for its existence in the universe.
For each one of us, our own reality.

Now I arrive at a critical point. I think I have to make a few things clear.

During the treatment or the apprenticeship, a topic of study can surge forward and become obsessive. It's like someone who discovers there's a secret in his family. He will dig into it, which is a healthy reaction but one that can, at a given moment, turn into an obsession. The search would then be transformed into illness and the person will be cut off from others and from the present.

What happened to me is not of this order, and the events get recorded in a stage that could be called an entry into the world of psychomagic. That means the pure approach of the form that arose in thought and its possible relationship with the invisible.

But the result is that in this period of apprenticeship I got into a mental loop. I perceived an inner phenomenon (the emergence of thought), and, instead of diving into this perception, I began to engage in reflection.

I began to think of thought. Perhaps it was something I had to go through. These zones of exploration, the territory of philosophers, seem dangerous for the ayahuasquero in the middle of a diet, and in rereading all these notebooks that I scribbled full at the time, I realize now that there's a lot of confusion. Certainly it remains a beautiful confusion and a great personal and intimate adventure. What could be more intimate than one's own thought?

Throughout this journey, of which I've selected the most meaningful segments, a state is reached that allows us to perceive where the plant can take someone, and it reminds us to be vigilant.

In the apprenticeship, you can bang your head against walls for years before you understand. Here you have an example of that.

THE SERPENT BREATHES OUT

The fledgling bird that has just plunged into the void is well advised to proceed by beating his wings rather than using them to cover his face.

TARIQ DEMENS

SOI PASTO, INSIDE THE MALOCA, NIGHT

A perception.
The serpent breathes out.
He enters and twists me, he moves in, along with the song.
My own thought . . .
vertigo
. . . is not my own.
terror

The serpent's breath dissolves it.
It forms again.
I am not my thought . . .
The song . . .
Terror again.
The song immediately extracts the fear.
A great shiver pulls it out in one spasm.
Thought returns.

From far away.
From the body?
From the space outside?
The song of the serpent dissolves it once again.
The game can begin again.
It lasts the whole night long.

NOTES FROM THE DAYS FOLLOWING

Is thought a sense?
The mind does not think; the mind perceives.
The mind perceives thought.

This morning the coffee machine is warming up. It's nuts how you can happily pass the night in survival mode then the next day calmly make a metaphysical assessment.

It's like going to movies. If someone were to film your face during the showing of the film, it's clear that you experience strong emotions, but when you leave you say, "Yes, not bad, not bad this film . . . but . . . blah, blah, blah." All that is very cool, and when you put it all together it's pretty funny. In fact, the phrase *not bad* really means *good*.

And the night's teachings?

Thought: positioned and positive, directed toward the good. But what is this thought; where does it come from? It seems linked to the other senses, to the emotions, to memory, to elements of the personality, to the culture, to language—to the unconscious, to the inner demons and angels. However, "thought" also seems to no longer be your only intimate and personal creation. That's what I saw, or believed I saw, that night—or perceived.

A terrifying perception.

It was a dizzying concept, which very quickly can lead to a brush with madness.

I know that this symptom belongs to the madman or the mystic—an inner voice is speaking to him, so watch out. Vigilance needs to be redoubled. I'm getting into dangerous territory. It's important to keep your feet on the ground. God, this is hard!

When I study the curanderos, with their sparing use of words, their silences, I see that for them words, and by extension thought, have a different place from the one we accord them. They take their time; they choose the thought that they want to transform into words, especially when the discussion bears on what happened the night before.

I try to convey my perception to Guillermo. I tell him that I was afraid because the intoxication was strong and that, for the first time, I had the impression that the thoughts moving through me were not my own nor were they his, and yet his song had guided me well and that he had literally driven out the fear that had me in its clutches. That night everything was clear. Now, everything is distant, in the mists of my return to "normalcy." After a time, he replies that it's an entry into the world of psychomagic, that I shouldn't worry, but that I must remain well centered and calm. Calm? That's a good one. I leave to go and reflect on all that.

Is thought where our sensory perceptions intersect? Or instead is it an additional perception. If so, we need to position the mind elsewhere, or perhaps define it as the territory of experience situated beyond thought? Maybe it's as simple as that.

I am fragile at this moment; I become sensitive. I've always been confident. I keep on going, but the next few nights might be rough. I feel it.

Precision is needed. Refine. Think thought—a self-reflexive exercise. No. You have to feel thought. Calm the thinking process and link it to the heart and the body. I put the exercise into practice. I seek calm. I lean against a tree; I breathe. The state of the night before returns. I slide into it gently, a meditation in Amazonian mode. Every ten minutes, make notes and define this state.

I am a universe.
A universe in movement.
Always changing.
Within this universe are my organs.
I feel them.
My limbs.
I feel them.

I take note. The intoxication climbs again. In the territory of the emotions it's my fears that manifest first.

My emotions. I feel them. Raw.
I breathe.
Then what?
Words make sentences, wave by wave.
At the center: me.
Who am I?
A little white guy covered in mosquito bites who really "got it" last
    night.
There you go!
That's it exactly.
Relax, little animal.

I go over the last sentence in order to taste the present moment. I'm a little white guy covered in mosquito bites. The good fellow really collected last night.

Presence.

I'm a being with atrophied ears who is trying to theorize about music having just heard his first sounds, when he's only just heard one melody.

A wave of thought is grasped: it's difficult for me to perceive this field of knowledge because it does not belong to the "world of ideas" I come from. Its mode of apprenticeship is in total opposition to the mode of functioning learned in the rest of my life. It's a mess—I'm not prepared. I'm fighting with myself, with the intellectualization, with the instant conceptualization of what I perceive. And I can't do otherwise. The toad with the scorpion on its back tries to cross the river of my psyche.

That night my thoughts were no longer my own. So whose thoughts were they?

The thoughts of the spirits?
Of the warrior?
Of my ancestors?

Of the dead?

Of my unconscious?

Stop, now!

The inner command is strong. A nausea rises up in my body. I feel sick, messed up, dirty. What's happening? I am sensitive. I see the inner dialogue as being too strong; thought runs away with me—or let's say that's how I feel it. I'm getting into dangerous territory, I feel that energetically.

Away you go now, trembling little white man. Close your notebook and go for a walk in the forest.

JUNGLE, NIGHT, CEREMONY

The serpent's breath opens the doors of the mind.

Thought . . .

The song—muffled, warrior-like and slow, seems to be saying to me:

"Do not seize your thought.

"Think well and let it go.

"Reconnect yourself."

After my vertigo I inwardly acquiesce. No, I am not going to seize my thought this evening. This evening I'm going to let it run. I set about that, immediately.

The song soars up. It becomes airy, feminine.

The visions are divine lights.

Worlds unfold and I climb.

My soul seems to fill me.

A few moments later I seem to be floating through the crossroads of space and time.

I am immense . . .

Without beginning or end.

From now on I know it.

I feel it now.
I am . . . immortal!
My thought is evidence.
It is truth brushing up against the absolute.

At this moment, the song becomes muffled. Guillermo returns to where he began. I receive a shock. My body is shaken up. I understand immediately.

I seized my thought!
In full awareness.
I grabbed it!
I didn't stay with my commitments.
I descend down a long visionary spiral, into the eye of the cyclone of my psyche.

We begin again at zero.

What happened?
Don't think about it!
I can't.

I seize a state. My atoms are the same age as the universe, but not me. I'm going to die one day.

Confusion.
The soul's perception.
The individual's perception.
Maelstrom.

My mind hangs on to the broken branches of its folly.
The song seems to be telling me, don't trust your thought that is telling you stories! Trust your feeling. Trust your heart.
I react inwardly through the deployment of great serpents that navigate through my visions.

"All right, I am not trusting my thought!"

Return of the song and the passing by of an even more impressive serpent.

Once again . . . thought.

Aaaaaaaah! What to do?

I wriggle.

I wriggle.

I'm a human being!

I think!

If I don't trust my thought, I turn insane.

If I trust my thought completely, I am in illusion.

No, no, little serpent.

Simple and well-placed thought. Body and mind united.

Until morning.

I wriggle and tremble, trying to escape my thought.

I CRACK UP

Jungle, Sunny Morning

Words describing the experience need to be examined carefully. Superlatives jump out immediately from a fresh memory. In daylight they run off with the night's experience: infinite, eternity, truth, absolute, and so on.

First task: eliminate part of this vocabulary. It's utopian language. The words are too strong and pop out too quickly. To use such terms is to exaggerate rather than accurately describe the experience. "All the idiots go to the city," as we say in the South of France. Or as another example, "On a hill, nitwits roll down."

I have trouble walking on the grass. I have the sense that I'm hurting it. The Shipibo laugh. The trees are looking at me. Hi guys!

I must look like a madman this morning. I'm going to skip a night of drinking the vine. I have to write down all these new ideas; otherwise I'm going to forget them. Even the idea of forgetting them drives me bananas. I'm afraid of forgetting what I've seen. I've already lost the feeling of mental clarity that I had during the night. All this new information is disappearing . . . Learn to accept the forgetting.

Poof! The great theoretician of music theory makes his comeback.

And then messes up! The demon of conceptualizing takes hold of me. I'm too tired to resist.

The five senses are the sensors and the channels that allow the human animal to perceive the surrounding reality, but in a limited range. Beyond a technology of survival, this information forms the outline of the human's world—the world that we can touch with our senses, the world that we share . . . the known.

Thought has nothing to do with the other senses. Thought reflects the inner world. In general, the process of the formation of thought is not perceived by the individual. We are happy to live in the universe of our thoughts. However, at the source of this inner universe you can come to a place where energy dances and is transformed, subtly linked to an external energy and to worlds that are perceptible and invisible for certain individuals. If my thought doesn't seem to be mine, it's because, at moments, I am really lucid.

Is the madman lucid?

Is the person who says he's lucid crazy?

Damn. I'm cracking up. I don't know anymore if what I'm writing has any meaning.

Goal for the ongoing nightly operations: try to become a bit lucid without swinging into madness.

Verify.

Recapitulation.

Are you in the process of becoming mad?

Yes: in the sense that I am swinging ever more deeply into a universe that is not referenced by my culture.

No: in the sense that everything seems coherent.

However, to himself, the madman's world seems coherent . . . Not very reassuring. Let's say that I feel that this world is shared by others but I have no verbal validation of it. That means there's still the danger that I will make an error of interpretation.

Evaluation of the physical and mental states.

Physical state:
    Positive: relaxation, hypersensitivity
    Negative: tiredness, hypersensitivity

Mental state:
    Positive: mystical ecstasy, exploration of consciousness, discoveries
        of the mystery
    Negative: primal fear, new terrors, metaphysical confusion.

The force of the ceremonies is on an exponential curve.
Operational mode to maintain: in daytime—rest and inner silence.
At night—concentration. Do what you can. But do it!
I have to hold on for about ten more nights.

(Note from the end of the journey: I held on.)

TWIN TOWERS

SEPTEMBER 10, 2001

We arrived late, Ariel and I. Our operational base is the Sunset Marquis. The shooting of the film *Blueberry* is getting close. We're going to sign up the American cast of the film: Juliette Lewis, Michael Madsen, and the others. Tomorrow we will be joined by Thomas Langmann and Lou di Djaimo, the director of casting.

Tired, I slip between the sheets.

SEPTEMBER 11, 2001

I am awakened by the phone—it's Ariel. Enigmatically, he tells me to turn on the television and to call him back afterward, when I feel the need to. I hang up and, half asleep, look for the remote. The screen comes to life and I see shots of Los Angeles airport, totally empty. I was there a few hours before. I think of chemical contamination, but the screen immediately goes straight to repeating images of the Boeing jet crashing into the tower. Like the majority of the inhabitants of this planet, I'm in wake-up mode. I don't know how it was for you coming upon these images, but for me it was stark naked, in bed, with my eyes half open.

I remember hesitating. My thoughts went in two directions at once: the first, the shock of the dramatic reality; the second, the shock of the fictional unreality of the scene, somewhat as if I were watching an action-flick disaster scene with the overdrawn panache of Hollywood scriptwriters. A shock enters into the content, coming from a mythological universe, the metal bird crashing into the temple of commerce, and the raw reality of a human and political drama that was going to change the world and, alas, in a not very wonderful way.

The plane bringing Thomas Langermann has to make a mid-Atlantic turnaround, and Lou di Djaimo's plane made an emergency landing in Arkansas. Everything stopped. Reality shifted. We were stuck here for an indefinite period. That same evening, I walked on Sunset Boulevard where giant screens were displaying the tense face of George Bush and cars were flying the American flag. People were crying. I caught whiffs of fear and loneliness. I returned to the hotel and meditated.

Confusion burst forth.
Death and violence.
My family far away.
The film is going to stop.

I concentrated on my emotions—nothing else to be done. I did my grieving for the film pretty quickly; then I reached a state of a very high vibratory level. It's true I was very sensitive, but there was something else—a great wave of peace, of love. How could that be? I imaged love and fear to be energies of opposite polarities, available in the space around us. At this point in time, fear was naturally very much in demand; few people were connecting to love, which was therefore fully available.

This is how I spent ten days alternating between Jacuzzi, pool, healthy food, and meditation (jungle-style but without the plants). No television. No excursions.

My thanks to ayahuasca, for it is she who has taught me this attitude—perfectly logical and simple, but actually difficult to stay with.

I tend to panic when I cannot find my keys or my credit card, when someone makes an unpleasant comment about me, when I'm late for an important meeting. When it comes to dealing with life's little inconveniences, ayahuasca has brought me a lot of benefit.

However, it is during big moments in one's life—September 11 being a prime example—that the benefits of working with plants and healers have their full effect. A death, a serious difficulty in a personal or professional relationship, a serious threat, and there we are once again, plunged into fragility, confusion, and fear. Ayahuasca teaches us to pull ourselves out of these states. The vine teaches transcendence and sometimes certain events of life bring us face-to-face with the need to transcend. So the teachings of my brother, the maestro, activate mechanisms implanted during the deep emotional disturbances that took place in a ceremony.

After about ten days the airports reopened, and I returned to Paris in great shape. The film was made; it was simply delayed a year.

LA CUCARACHA

Difficult ceremony, bad spirits. Each time the visions open and I see the spiritual world, a discharge runs through my body, then the visions disappear and I feel intense bodily pain. Impossible to properly open the intoxication, the mareación. Ricardo looks after me well; he sings a long time for me, cleansing my body and mind.

Rama kano abano
I'm going to open the visions

jaconmabo canobo
the bad visions

jaconmabo behabo
the bad songs of the sorcerers

jaconmabo cushonbo
the bad whisperings

jacombabo bomanbo
the bad intentions

jaconmabo shitanabora;
the bad energies;

pisha, pisha vainqui
reject them, reject them

103

sua, sua vainquin
wash, clean

payan, payan vainquin
air out, ventilate

queyo queyo vainquin
be done with them, be done with them

Be done with them? It's not going to be this evening, maybe never; but that's okay, the treatment is effective. Ricardo says to me: *"Falta más, vamos a terminar mañana."* (Some things are still missing; we'll finish tomorrow.)

Right, right . . . He tells me that every day.

Guillermo is in Lima. All of a sudden, the scientific experiment moves to the back burner.

THE NEXT DAY

This evening no ceremony; nothing worth noting.

THE DAY AFTER THAT

Difficult again. Negative energy; it's working away, it begins to tire me. Ricardo takes care of me. I take advantage of a very strong treatment he does for his wife, a great song of taking on strength, of cleansing the mind. She has not taken ayahuasca. I am nearby. I vibrate.

Cushi cushi medicinama
All the strength of my medicine

medicina maquecan
is going to enter your body

maquecanra acai;
along with the singing;

shinan hueshenibora
thoughts blocked

churo, churo vanquin.
reject them, send them away.

Rama punteyonbanon
Now I'm going to center

jacon aquin punteque
nicely align (center)

shina cano puntequen
align the five senses and the intellect

senen paramanyonnan
harmoniously

caya yahi puntequen
align your soul

yora yabi puntequen
align your body

joe yabi puntequen
align all of your light

yora kuchi ayonan
reinforce your body

shinan kuchi ayonan
reinforce your mind

puno cushiayonnan
right to the farthest reaches of your nerves

cushi ayonshamanan
reinforce your whole being, mind, senses, and body

senen paramanyonnan
harmoniously

paramayonshamanan
in a harmonious way

senen paramanyonnan.
with harmony.

I feel the strength and the specific love that Ricardo sends to his wife. His singing is based on their love connection. Singing for a life companion is the most beautiful of energies. I take advantage of this round of good energy to go to sleep.

Tomorrow Ricardo is going to rest; he's exhausted. There won't be any ceremony at the center. It's a general rest period.

Good. As for rest, it will have to be some other time. James Arévalo (Panshin Copé) invites me to the weekly ceremony at Luz Kósmika, the center for apprentices. There are eight of them. James suggests I sit beside him, opposite them.

I met James ten years ago; his apprenticeship has been difficult. Today he's a good healer. He named his son Jan.

This evening is unusual; Guillermo is not there. Panshin Copé is the master at the helm. At the end of the ceremony, the apprentices sing their ícaros. What joy to discover the ícaros of my French friends. So fine. Each one has his own sensitivity. Teddy is navigator of the depths, Benoît is astralman, and Yann is another acrobat of the medicina. Future curanderos?

BRIEF DIGRESSION

Stories about Western Curanderos

There is a new category of curanderos—the Westerners. Among them, one person greatly helped me to advance these past few years, François Demange (Metsa Niwue is his Shipibo name), who has been learning traditional medicine for fifteen years. He is the only student of Guillermo who I know to be involved in the medicina longer than me. He helped Guillermo a lot in the setting up of his clinic of Amazonian medicine.

That makes two Frenchmen working with Guillermo, and now there is a third with Dr. Aziz Kharzai, an apprentice.

My meeting with François is recent—barely three years ago. Our friendship was immediate. What a pleasure to discover a Frenchman who was familiar with the experience in a deeper way! It wasn't long before, in the maloca, I became aware of his strength. He offered to have me accompany him on a journey with toé (datura). I refused, even if Guillermo was to be present. Toé has a devilish reputation. It's a plant that has to be handled with the utmost caution; it's relentless and requires a lot of experience. Even though I appreciated François, I did not have total confidence in his ability to sustain me in the worlds of toé—the prudence of an ayahuasquero.

Another evening, a healer came and sang for me in Shipibo. I was in full intoxication and during the song, which was very precise and very strong, I wondered who was singing. It wasn't either Guillermo or Ricardo. I took a peek and saw it was François.

Little by little I gained a more accurate assessment of his abilities, and one day, when Guillermo was absent, he presented me with toé, and naturally I drank it. The moment had come. Then, after the toé came other plants. That established our connection in a more concrete way, and I accepted what he offered me in a generous way during the ceremony.

Toé is fuerte!

François and Guillermo together in a ceremony—that's something. When Guillermo, Ricardo, and Maria are together, chatting in Shipibo, I follow very little of the conversation. And sometimes when I hear the tone of their voices or their laughter, I would really like to take part. With François and Guillermo I can follow, and I'll take advantage of that to recount a little more.

After a lengthy song from Guillermo for a dieter, who cried out every last tear from his body, the dieter, stumbling around, is led back to his place by an assistant. Guillermo quietly speaks a short sentence. It makes François laugh, and he turns to me, his eyes twinkling. He had trouble speaking. I pull myself out of my visions and lean toward him. He repeats to me what Guillermo had said, "Don't be sad. Tomorrow you'll eat an apple!" I laughed hard. You're wondering? It's an ayahuasquero's joke, or even a dieter's joke. Oh yes! A slight deviation from the diet, and you pay for it in spades.

Another time it's the reverse. François, Guillermo, and I are in ceremony. It is a very big intoxication. I am vitrified by the visions. In silence. No one has begun to sing. I hear Guillermo's voice speaking to François. I turn around. François is seated straight as a post, a sign of a big mareación. Guillermo: "Go ahead, François. Sing!" Silence. François doesn't budge. I say to myself, "If he asked me to sing now I'd explode. I'm right where I belong!"

I sympathize. The maestro and the apprentice.

Silence.

GUILLERMO: Go ahead, François, sing something!

Silence.

GUILLERMO: Sing any old thing, even "La Cucaracha" if you want to.

And, at that point, in spite of a big intoxication—those who are familiar with it know that there is nothing amusing in that state—a burst of laughter later, François begins to sing.

I also have a diet story connected with François. It was the final evening. I was closing my diet; the intoxication, as usual, is very strong. Guillermo does the song for me that closes the diet—very hard and strong. He puts the protections in place. Twenty minutes later, moving on all fours (I only had to move six feet, so why stand up?), returning to my place, I pass by François, who stops me. Starting all over again, he takes his turn singing for me, for a long time, putting in place a second protection. Then I sit down. I've just had a good half hour of songs. It's late; the ceremony is entering into its last quarter. François turns to me and says, "Guillermo and I are going to drink again. Will you join us?" How could I refuse? We drink. The mareación climbs like a shot. At that point I understand. My diet has just been closed. I have a brand-new cockpit, refurbished motors, and the tanks are full up with nitromethane.

The jokers. Drink again right after closing a diet. Instead of Cape Canaveral, that's Cape Anaconda—cosmic blastoff from the depths of myself. Trembling everywhere, but the vessel holds together. I'm able to go further. With nothing more than describing that moment now, today, I feel its special intoxication climb. So, in short, if a healer whom you have your own reasons to trust asks you, "Do you want to take ayahuasca again?" it's up to you to do it or not. You can refuse—everything depends on your state. The healer may say to you (and here are the three types of offers I have received): "Do you want to take ayahuasca again with me?" or "I'm going to take ayahuasca again. Will you join me?" or "If you like, I would like to take it again with you." Once again, it's up to you to refuse or agree. However, I advise you to accept, regardless of your state at the moment. If your state requires that information be communicated, tell the healer beforehand. These invitations are part of the general sharing.

Let's speak about the third Frenchman, Aziz, the surgeon. He embarked on long apprenticeship diets five years ago and has spent a large part of his time at the center. He suffered on the big diets. With several years of sacrifice and intense work, he became a good Western curandero. Right from the first ícaro of his that I heard in the maloca last year, I understood him. He has a very strong song and also a personal style consistent with traditional Shipibo medicine.

RETURN TO THE MALOCA, LUZ KÓSMIKA

This evening I listened to the potential future curanderos. The paths of apprenticeship are difficult—some give up en route as in any rough discipline. However, the movement has been launched. Bastien, who is living at the center, is also making progress in the medicina, and I take advantage of that with joy.

The next morning I taste the noisy jungle of Luz Kósmika. I will see the apprentices and congratulate them—their long diet has given them much strength. The conversation shifts to cinema. Their enthusiasm on the subject is catching—I remember that I'm a filmmaker and that's good. As Guillermo sometimes says when introducing me to someone while miming a camera: *Jan, el cineasta ayahuasquero.* That's what I've become. I'm very lucky to be able to make films. It's an art that is truly full of magic.

AYAHUASCA MOVIE AT THE CANNES FESTIVAL

MEMORIES, A FEW WEEKS EARLIER

Different energy and different ambiance. Joy and stress: my film *Coco Chanel & Igor Stravinsky* will, in a few days, be the closing film of the festival. Today, accompanied by my companion Anne Paris, Vincent Ravalec, and Marc Caro, I'm skipping interviews in order to see *Enter the Void,* Gaspar Noé's film.

Superb.

We are all seated together except Gaspar, who is two rows behind us. The film takes us back to our trip in the jungle, ten years ago almost to the day.

A band of arts people wandering around at Kestenbetsa's place. It was at the time of my first journeys there. One day my entertainer friends went with me. The funniest was Vincent Ravalec, whom I knew very little. I ran into him at Ajoz Films, the production company of Ariel Zeitoun where we were working on *Blueberry,* and at his request I told him briefly where I was going for about ten days. Before I even finished my story, there he was telling me, "Great! I'll join you down there." A bit surprised, I dish out the dates and locations for him and he takes his leave. Needless to say I was no longer thinking about him when I ran into him in the transit area of the airport in Atlanta. He was arriving from New York and was on the same flight as us to Lima, calm and not very surprised. That's Vincent. So there we were—a small group: a few patients, two doctors, and people from the entertainment world.

It was about ten days of madness in which each person traveled far.

One evening over a period of six hours, Gaspar climbed back down the scale of evolution ending up in the state of a mollusk and stagnated there in a bad trip that had no escape but was rich in teachings—a version of *Altered States* in Noé style. The next evening, before drinking once again he said to me, "I don't know what there is beyond a mollusk, but one thing is certain, this vine is not something to put in just anybody's hands!" (Glug glug.) Vincent went into a tailspin, but with class and Zen—keeping through it all an aspect of "Tintin* with the Shipibo." He told me to "download" some programs coming from the curanderos. Anne vibrated too much (for a human being) in transforming herself into a siren. "It was so very beautiful, but so very much too strong!" I remember Marc asking me one morning at the end of the ceremony: "Why are we still doing movies?" What I've done is put my rushes through the centrifuge.

Even though she wanted to slow down, I remember having insisted that Anne participate in the final ceremony. I asked in front of Guillermo if it was all right that she come. In short, I insisted; he replied, "Yes." Jan: "Come on, Anne, we're all together. It's the last night; it'll be terrific." In the end she agreed. And ka-boom! I speak about my experience later in "Remembering the Closing Diet."† What I don't talk about there is that at the end of the last ceremony, in the early hours of the morning, Anne was no longer in the maloca. I experienced a small freak-out. Feeling doubly responsible, I start looking for her. A bit intoxicated, I look around in Guillermo's garden, then going back past the maloca, I see Guillermo standing still, smoking his pipe of mapacho. I ask him if he knows where Anne is. With a finger, he indicates the other side of the house. I find her flopped down in a bush, groaning softly. Phew! All is well. Er, not yet, but soon.

The next day, everyone happy, we left for Lima. In the car on the

---

*[The *Adventures of Tintin* is an extremely popular series of comic albums that have sold more than 200 million copies in seventy languages. —*Trans.*]

†See page 127.

way to the airport Gaspar laughingly cried out, "We are alive, alive!" Yes, alive and in top shape.

We were all there, seated side by side in front of the most beautiful cinema screen in the world, and Gaspar was showing us his opus. In any case, his film took us back to the jungle we remembered. I heard Anne softly chanting a little serpent melody to bring calm to herself in the most difficult moments.

As we exit, dazed and unsettled, we all agree: a unique film, an accomplished director. We also agree that it's the bad-trip version of our expedition. Walking down the steps of Palais des Festivals with them, still drifting in the film, I think of the artistic impact of this journey. It resonates with *Enter the Void* and *Dante 01,* Marc Caro's film. Vincent Ravalec wrote several books as a follow-up to his adventures in Gabon with iboga.* And, in my case, I made three films and wrote books, and now we have Gaspar, ten years later, bringing out his film. It's the most fantastic to be sure!

I find this whole adventure marvelous in fact, and I'm aware of the common wave that connects us, that awakens our creativity and our consciousness. It moves forward like an object that has weight: you take an artist, you dip him in the juice of the vine; inevitably that changes his creation, or let's say rather that he's going to participate. Something is going to change; it makes sense. I was aware of the collective demonstration of it as we walked down the steps of the Palais. The Palme d'Or prize goes to Gaspar for the journey to Peru.

Now there's still another creative work to be done: that of Anne Paris. Her scenario with the evocative title of *Elixir* is almost done. The artistic adventure continues. For her, the theme will be desire, in a film of erotic anticipation.

At Cannes, I am back once again in the universe of the vine when my friend François Demange (Metsa Niwue) shows up for the closing. He is at ease like a fish in water, and his eyes shine in jubilation at the idea of walking up the steps with me—all this contributes to my relaxation before the ceremony.

---

*Iboga is a rainforest shrub native to western Central Africa that has psychedelic properties.

Preparing yourself for a ceremony is a bit different at Cannes. You don't check your flashlight or put on bug spray. It's more like don't crease your tux. And you have a bow tie in your pocket instead of Agua Florida. On the other hand, the two are somewhat alike at an emotional level. Thoughts go through my mind of the type: What type of sauce am I going to stuff my face with tonight? Will good spirits be there? Will the *yoshin*-critics* hoot at me? So I was a little tense, shaken by emotion, like just before drinking the eight plants. Anne offered me a little yoga and a foot massage, which brought immediate calm. Suddenly, I thought—too late—I should also have asked François for a little ícaro. Nothing of the sort! The two of us are so connected that it works by itself. Never mind. If it goes badly I'll sing in my little head an ícaro of aligning the thoughts and the senses.

The ballet of the cars, the ascent of the steps. I arrive in the hall having managed not to step on Anna Mouglalis's long dress and without losing my pants. Stress is truly peculiar: at one moment in the limo that took us to the Palais des Festivals, I thought that at least I didn't have to lose my pants. We had a good laugh with Anne; it was "the idiot's anguish going up the steps."

I found myself seated next to Anna, Mads Mikkelsen, and Elena Morozova, the main actors in the film. I felt the tension we shared, especially since Elena and Mads, like the public, were seeing the film for the first time. The last time I had seen it was to verify a copy in a small Parisian viewing room. Tonight the hall is full and the public not necessarily kind.

Fortunately, family members were there with us. My mother and my brother, my producers Claudie Ossard and Chris Bolzni, the technicians, some of them long-standing friends, and, of course, Anne. The lights go down. Thierry Frémaux, the film selector and a Cannes bigwig, shows up and surprises me by putting his hands on my shoulders with an impish grin. He drills his gaze into mine, a lively and discrete embrace, a kind of *haka*† from Cannes that I imagine is of his own invention. He whispers, "It's traditional." His gesture makes me feel like it's a game,

*In Shipibo, a *yoshin* is a bad spirit or bad energy.
†A *haka* is a traditional Maori dance that can serve a variety of functions, including that of a ceremonial welcome.

a strong and direct support, like a good hit of mapacho. After all, if I'm there it's because of the choice made by the selection committee. So enjoy!

I didn't have time to return his smile; he just vanished. We're off.

People shout, others applaud, someone whistles. In short, it was percolating from the moment the fractals of the credits splashed across the screen. All in all, it was a beautiful ceremony.

STAR WARS IN THE MALOCA

ESPÍRITU DE ANACONDA

Ricardo warned Guillermo that the energy was heavy these past few days. Back from Lima, smiling, the maestro says that he'll take care of it. He sends great clouds of tobacco smoke over all the patients and apprentices; the vessel will be taking off soon.

Guillermo opens the ceremony; but it resists. Big blockage. He stops in the middle of his song. I see Ricardo wavering, and as for me I dig into my resources in order to traverse the somewhat unwelcoming universes that are in the process of being deployed. I don't flinch, and I adopt my Rascar Capac* pose. Guillermo does not vomit, staggers, then picks up and continues his song. I latch on to it, without any thought of mentally asking him for assistance. I move through and maintain my position all night long. Ricardo is not doing well. Guillermo begins with a big treatment for him, then the two of them call the patients and the dance begins.

Through my intoxication I see the treatments. Visions emanate from the healer and interact with those coming out of the patient. It's impressive. I recognize the stages that I experienced in receiving a song from him.

When I'm receiving a song myself, it's as though I were seated in the front row of a big movie house, a partial and crushing vision with

*Rascar Capac was an Incan mummy featured in one of the comics from the *Adventures of Tintin*.

which one struggles. This time, I'm at the back of the room and I have a little distance. I hang on to Guillermo's songs, which transport me, somewhat like an experienced driver who drives in the slipstream of the car in front of him. I unwind the ícaros in my mind to increase my concentration. The night goes on; the energy becomes more airy. Peace gets installed in the maloca. Guillermo once again provides a big treatment for Ricardo. He turns toward me after not having been concerned about me all evening. "¿Cómo estás, hermano?" "Tranquil," I reply (which, on that occasion, was true). Along with Ricardo, the two of them begin to giggle like kids telling each other about the dreadful visions, their strong intoxication, and the difficulty at the beginning of the ceremony. Still in the intoxication and somewhat astonished, I say to him, "Hey, it was really hard this evening and you're laughing." He replies, "Of course we're laughing. We succeeded—that's good reason to be happy isn't it?" True. I recall the motorcycle stuntman in *99 Francs** picking himself up from the crash after flying at fifty miles per hour and sliding thirty yards. He had succeeded, and he had exactly the same smile. I would never have thought it possible to establish an emotional rapport between a Parisian movie stuntman and a traditional indigenous Amazonian healer.

MORNING, ALSO JULY 2009

I run into Guillermo. He's caring for his teeth by chewing plants all day long. I suggest he go to a dentist. After all, when he needs to, he goes to see allopathic doctors. Why forego it in this case? He prefers to resolve his problem using plants. I ask him what he thinks of my idea of continuing my diet in France. He likes the idea. Three months would be good.

Three months? I'm going to ask my sweetheart first.

Exchange of e-mails; rapid reply.

Back in Paris this means: no salt (okay), no sugar (harder, but good), no meat (easy), no alcohol (done for years now), and no sex (*oh* là là

**99 Francs* is a 2007 film directed by Jan Kounen based on the novel of the same name by Frédéric Beigbeder.

. . . much harder, we have a joyful rhythm). Good. I'm happy she has accepted. It'll be a harsh cleansing. I should say that it's not just a matter of not having sexual relations when on the apprenticeship diet, it means also not having sexual thoughts or sexual dreams! So you really have to pay attention. Otherwise you gain nothing. I am well established in my diet. I will continue and reach my cruising altitude, a sort of leap, before returning to France, where it will be more difficult. That having been said, all is well: I've had signs that the diet is well established. Two days before, I began having an erotic dream, and within the dream, I withdrew to protect my diet.

Guillermo lets me know that a group of Chinese yogis arrive today, and he wants me to be the translator during the debriefings. That calls me. Given my state of high vibration, I'd really like to do yoga. They arrive around noon and surprise! I know their boss. It's Matej Jurenka, a fine Slovak with an intense look and long dreadlocks, a great yogi. He came with his student Shiu-an, a very pretty, tiny Chinese woman with a great, luminous smile. I had already seen them the year before at the center. The others will arrive the next day, but there will only be two more instead of ten because of last-minute visa problems for the other Chinese.

MALOCA, EVENING INSIDE, CEREMONY

We are back in the maloca. At the last moment Guillermo doesn't come. I am beginning to tire. I serve myself only a small glass; the ceremony is calm, so nothing in particular to report. It is a sort of interlude in which I take a look at my present life, my lady, my children, my family, and my friends. I send them all nice thoughts.

MORNING

After a big breakfast I lounge in the hammock and I see Matej's two students arrive: a beautiful Indian woman—fine and tall—and his Slovak compatriot, Martin.

First meeting with the group that I'm translating for. It's the first time for Kania and Martin. Matej lets Guillermo know that the group will do a ceremony every other night and that the preparation that he had taken the previous night was not strong enough. He would like a much more concentrated one for his students. Gulp. That preparation was just fine!

Grabbed by hesitation for a second, I end up turning to Guillermo and translating. You should know that I'd heard this kind of thing before and the story is always the same. Guillermo would reply, "Very good, we'll look after that." Later, when such a person drinks . . . the result is a big experience and the extreme intensity of it will sometimes bring that person regret for such recklessness all night long.

Guillermo is looking at me as I finish my sentence, and I feel that he can read me. I must have one eyebrow slightly higher than the other, meaning, "The poor creatures, they have no idea, don't listen to them my brother!" His impish eyes wrinkle for a second; he replies, "Since that is your wish, we will take care of it." Matej doesn't flinch. The others don't understand what he's just arranged for them—they smile in satisfaction. Tomorrow night we're going to rock in the maloca. The goals of each person are important. Guillermo keeps track of everything and with a big and gentle smile announces that the meeting is over.

I smile too, remembering that I experienced something similar last year with François: a case where the guy, in full intoxication, tells himself, "Frankly, they've given me too much, I'm going to explode, they've gone overboard," before remembering that the person who served him was himself. And I've no one to blame except myself.

Matej invites me to do yoga this afternoon and tomorrow morning. Perfect.

I watch the postures. I try to follow with let's say about fifteen percent of the curvature (take a look at Matej on YouTube and you'll understand). But it goes off smoothly. The students are at a very nice level. After an hour and a half, sweating, the neophyte that I am lies down. The benefits of the work spread through my whole relaxed body and my mind. I feel the very beautiful alchemy between the plants and the physical work of the yoga circulating in my body. I close my eyes.

When I wake up I am alone and it's already dark. A little worried about the time, I head for the maloca. It's empty. No mattresses, nobody there. I head for the cleared area in the jungle. Everything has been set up outdoors. They're all there. My stuff has been placed beside Guillermo. I just have to sit down and drink. I am to be awakened once again by the dew, and this time it will be very pleasant.

MORNING

I feel the work from the yoga; I feel it so well that I'm not going to repeat it this morning, otherwise I'll be a mollusk tonight. Doing it every other day is going to be better. The year before, I had worked with a yoga teacher. I practiced in the maloca every morning, and that was really cool.

Breakfast. Guillermo asks me to come. He's having the Russian brought over and wants me to translate. My curiosity is suddenly stirred. The Russian arrives. It's been several days now that he hasn't eaten but only drunk water. He's almost at the end of his treatment. I study him, fascinated. He is very different. The fear has gone from his look; he is collected, calm, his body is moving more slowly. He says he is doing well, he's not hungry. The conversation is brief. He returns to the forest. I will be gone when he leaves but I know already that things are going well for him.

Guillermo confirms it for me, laconically and mischievously. "This man is strong and he will succeed in achieving the goals he has set himself." I reply by saying that the center is going to have a new clientele of traders and brokers who have succumbed to the crisis! He opens his arms and says, "Everyone is welcome to receive a good treatment!" We burst out with laughs as big as whales. I imagine Wall Street men in suits lined up in the maloca, each one in front of a five-gallon bucket, ready to vomit up their hedge funds.

Oh, how I love this hammock!

I'm thinking once again that you could make a beautiful comedy movie on this topic, or a play for the theater. I drift along happily remembering pithy little anecdotes. Like this little story for example: When I was shooting *D'autres mondes,* one of my collaborators took advantage of the shoot to try out the pranks of the magic vine. At Pucallpa the boy walked out of the first maloca, a little cabin in Guillermo's garden, impelled by an inner urgency. He was searching, as you can guess, for the toilets—at night, without a flashlight, and without having gotten his bearings ahead of time. (He hadn't read the manual.) Groping his way, because he was very intoxicated, he finally found the makeshift toilet. (This man is a great storyteller, and in his own words the anecdote is really something.) He managed acrobatically to discharge the liquid that desperately clamored for an exit from his body. The operation was a success without too much collateral damage. But he didn't have any toilet paper. In the dark and the intoxication he found—what a miracle!—some carefully folded sheets at the bottom of his pocket. So he was saved. Alas, he noticed too late that the paper he had used was his only copy of the work contract he had negotiated with such difficulty.

Some weeks later, while I was working in the production facilities preparing for *Blueberry,* the secretary hung up her phone and called the accountant saying, "Mr. X's contract has gone missing, we need to send him another one. I think no one understood why I burst out laughing. They must have thought that Peru had made me a little strange . . .

I take advantage of the day to repeat a test on the PC so that the scientific experiment can be conducted two days from now. After several attempts, e-mail communication with the technicians has finally allowed me to restart the software; everything is finally ready.

MALOCA, EVENING INSIDE, CEREMONY

The maloca is crowded—around twenty-five people. I am on Guillermo's right. To his left, Ricardo serves the drink. At the end, the yogis seated opposite us took their turn. The liquid they are drinking is superconcentrated and looks like melted chocolate. Just looking at it makes me want to throw up. Matej asks Ricardo, who didn't need to be asked twice, to please serve his students.

When I see Kania drink I experience a burst of great compassion and a shiver down my spine; what's coming for her is going to be violent, and it takes me back to my own experience ten years before. I remember Guillermo serving me a plant that wasn't ayahuasca, something much stronger. As he was pouring, he asked me, "Why are you drinking?" and I replied, "I want to know." He then poured me a big glassful. I received a shock, but what a shock!* I collided with my beliefs, my feelings, the spirits, the mystery, the culture, the jungle.

The next day I was different—different forever. Even though later I experienced stronger ceremonies, the extent or perhaps we could say the differential between before and after was never again that strong. I experienced a change of paradigm.

I watch the beautiful Kania empty her glass and say a prayer inside that all will go well for her. The rest of us are taking the regular preparation. I serve myself and take the normal dose. I feel strange for an hour. Guillermo is avoiding me; he remains there, does not move, concentrating. I'm upset. At the moment of drinking I disturb his concentration and tell him that I still don't have answers to my questions. He answers me directly, "You have to drink more." Okay. I ask Ricardo for a big glass. Tonight we're all going to fly. In fact, it's starting fast. The yogis purge silently, except for Kania, who enters the terror: "Help. Help me, Guillermo. I wanna go home. Please, help." The poor dear, she took a jugful. Her repeated plea, piercing, endless, is stamped with a sacred terror that makes everyone's blood run cold. Well, *everyone* meaning the others and me! My intoxication is blocked. Guillermo gets up and goes to sing for Kania, he spends a part of the whole night doing that. Gentle, profound songs—he stops then begins again. Kania's intoxication is such that it seems to me to be greater than Guillermo's.

I work quietly to align my thoughts and senses properly. There is vomiting everywhere. The heavy ship takes off gently. At the end of the runway, its long belly seems to brush the treetops.

Guillermo returns; he's calling me for a song. I receive it, well centered. He connects me to the medicinal world of the vine; I hear in the

---

*Shock comes from *chocar,* meaning "to collide with," a local term of the ayahuasqueros, which usually applies to diets. You can say, "I shocked my diet," which means "I mishandled it, shook it up." For example, I once found myself moved along in spite of myself in a National Front march because of all the very dark energy of those people shocked by diets of piñon blanco (see the discussion of diets on page 144).

words that he is connecting me to *Nete Ibo Riosqui,* the world of the dean of the universe. Wow! The intoxication jumps up a notch!

First of all I descend into the depths. Tension, relaxation, tension, relaxation, the loops get larger, and then the madre of ayahuasca appears; a clear vision. She is standing and, with her arms open above her head, she is holding up the medicinal world. This world is immense, and I penetrate into it. In this way I receive her treatment. Then it's sky, a sky like those in religious paintings. A feeling, airy and strong, of gentle, powerful well-being. The world of love . . . In fact, I don't want to describe what took place next. Perhaps one day I'll have the opportunity to picture it in a film. Let's just say that I found once again the great strength of the five senses, a strength that I had lost.

How to speak about this?

After a series of very luminous episodes, I saw the immense houses of medicina in the room—they filled the maloca. And I had my eyes open. I experienced an intense joy, very precise, the joy of one who has found once again an intimate connection with the creator. And everything coming from these houses of the medicina was simple.

I was drifting in an airy feeling, the air seemed perfumed. And thoughts seemed to enter into me from outside. Everything seemed logical. Crystalline.

Childlike.

I see clearly, through the vision, the meaning of the diets.

I didn't expect this kind of information.

In order to connect to the light of Ibo Riosqui, to the medicinal force that seems to come from higher up, we pass through the world of nature, through the plants—through the medicinal world of the plants.

The diets lock in the connection to the luminous world of the medicina of the plant. In order to remain connected to the luminous part of this world, the diet is the path.

Everything seems simple to me, the visions are in place in the maloca; I feel like an aboriginal who has taken a full jugful of salvation. I am laughing inside. I have the impression that I am inhabiting my body with a strength that is lively and clear.

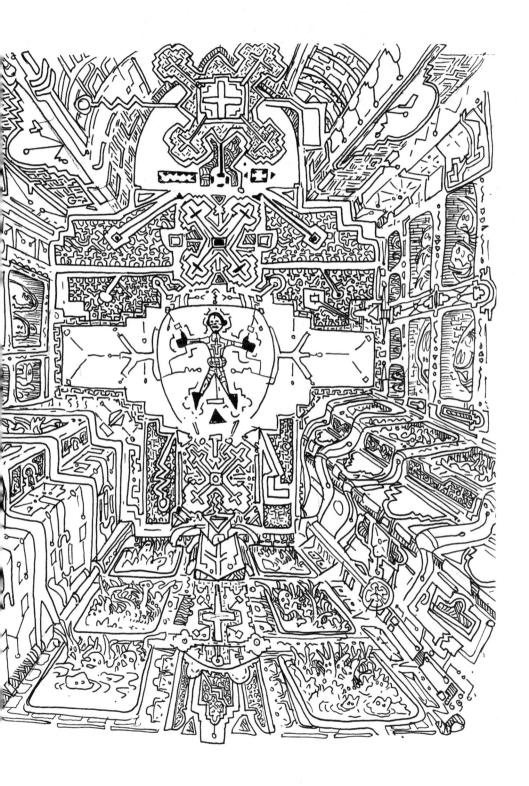

I go back and sit down. Being connected to the ayahuasca, the plant seems to be whispering to me the title of the comic strip that I've been drawing since the beginning. It's to be "Doctor Ayahuasca" (see page 123). I smile, it's a nice title.

Leaving the maloca (be careful: unless you have acquired a solid practice, you should never do what I'm describing here in the midst of a ceremony), I moved into the forest, not very far, but enough to be alone, and I sat down under a big tree. I listened to the songs of the birds and the cries of the monkeys; then I looked at the stars. And, from within my intoxication, I sang softly for nature. I saw spirits in the trees who seemed to be observing me quietly. I stayed there almost an hour and then reintegrated myself back into the maloca.

Guillermo had returned to singing for the group of yogis. After a while, he came back, threw down his cushion, and sighed with a smile. The work had been accomplished, but he was tired. He took off his t-shirt, stretched out on his stomach, and asked me to put a stone on his shoulder at a very precise spot. I did, surprised. I had never seen him work with stones on his body. He must have had a rough time energetically. A wave of admiration passed through me for the work of a healer, his work to help others.

MORNING

At breakfast I learn that there will not be a ceremony tonight—everyone has worked hard; it's time for a break. I run into Guillermo, who suggests that I go with him to a ceremony at Luz Kósmika with the apprentices. But now it's time to get together with the group of yogis. Everyone survived. I set about listening and translating. Matej is concise, precise, and short in what he's willing to share. He's now a solid ayahuasquero. Kania tells her story, which I can't write about because it's very personal, but let's just say that it's a grandiose introduction to the deep sacred wisdom of the medicina. I am captivated by all that I'm hearing, and I revise my judgment. Clearly the dose was very strong and one could not escape the experience, but it was a beautiful ceremony for her and for all the other yogis as well. Everyone has the sparkling look of someone who has passed through the veil to the other side. Guillermo ends the meeting with a big smile, "You're all new; tomorrow we're going further."

I run off for a moment to make these notes, because if tonight's ceremony is as strong as the last one with eight plants, I will have forgotten everything by tomorrow.

EVENING, LUZ KÓSMIKA, CEREMONY

I prepare myself to take a hit; it's the return of the special brew, cooked up by some of his pupils. Ricardo is there too. Ricardo, Guillermo, James, and I are seated facing the nine apprentices. I drink. I see the benefits of my diet, but the preparation lacks strength. We begin again. Nothing works, we don't take off. Tired, I watch Ricardo fall asleep and then fall asleep myself while Guillermo and James take care of the students.

MORNING

Return to Espíritu. I set to work painting again. I paid for construction of a house there, although it belongs to the center. I paint colored anacondas on the wall. But something is bothering me; I have an idea that my plane is early on the day after tomorrow. Is it really the day after tomorrow? I check and discover that my flight is the next day at 8:00 a.m.!

Tonight will be my last ceremony then, and I'm going to have to run directly to the airport at 6:00 a.m. Everything speeds up. The sky is black. I jump on my bike and dash to town to buy little articles of clothing that my daughter is crazy about, a few bottles of Agua Florida, and some mapacho.

I manage to get back before the rain. I throw things in my bag and arrange a departure with a motocaro for 6:00 a.m. By nightfall it's all in place. I check the PC, the installation. It's ready. I get set up in the maloca. Everybody stares at the mysterious machine that I place beside Guillermo. It's the last chance to do the experiment. Nobody asks me any questions, but later I find out that Ricardo said that it was a machine belonging to the director ayahuasquero Jan Kounen and that it would record Guillermo's visions!

I stretch out and let my mind wander.

■ ■ ■

This evening, as at the end of each visit, memories start coming back. On the path with the curanderos. The journey that I've been on with Guillermo is an incredible journey that will end in my death, or in his, or will continue into the hereafter. I recall the moment when I came back to see him a few years before in order to die. Jostled around in my thoughts, in my life, and in my apprenticeship, I did in fact return there, thinking I was going to die, telling myself that they—the healers— would look after my soul. I was very much out there psychologically. I had a premonition of what was going to happen, that I was going to die. However, even though it was intense and experienced to the full, the death was only symbolic.

I thought back to the first discussion with Guillermo, after the first three ceremonies, ten years before. Having difficulty containing my emotion, I had asked him if he would stay with me. I had promised to help him achieve his goals. I had also told him that we needed to do scientific experiments!

I smoke mapacho thinking of all that.

My aboriginal brother.

My friend.

Sometimes the closing of a diet can be a painful moment. During the diet the energies of the plants accumulate around the patient. When the diet is being closed, the healer causes the healing energies to penetrate into the patient's body. Then, using another song, the healer will protect the patient by positioning protections outside the patient (don't ask me how that is done). This operation is very strong for the person receiving it. Closing a diet can take several days. Little by little, the energy is positioned inside, harmonized, then the closing has been carried out and locked in by the song of protection. In general, only right at the very end do you feel really good as you wake up in the morning. Sometimes you have to wait several days to feel the effects.

I remember the very difficult closing of my first diet, before and after, when I didn't realize that my diet was *him*.

REMEMBERING
THE CLOSING DIET

THIRD JOURNEY

In December 1999 I made my third journey. I returned for a stay of a few weeks along with my friends Gaspar, Vincent, Anne, and a few others.

After several ceremonies Guillermo said to me privately, "It's good—you are ready. During this stay, I will transmit my knowledge to you." Then very quickly everything is spoiled. I suffer. In the following sessions I have only dark visions. It gets worse and worse. I think that Guillermo wants to steal my soul. I have terrifying thoughts about the man I've elevated to the rank of spiritual father. We leave on an eight-hour pirogue trip to the community of Paoyan. During the night on the river I tremble in the darkness—an irrational fear of the jungle. I look at him, he's no longer smiling; I have a cold-blooded anaconda facing me. This trip is unreason, it is terror. The ceremonies continue and my state of paranoia worsens. One morning I try to catch Guillermo in order to speak with him, because I no longer see him except during the ceremonies. I slip and fall in the mud. He turns around. I lift my hand. It's a movie! I ask him for mercy.

The anaconda looks at me, then continues on his way.

Very hard moment. My confidence is put to the test.

What keeps me from fleeing, from taking the first plane out, is the nature of the moments spent in other worlds with this man who had, from the first day, opened his inner world to me. I saw who he was. From the first ceremony, from the first song he sang, I knew that our destinies were linked, that I was home, that he would be my maestro. My history with him was obvious, everything played out in ten short minutes. So the harshness of what I'm suffering is new. But this is the path. I cling desperately to this last thought. It would be just stupid to give up on everything now.

There's nothing I can share with my friends. My solitude is immense even though I try to put on a brave face.

JUNGLE, NIGHT, CEREMONY

The preparation is too strong, or to be more exact—too strong for me. My friends are simmering nicely. The Indians are not at all fazed by it. I have visions with my eyes wide open in the room. I'm not holding it together. When the songs end, I leave the room—there is too much energy in the maloca. I literally hang on to the branches of the closest tree. I look up at the sky. At the sight of the canopy of heaven I feel that the world is upside down and that I'm going to fall into the sky, fall endlessly toward the stars, dissolve completely.

I am Icarus, my wings are burning up.

My goal as I see it is to be plummeting. To survive: kneel down, hold this tree in my arms, and wait for dawn.

A FEW INSANE NIGHTS LATER

Before the ceremony on the second to last evening of our stay, when I'm in Guillermo's garden with Anne, he says to me, "This evening, I'm going to transmit my knowledge to you." Anne is surprised to hear these words. As for me, I am relieved. I had held on; it was time for the payback. Right away I start to imagine that I'm going to have the navigation keys to other realities. I sit down, confident, in the maloca. We drink. The ceremony begins.

Nothing.

No effect.

At the end of forty-five minutes I look around me. I have a somewhat pathetic feeling with respect to my nighttime companions.

Guillermo sings and treats people one by one. This particular evening he doesn't call me. I look at the curanderos and see them as poor beings lost in old, supernatural beliefs. I am terrified by these sensations and these thoughts. How is this possible? An hour before, there I was living in a magical and terrifying world; now I am confronted by the reality of what I perceive with the whole of my being. For us, little white men, it's all very clear: these journeys are nothing but illusions. I try to escape from these thoughts. It's impossible. A terrible sadness rises up slowly over the course of the night. Disgust with myself increases inexorably. I let it invade me and a wave of thoughts wells up and overtakes me. "The whole thing is false; everything I've experienced is an illusion."

Then I latch on to this thought: what I experienced was magnificent. For a moment, I believed it. I need to cherish the memory of what I believed in. It was a magic spell of salvation, pure and beautiful, full of mercy and madness. In this way, little by little, I regain my self-esteem. The world is no longer magic, but for months I believed that it was, a sort of Santa Claus for adults. And I had to cherish this memory like a precious gift.

I distance myself from the songs, from the journey, and I literally latch on to this thought all night long. Then in the early hours of the morning I get up and move to make a gesture of acknowledgment to Guillermo before going home to bed. I grit my teeth. He looks at me and tosses me an *adiós*. I read his look as, "Make your choices; return or never return. You are free, as I am free toward you."

I have never been so sad.

I go back to my room, but I'm unable to sleep. Anne comes to see me and instinctively takes me in her arms. I cry like a child. I was the one who advised her to take this trip. She is a director, and I wanted her sensitivity to be part of *D'autres mondes*. I thought too that an encounter with the vine would be positive for her. Never could I have imagined that she would pull me out of this state, nor that I would fall insanely in love with her during this journey. I weep, my body relaxes, and the visions open. I see a blue hummingbird fly out of my heart, I feel a great relaxation, and then I fall asleep.

In the morning I am okay, suddenly freed of my thoughts and

desires connected to the idea of becoming a curandero. They went up in smoke.

I am surprised and happy to savor this new relaxation—a peace I hadn't known for months. That particular morning, for the first time, I no longer questioned the nature of the experiences. The day is peaceful, and in a state of calm I go to take the boat to Yarinacocha.

YARINACOCHA, LAST CEREMONY BEFORE RETURNING TO PARIS

In front of Guillermo once again, I thank him for the night before and explain to him that from now on I am freed. I have understood that it is not my calling to be a curandero. I am happy to accompany him humbly in this final ceremony. He replies that everyone is needed in making the world: healers, movie directors, fishermen, scientists. Each one has his own importance.

We are drinking a new preparation. The special farewell cocktail, ayahuasca and chacruna, was cooked with cane sugar. It's the sugar I think that accelerates and amplifies the release in the brain of the sacred molecules. Guillermo calls me.

He begins to sing.

I am thunderstruck.

My eyes are wide open.

Luminous spirits are around Guillermo and above me. A crown of light descends on my head. As a multicolored shawl literally winds around my neck, luminous panels are placed on my body. A great feeling of respect floods into me, respect for the plants and for the Indian world—a lineage, a coming to fruition.

Sonia, Guillermo's wife, is at his side. I hear her murmur, "Look. He sees."

I move into a vortex of images of powerful spirits who introduce themselves to me. After that I have no further memory of what I experienced. I am proud, though, that I remained conscious. My friends told me that I lost consciousness for half an hour, then I had jumped up and resumed my initial position—legs bent in front of me and my arms wrapped around them, like Rascar Capac.

■ ■ ■

In the morning Guillermo says to me, "I've put protections in place for you. The diet is finished for you." As for me, I was not aware of anything to do with diets, but for a few weeks I had been eating almost nothing—a little rice. I was weak; even Guillermo encouraged me to eat more.

The last two ceremonies were a huge shower that repeatedly turned hot and cold. But I didn't think about it any longer. It was only some months later that my interpretation of what I had lived through the day before this ceremony—the meaning of Guillermo's attitude—became coherent. He had transmitted his knowledge to me—to remember that in oneself, in every man, the one who judges and doesn't believe in anything is always there, lying in wait, ready to jump in. He had plunged me totally into this feeling so that I could see that part of myself, a part capable of dominating the whole being.

Knowledge is not a pilot's manual for the mind, for the soul. It's self-knowledge—the knowledge of the forces that lie dormant in the being. It's remembering to hang on to one's faith when all your thoughts are telling you the opposite, when you are submerged in negative energy. It's working to be connected to your heart and in doing so cleansing your mind deeply.

He had shown me the way. The outcome had the effect of realigning my shamanic ambitions. I was not being led by the desire to become a curandero for the wrong reasons but was now simply accepting the adventure that I was offered in order to expand my perception of the world and develop connections to other worlds, and in this way move forward. My role with traditional medicine is in a different direction.

That day, my confidence in Guillermo grew. I thought of Castaneda and impeccability.* Guillermo took the risk that I would leave. Afterward he showed me the light, but first he had to make me go through the darkness.

He did not cheat on his tradition, on the teaching.

---

*According to anthropologist and author Carlos Castaneda, impeccability is doing one's best in any endeavor, free of self-importance, assumptions, and preconceptions.

In all his actions he also dissolved the misplaced feeling of a father that I had constructed around him. I already had a father whom I needed to find once again. He assumed the position, which has not changed up to today, of an older brother. Sometimes I wonder if he was certain that I would come back to see him. I think so. In any case, after that I often saw apprentices disappear on that very day, the day before receiving. It's a little sad sometimes.

With joy I again found my place as an artist-entertainer. The dimensions of our feelings are tangible worlds. The imaginary, like dreams, is a real world of experience. Denying that is to reject our potential as creators.

END OF NOTES ON THIS JOURNEY,
DECEMBER 1999

I WANNA GO HOME

LAST CEREMONY

Guillermo has just sat down. Immediately I tell him that I was mistaken and that I leave the next morning at 6:00 a.m. He puts on a surprised look, "My brother, you're leaving already. It's sad." We joke about it. I show him the setup for the experiment. "Here's the machine. The idea is that you enter into the experiment when you want to. The machine will run for six hours." He says, "I'll do it at the beginning, when my intoxication is really strong." Okay. I press *start* and the program begins running. During this time Ricardo has had everyone drink, and once again it's a big dose for the yogis. My admiration for them increases. Now they're drinking the melted chocolate in full knowledge of what they're doing. Respect!

RICARDO: What are you going to take this evening—the normal dose or what the yogis are taking?

JAN: (a quick cycle goes around in my head) Er . . . And you, what are you taking?

RICARDO: Guillermo and I are taking the same dose as the yogis.

JAN: (wrinkling the eyebrows) Okay. The same as you then . . .

Ricardo begins to pour, but so quickly that the glass is half full very soon. It looks like the chocolate liquid has already reached at least four times the normal dose. My hand goes up to tell him to stop. He looks at me, amused.

RICARDO: (surprised) You're afraid?

He bursts out laughing. I smile and say to myself, "Okay. Anyway, all is well up to here, and then shit happens." I tell him to continue. He adds some more. I think of the famous "one mouthful too many" and drink. The preparation is terrible; it's so concentrated that it flows slowly down my esophagus. I go back to my place.

After only about ten minutes, Kania restarts her litany of the evening before: "Help me, Guillermo, I wanna go home . . ." Immediately I have this very special feeling, or this thought: "Now what've I done?" I'm joking, but it wasn't funny. Beside me I hear the voice of a patient, "Oh, no! Not again . . ." Everyone is thinking the same thing: "No, Kania, pull yourself together." Then it begins to pitch and sway and vomit. The intoxication twists me. Guillermo doesn't move. I concentrate on centering myself. This time he doesn't get up and go to help Kania. After a moment, it's Matej, stumbling in his strong intoxication, who leads her up to Guillermo. She's trembling and hangs onto his feet, "Help me!" Ricardo vomits a lot. I'm in a serious tailspin. Her energy flows toward us. Guillermo begins to sing to relieve her. We're off.

My intoxication explodes; everybody begins to simmer.

I remember feeling the nausea just behind my lips for a long time after Kania returned to her place. I remember especially that in the middle of the ceremony Guillermo called me and that I was surprised. "Yes? What?" "Come!"

I had forgotten that this was the last evening; I even think that I didn't remember until he began to sing. I will not describe the visions. They were very strong. Light! Instead, I'd rather speak of the feeling that I experienced and that I will remember for all time.

Rising up through the worlds of the medicina toward harmony; within a half hour, peace settles in. Then, joy—an immense, irresistible joy. I clench my teeth so as not to laugh, to keep my concentration. The joy of life spreads with new strength through my whole being.

Paratatoninbi chono joyomatana je
From down there, I install the swallows*

Swallows refers to "pretty young girls."

Chono joyomatana, mestamayontana;
In leading in the swallows, I adorn them;

akin shamanra, jakon akin shamanra
I set myself to do this

nete metsaayona, metsaayonbanori
I adorn the universe, I adorn it so much

nokon joi ronrona, ronronaitoninra;
my words resound, how they resound;

nete soi ayona, paro soi ayona
I adorn the universe, I illuminate the river

en toninra, soiyatoninra je
at this moment

noma kakaira je
the multitude of doves

senen parabetanai je
arrive in ordered fashion

nete raromanona (repeat two times)
by brightening life in a resounding way

raromayontana
by brightening it

pishamanra, metsatishamanra
life becomes very beautiful

nete machiankiri;
the whole universe is illumined;

metsaabetanai
they come in as they adorn (repeat two times)

nete sheka kanonra;
these forces of the universe;

nete raromayonke, mai raromayonke
I have brightened the universe, I have brightened the earth

paro raromayonke
I have brightened the river

nete senemayona je
the universe becomes harmonized

joi senemayona je
the word becomes fulfilled

kayan kayanra je
and this, and this

shaman kayan kayanra je.
and this, until infinity.

The song ends; I remain floating in the joy of life. A universal joy that I had forgotten?

Yes.

I was good, centered, but I had forgotten.

The quintessence of the human—pure joy. Love.

Forgotten that the source of all strength is love.

Love in joy.

Joy and love.

Protection—joy protects my being.

It nourishes my being; it aligns its thoughts and its actions.

Joy.

Happy are those who are blessed . . .

The great strength of the five senses. A big joy.

A sacred joy.

I bite my lip so as not to laugh at the simplicity and the obviousness, and yet I've known this from the first time. Guillermo gets up and goes about continuing his work. Meanwhile, I am crumpled into my strong intoxication. The worlds of the medicina spread through the maloca and the maloca rises into the cosmos. I follow the worlds in the ícaros. The songs intersect with the harmony. I apply my songs over theirs, which for me further opens the worlds of the *medicina*. Ricardo calls me and does a song of protection for my diet. The ceremony is coming to a close. Guillermo comes back to sit down and says to me, "So, *carapate cósmica*, how are you doing?" I explode with laughter. I need to say that *Jan* in Shipibo means "centipede" (*carapate*). Ricardo puts together a great song for Guillermo, a hypersensitive song such as I had never heard done before. I see luminous spirits descend, rivers of love that flow onto him and onto me, because I am right beside him and very connected to his journey. This is my final gift.

The sun rises, I am very intoxicated, and in two hours I will leave for the airport. I sit down on a bench; it's working away hard in my body. The second Kiss Cool* effect: bile and saliva flow in great quantities from my mouth. This is a new experience (final cleansing). Guillermo is having conversations with the patients. Ricardo, still very intoxicated, a mapacho cigarette in his mouth, comes up and sticks his face a couple of inches away from mine. We talk a bit, laughing about the force of the ceremony. He asks me what time I'm leaving. Later on he comes back to say good-bye and to bring me a very beautiful, traditional painted fabric.

I love this man. Our friendship has taken years to be formed. I met him when he was only a young apprentice healer, and over the years I watched him get involved in the medicina, embark on long diets, and gain a great deal of strength. This summer with him I often worked on the songs, and I learned many things. Most importantly, he put a lot of energy into cleansing for me so I could connect high up and strongly.

I watch him get up, stumbling a bit.

RICARDO: See you soon! I still have a bit of intoxication; I'm going to sing for my son.

I realize that I'm still very deep. I hum a melody. I start up my mareación again. Soon, I'll be at the airport. I feel good.

---

*[This is a reference to a French advertising jingle for a breath mint named Kiss Cool: "The first effect is cool; the second effect is pretty good too." —*Trans.*]

I gather up my things and discover all the scientific equipment, which I'd completely forgotten about, really and completely forgotten about. I laugh about it. I secretly hope that Guillermo will have something to say to me about it. There is just time to give hugs all around, and then I jump into the motocaro.

JAN: Guillermo, I forgot to ask you. Were you able to do the experiment?

GUILLERMO: I began to do it when Kania came and held onto my leg, and then I was carried away by the work. I forgot!

We laugh. It will be for another time. When the motocaro takes me away I have some compassionate thoughts for the scientists in France who were waiting for results.

The return trip went off peacefully (I have my plastic lunch box containing food for my diet). I'm in economy class, but I have the feeling I'm in first class on Anaconda Airlines. I write up my final notes and then sleep for the whole trip. On arrival I add these last words, "A stream of fresh water flows in me."

I reenter my life on the other side, my companion Anne. I feel my love for her and watch out for the sensual orientation of my thoughts, but the diet is well protected. To my great surprise, desire does not arise to disturb me. I'm back with Douglas, my big boy, and Biri, our darling daughter, relatives, and the warm support of friends. Great happiness— a month's vacation in Corsica! The sun is shining on my planet.

END OF NOTEBOOK,
AUGUST 2009

EPILOGUE

This year I spent a lot of time in Peru. I've just come back to close a new diet. The plan was that once back I would review the book, which in the meantime had been corrected. Having done that, I realize that I haven't really spoken about the carnal desire and the amorous adventures that the plants awakened me to—a desire that is no doubt linked to the effects of the diet.

Have I really addressed the question, "What has the medicina done for me?" Yes, in rereading the book I believe I have.

People often ask me that question, and there is always a silence before I can speak. Perhaps there's too much to say?

What to add?

I would say that this medicine reconciled me with myself, it allowed me to come into contact with myself, and then to relax as I faced life. Initially it shook me up, and afterward it calmed me down. On the creative front, it extended the reach of my artistic endeavors and moderated, channeled, my passion for the cinema. And the most important thing—it opened me to life. I would like to live to be old, to watch my children grow up for as long as possible, but if I die, I can today thank all those whose paths I've crossed—for my welfare, for my misfortune, for the joy, and for the hurt. I feel that up to now I've had a very full life, joyful and crazy—a beautiful entertainer's life.

AYAHUASCA MEDICINA, A MANUAL

Forty Questions and Answers

So, I write down: what happens is indescribable.

THE BASICS

Ayahuasca Medicine, Diets, and Songs

This little manual offers answers to questions that I have been repeatedly asked and that, I imagine, you will have if you make the journey.

As with the "Inner Journey Notebooks," I've made an effort to instill a bit of humor into my answers.

Let's first tackle the heart of the subject: the experience.

Practical details will be found at the end.

⚔ What is this medicine? How does it work?

First of all, we have to set ayahuasca aside for a moment and speak of traditional Shipibo medicine. At the heart of this medicine we find the teaching plants (you'll find a list of them in the "Glossary of Plants"). Most of the medicinal plants and teaching plants are not psychotropic.

Let's start with how that works for the patient.

The person coming for a consultation has a difficulty that may be physical, psychological, or spiritual. The healer, having taken ayahuasca so as to see the problem in a precise way, will examine the person during a ceremony. The healer will then will sing ícaros (see page 154) to reharmonize the person's energy.

Ayahuasca is a diagnostic tool for the healer. There is no necessity for the patient to take it.

Certain sufficiently advanced healers no longer need a ceremony in order to know how to treat an affliction; they are able to "read" patients without that tool.

Once the diagnosis has been established, the patient can begin a diet—dieting with a particular plant given by the curandero.

⚔ A diet? You get put on a diet?

Plant diets are at the heart of traditional medicine. Plants are the secret knowledge and the basis of the therapeutic treatment.

It is essential to choose a good curandero in order to be well connected to the medicinal world of plants.

Diet: The Curandero's Instrument for Healing

Through diets followed for many long years, the healer has acquired knowledge and strength. When treating a patient, a curandero has visions and, according to the visions, will use songs to call to the world of a plant that the healer has dieted with, in order to transform the visions and harmonize them, and by doing that, treats the patient. Based on the pathology that is to be treated, the healer will choose a diet for the patient.

The Diet Is the Patient's Treatment

During the diet, one ingests a plant-based drink.

The plants that are recommended as diets are teaching and healing plants. Most are not psychotropic: piri piri, ajo sacha, ojé, chay, bobinsana, piñon blanco, piñon colorado, aire sacha, marosa, renaco. Some others are psychotropic: coca, tobacco, toé (datura), ayahuasca, sky ayahuasca. Each one of these plants contains several worlds, one of which is a medicinal world.

The patient drinks the diet plant once a day, either upon waking and before eating, or at the end of the afternoon. The curandero, using the songs, orients, directs, and intensifies the action of the plant.

Opening the Diet

The diet has to be "opened" by the healer during a ceremony. At the beginning of the ceremony, the patient takes a glass of the diet plant, often followed by a glass of ayahuasca (but the ayahuasca is not obligatory). It is not necessary to take the ayahuasca for therapeutic reasons. This is something that can be discussed between you and your healer. During the night, at the appropriate moment, the healer will sing a particular song to open the energy of the plant in the body and in the mind of the patient.

Sequestering

During the diet, ideally, the patient is sequestered in the forest in a tumbo in order to limit conversation, mental agitation, and to stay in the dieter's own "juice" and the juice of the diet plant. Little by little the dream world will open up for the dieter and spirits will appear in dreams during half-awakened periods.

Dietary Restrictions

Each plant requires that the dieter follow a particular dietary regimen. Some are more limiting than others, but let's say that the basics are: no salt, no sugar, little or no grease, no red meat, absolutely no pork, no alcohol, and no sex.

You can understand that salt, sugar, and alcohol can be in conflict with the diet plant; after all, in our Western medicine contraindications exist for most medications.

But sex?

Sex is a powerful physical and mental energy. Therefore there must be no sex with others or . . . oneself. Otherwise, a shock or conflict will happen with the plant's energy.

Don't Break Your Diet

For the diet to be effective you have to follow the curandero's directions. If you feel that it's too hard, you need to ask for it to be closed rather than risk breaking it.

You need to know that if you break your diet or if you "bend" it, you're making more work for the healer who opened it.

Respect your diet. It's not a big deal in the Amazon and is fairly easy to maintain because it's all organized that way. However, the lack of forbidden food sometimes makes itself felt in the visions, especially in diets that are long. According to different reports, during the ayahuasca ceremonies you may have dreams or even visions of butter and jam or chocolate cakes floating by in front of you; for Americans, it may be hamburgers and cheesecake; and for many people, at times, it may be erotic images.

So long as the diet is not closed you are open energetically. The dieter is sensitive and fragile during treatment. The required asceticism can seem a bit doctrinal, especially for the sex. But it's not; it's an energetic issue.

Now you're going to tell me, for sex, okay, I'll manage. But what if, without realizing it, I eat some forbidden food, what if I bend my diet accidently? That's not as serious; the curandero can straighten out your diet. That's why it's difficult to do diets in an urban environment or to follow a diet in the West.

I've even tested going off the diet myself—it's very painful. All you need to do is to go to a restaurant and eat some fish cooked with salt to feel bowled over, have cold sweats, and vomit your guts out, shaking like a leaf, whereas a few minutes before you were in fine form. As for sex, it stands to reason that the result is even worse; I've never had it happen.

If you feel you're not going to be able to stick to the diet, it's much better not to do it; it's safer.

Closing the Diet

At the end of the diet, the healer will devote a song to it during a new ayahuasca ceremony and close the diet. That means deeply implanting the energy of the plants in you, and then putting in place an energetic protection. It's somewhat like putting a roof on a house that was under construction and had been open to the sky for a few weeks. Now it can rain salt, meat, and sex and the house will be protected.

Continue to be careful during this last stage! You don't have to run off the day after the closing to chow down a dish of salted lentils with a pint of beer and end up in bed with the first person you come across.

You need to reintroduce food progressively and carefully and be sensitive when it comes to sex, especially if the diet has been long.

To complement the diet and the ceremonies you can receive various treatments: massage (generally it's Shipibo women who practice this art), plant baths, and steam baths with plants.

The minimum length for a diet is two weeks, but they can extend to several months or even years.

Apprenticeship Diet

If you want to be trained in Amazonian medicine—that is, do an apprenticeship—it's the same principle: the curandero opens your diet, but the diet is much more powerful and much longer, between three months and a year minimum. And with apprenticeship diets, you must have no thoughts about sex and exercise control of your dreams!

BONUS

Here is a little story about diets. One morning a friend on a diet in Peru cracks up. He leaves the center and takes off for Iquitos. He settles himself comfortably in a restaurant and orders a hamburger. Just as he's biting into it, he feels a hand on his shoulder. My friend turns around and, petrified, cries out in surprise: right beside him, there is Guillermo, full of smiles. Guillermo bestows on him a *"Holá, ¿qué tal?"* and then moves away and sits down some distance away. My friend looked at his hamburger, and of course he no longer had the courage and was not reckless enough to eat it. The good had rescued him.

Personally, I never heard diets spoken about during my first four years. Guillermo knew that I wanted to learn. From time to time during the ceremonies he would give me preparations of special plants to drink after the ayahuasca, but he never gave me any information on the diets. Sometimes he would say, "This evening, you're going to encounter something." It was partly my fault. In fact, after my first three ceremonies, I said to him, through my buddy Fred since I did not understand Spanish, "I want to learn with you. I don't want to learn Spanish, because we don't need it. You speak to me in my mind during the ceremonies. Everything has to take place there; this will be a proof of the effectiveness of your teaching." Afterward I really regretted saying this. Of course, I did learn Spanish. I speak it like a French cow, but it's needed for communication outside of the ceremonies. And, as for Guillermo, he almost never said anything to me anymore. That's how I came to set up the modalities of our relationship.

So, I received no information on diets.

Then I began to diet without knowing it. I couldn't make love any more, no desire; I began to smoke a lot of mapacho; and I ate very little, no meat at all. This lasted up until the last ceremony when Guillermo said to me, "Your strong diets are over from now on." I understood, because in the early hours of the morning I had gotten hungry and desire came back full-blown.

And then a few years later I show up for the first time at Espíritu and discover that diets are being suggested. Strange. Everyone is talking about their diets, but I remain skeptical. I even wonder what good it does to mix diet plants with ayahuasca from the first ceremonies on. Then, little by little, I came to understand why people were interested, thanks especially to François, who explained their importance to me in apprenticeship. I run off to see Guillermo, "Hey, you never spoke to me about that! I want to take my turn at dieting!" He replied, "In your case, you're getting a special treatment. I'm sharing my knowledge with you; I'm giving it to you almost without a diet."

During the following two years, he gave me various diets that never lasted more than three months, mainly piñon blanco, tobacco, and aire sacha. So I'm not the best qualified person to be talking about diets. Some of the apprentices have several years of dieting behind them and an extensive knowledge of procedures.

⚔ But what does this ayahuasca do anyway?

Yikes! I always dread that question, because you could talk about it for years.

So, today's assignment: answer it with just a few lines.

Let's set aside for a moment the visions, the spirits, and the cosmology and try to approach this question in the most practical way possible.

This medicine is going to launch you into a new experience. You're going to be in a state of consciousness that you likely have seldom or perhaps never known in your life, or solely in extreme situations. You will experience the climax of certain pairs of emotions: pleasant/unpleasant, ecstatic/terrifying, joyful/sad.

The medicina is going to toss you into extreme positions of your emotional, feeling, recollective, and cognitive cursors—the whole thing really. Why? For your own good.

Let me explain. If the experience of terror is virtual, which means that it is not connected directly to an actual mortal danger, becoming familiar with this state will allow you to better master this emotion should you run into it again.

Ecstasy . . . Master it and learn to let go of it; learn not to hold on to it. In this way, you will not be taken over by suffering, disappointment, sadness, and confusion when you come upon your mental projection that was generated during your ecstasy, or simply at the moment when that ecstasy disappears.

Diving into negative emotions is also a way of expunging them through catharsis. The positive will have flourished and will be anchored in. By finding your way through certain states you will be less overwhelmed by them in the future and will become a little animal that is more conscious of what you are and what you are experiencing. So, move your cursor to the outer edges of the two sides of emotion to enlarge your spectrum of self-knowledge. An extended spectrum means leaving behind childhood fears and recovering the pure joy that you knew then but have somehow forgotten.

It's true that the therapy is somewhat warlike, because it came from people living in the jungle. Initially their intentions were connected to survival. Your body is going to be shaken up: you know that ayahuasca is a powerful purgative; you're likely to vomit and have diarrhea. At a therapeutic dosage, which means one that stimulates a strong experience, the vine is unforgiving; if you have fear or a problem, it's going to go right after it.

And that's why you need to go see those with the knowledge, those who can guide you through this inner apprenticeship. What I'm telling you may seem simplistic, but I find that too often we forget this straightforward view of ayahuasca.

⚔ Isn't it really just an excuse to take drugs?

This is a question I was asked during discussions following the screening of my film *D'autres mondes*. I must confess that, after the film and more than an hour of discussion, I was saying to myself, "Some people are really hardheaded."

This is what I found when I took a little tour of Wikipedia, typing in *psychotropic* and *drug*. Selected passages:

The term *psychotropic* means literally "that which gives a direction" (from the Greek *trope*) "to the mind or to behavior" (*psycho*).

A substance is called psychotropic when its chemical composition, be it of natural or artificial origin, has a psychological *tropism*, that is, it has the ability to modify mental activity, regardless of the type of modification that might be.

The effect that is felt when a psychotropic substance is used is sometimes called a psychotropic effect. While it is generally understood that the psychotropic effect can be induced by a psychotropic substance, this effect can also be achieved by spirituality, meditation, or through art.

Drug: A substance whose psychotropic effects give rise to sensations related to pleasure, causing repeated usage to make the effect last permanently and to ward off the psychological distress (psychological dependence) or even the physical distress (physical dependence) that would arise if the ingestion were discontinued, thus turning the ingestion into a need.

Ayahuasca is neither poisonous nor addictive, and taking it is not always a picnic—more often it's an act of courage. It's true that it's a powerful psychotropic substance. So it should perhaps be categorized as a "psychotropic medication," but I don't much like the idea of seeing it associated with antidepressants—Prozac or its brothers and sisters— the consumption of which we in France are world champions at.* No, it belongs somewhere else, somewhere not so easy to find.

---

*A study published June 19, 2013, suggests that the use of antidepressants has been on the rise in Europe, with U.K. use increasing 495% between 1991 and 2009. (Ricardo Gusmão, et al., "Antidepressant Utilization and Suicide in Europe: An Ecological Multi-National Study," *PLoS ONE* 8, no. 6 (2013): e66455, doi:10.1371/journal.pone.0066455.) Similarly, "From 1988–1994 through 2005–2008, the rate of antidepressant use in the United States among all ages increased nearly 400%." (Laura Pratt, et al., "Antidepressant Use in Persons Aged 12 and Over: United States, 2005–2008," *NCHS Data Brief*, no. 76, October 2011.)

In France, it was added to the list of narcotics.

Ayahuasca is sometimes associated with religious practices, notably in the Santo Daime churches (recognized in Spain, Portugal, United Kingdom, Canada, the Netherlands, and the United States), the União do Vegetal, and other eclectic organizations. Are the faithful having their minds manipulated? Could that spill over into our own homes? Maybe that's the kind of questions the legislators asked themselves. Uncertain, they banned the vine, using as an excuse, I believe, laboratory tests in which mice staggered around under the influence of this plant. Mice stuffed with ayahuasca—how surprising that they were staggering around! Poor dears, not a single curandero to help you?

> "Center yourself, my dear little mouse.
> Center yourself well in your intoxication.
> No help is going to come to you from outside."

Now what's happening for the mouse? The drink opens her mind. Suddenly she perceives completely differently. In the quantum leap of the opening of her consciousness, the little white mouse discovers that she is in fact in a laboratory or treatment center belonging to a higher intelligence. What she believed to be wild nature, the frontier of her world, is in reality a space created by very strange, gigantic creatures— the *viviseccionos* (vivisectionists). They possess a much higher consciousness than hers. What a fascinating discovery! In fact, they are in the process of establishing contact with her. Using this miraculous substance that must have come from their knowledge, the viviseccionos open her mind. She is the chosen one, the very mouse who will establish contact with them. A bit freaked out by this new responsibility, upset by the nausea and the intoxication, the little white mouse stumbles. She needs to find a way to get information through to them. To tell them that "yes, it works" and that a new era between humans and mice is going to open up. At the same time, there is another phenomenon happening: she is getting new information about herself. She is suddenly aware that she is a living being destined to die. This is not a very pleasant discovery. Trembling, she wonders what there is before and after death. Visions spring up in her mind that tell the tale of the history of mice and men. And at that point she says to herself that humans, and more particularly those around her belonging to the caste of viviseccionos, have not come to this experiment with her welfare at heart—even that they perhaps have other goals. All that becomes really upsetting.

And yet, they really seem so much more intelligent. How is this possible?

The little mouse is overcome by intense fear, but she says to herself that she needs to convey a sign to them, tell them that it works. And later, solutions will be found.

Everything comes together in her now-opened mind. Wandering around and falling down, she looks for a solution and finally finds one: "I'm going to lie down on my back and wiggle my feet. They will see that this is not my usual behavior, and they'll understand that something is happening. Yes!" With great effort, since she's still very intoxicated, she turns over and wiggles and wiggles . . . Images of her mother, of her ancestors, rise up in her mind in a new way, and she takes a new energy from that. Stretched out on her back, she waves her legs nonstop.

The human bends over the little mouse. He sees the legs that are waving at greater and greater speed. His lips purse and he writes, "Total loss of orientation, possible intense suffering." He thinks, "I wouldn't like to be in her place!"

Conclusion: dangerous psychotropic substance.

Instead of conducting experiments on poor little mice, the scientists should have developed a study protocol with human ayahuasqueros. There are thousands of people who take ayahuasca every evening in South America. Don't you think such a course would be scientifically more convincing in terms of both communication and accuracy?

I'm going to surprise you: even though this ban is perfectly ridiculous given the nature of the subject (inside you, your inner space, no one will hear your cries, and not just because you're a mouse), there are nevertheless certain positive aspects connected to the banning of ayahuasca.

Although ayahuasca is not a drug, and even though I'm going to amuse you in describing its effects, the experience must be taken seriously.

Banning it will dissuade those who might otherwise take the vine as a recreational drug or as a medication that they can order on the Internet and take all alone.

The ban will push the most determined individuals to travel and meet native peoples for whom ayahuasca is a medicine. They are the practitioners, the specialists in the matter. That's the really positive aspect of the ban.

In France ayahuasca is considered to be a very dangerous drug. Whereas in Peru it has become, by decree, a national patrimony of the Peruvian people (see page xviii).

There are those who know and those who don't.

Those who have drunk and those who make mice drink.

It's all very clear. I'm sorry, but you're going to have to save your pennies and set out for South America to be with the aboriginals. But in the end it's best that way.

⚑ But if you've taken this plant, how does the healer guide you?

It's very simple and yet complicated at the same time.

It's hard to know really—it's a cultural question. An aboriginal can understand how a pilot makes a plane fly or how the pilot flies, but to really know everything that is taking place during flight, one must assimilate the history of aviation and understand the physics and mathematics of flight. In short, the whole thing remains somewhat mysterious, but the pilot is still capable of making the plane fly.

So I'm going to play the role of an aboriginal who has made a bunch of flights and who has been given the control stick. I'm going to explain to you how the pilot revs up the motors, talks to the control tower, and keeps the plane balanced and in trim. But I'm not going to tell you how the motors work and, essentially, how this pile of scrap metal manages to stay up in the air.

The healer takes the drink and allows the intoxication to climb. When the intoxication is strong the healer pulls back on the control stick while singing to open the intoxication with force and care. This is done for the healer and also for all the patients/passengers. This work is done to align the intoxication well and to harmoniously direct the collective energy of the group.

The healer's awareness of his own intoxication is like a surfer on a stormy sea with big breakers dancing around. To enable the consciousness to slide and manage the intoxication, a surfboard is needed. The song is the surfboard, slip sliding on the big wave of the healer's intoxication where the foam of his thoughts crashes away. The song will focus and concentrate the healer.

The intoxication is then an internal wave; he slides over it, he lets it fill him. The healer is a surfer of intoxication, taking you along with him. Together you climb up onto the surf; sometimes you are hanging on like a cat with its claws digging in, and you are with him as long as your thought doesn't take you away.

He draws arabesques on the wave of his sadness, blows away the foam of his fears. The healer knows the way. Guided by visions, he brings your own path alive through them and, all at once, dives into your intoxication, your world. A curandero is able to dive into this great vertigo, enter into this world and sing there, nausea just behind the lips, because he has traveled far in his fear, in the great metaphysical terrors as well as in his ecstasies. The curandero has acquired knowledge through long diets so he can, while you are there trembling, travel through the same state as you, but calmly.

Reports from several Shipibo healers indicate that during the song they take a reading of the patient in which they see various events in the person's life appear before them. They go back through these events, as in a film, toward the origin of the illness. Once the origin has been identified they will wait to see the same vision a second time in order to confirm the diagnosis. Then they will have the information they need: how to heal the patient, with which plant, and how long it will take.

Several times you have spoken of songs, of *icaros*. What are they for? Can they be understood?

The songs are the main therapeutic tool. They arise from the concepts of the medicina but also sometimes directly from spirits who position themselves and sing in the ear of a healer who then has only to sing what is heard. During apprenticeship diets it also happens that the songs arrive out of context. Or else it comes from the thought process of the healer, who, by association, goes looking for the energy of a plant with the song. In short, you see, there are a thousand and one kinds of song.

The curandero uses them to guide and care for the patient. However, this is done in the curandero's own language and, even though the patient may feel in the melody the intention of the traditional doctor, understanding the meaning of the words, and therefore the concepts, does help the patient who is receiving the song.

If you understand, even if only a little, about what the song is saying, it's better. I have myself explored the sharing of this understanding and have had impressive results. In fact, I have seen changes in the nature of what I was experiencing by understanding the songs—not all the words of course, because I don't speak the language, but enough to recognize at key moments the nature of the way the healer was operating. I had occasion to have this experience with others. During a ceremony with French ayahuasquero friends, someone suggested I sing and I did so in Shipibo and in French. Something different took place for them when the songs were in their mother tongue. From the moment I began to sing an ícaro in French, the person who received it was immediately connected to the work, and almost all the others who were present in the maloca as well. The visions were harmonized in the same worlds I had described.

If you hear, "I descend into my intoxication . . ." or "I align my senses . . . I align my thoughts, or my body," you concentrate yourself in your intoxication, in your senses, in your thoughts, or in your body. No longer are you going to think, "Oh my gawd! Where am I, what is he dragging me into?" You have an object to direct your mind to.

If you hear, "I open for you the world of ayahuasca, and I do it nicely," you're going to relax because you know it is not a call to great, esoteric forces, which is what you might otherwise be thinking, since, with the opening of the world of ayahuasca, spirits come tumbling out.

However, it is not always possible to hear the ícaros sung in your native tongue, which is why it's valuable to be able to grasp the structure and a few Shipibo words in order to connect to the meaning of the songs.

I return to this subject in more detail in the preface to *La Danse du serpent* (The Dance of the Serpent), the book by Romuald Leterrier with whom I made this discovery. I recommend his book because, while it's not a sequel to Jeremy Narby's *Cosmic Serpent* (the explosive book that connected me to the vine), it is a passionate and novel exploration of a multitude of bridges between science and traditional medicine, and it includes reports and theories on the nature of phenomena that are cognitive or poetic.*

BONUS

Here is a short, basic word list of traditional concepts that will help you comprehend the ícaros.

>*Nocon:* If the verse of the ícaro begins with *nocon,* the singing is being directed toward the healer. This can be done at any moment in the song and for a variety of reasons. At the beginning of the treatment the curandero needs to gather strength and to center it, a bit like preparing for a race or an inner runway takeoff.
>
>*Mi:* If it's *mi* that is at the beginning, then the healer is singing for you and is leaving the runway and beginning the treatment.

For example (with a rough translation describing the attitude):

Nocon shinan punteque.
I center myself—in my mind and in my senses. I align myself.

Nocon yora kuchi ayonban.
I center myself strongly in my body and in doing this I give it strength. I align it.

Nocon kuchi pae punteque.
I center myself in the strong intoxication of the ayahuasca.
    (I don't try to run away from it; instead I let it unfurl.)
I align the intoxication.

La Danse du serpent is available, in French, as an e-book at: www.chamanisme.net.

If the healer sings:

Mi shinan punteque

this becomes

I center you in your mind and in your senses.

In a way, the healer is aligning your intoxication and beginning to harmonize your inner worlds by diving into your world of visions and basing this on the stability of the curandero's own state.

The healer may move back and forth from *nocon* to *mi* in the course of the song because, assuming that the flight has taken off, the treatment will begin and then the flight is dragged into the patient's emotions. The curandero can chocar (collide with) negative energies, just as lightning can strike a plane, and then has to reset the trim—that is, level out the angle of flight. By turning the song back inward the healer again becomes centered inside the song, gathers up drive once again, and once more takes off to tackle the clouds. Planes are intended to withstand lightning, healers are used to "shocking up against" energy. So don't be upset—especially if the song turns to the healer (nocon, nocon, nocon). The storm may have its source in you, but you still have your seat in the plane. When curanderos align their intoxication and sing for themselves, the patients benefit by that too. It's all part of the treatment.

If the healer sings *Akon shaman akindra,* that means "I do it nicely, I do it well, I do it with attention." It's always good to remember this, because of course it's a phrase that recurs often. It is a beautiful intention.

If you hear the words *choro, pisha, sua,* it means that the cleansing phase is beginning. That means throwing out, cleansing, evacuating, having done with it.

These words are often associated with *vainquin* and *vainchon* and *ramacayara.*

Throw out, clean, do it now.

Remember this, because there's a good chance you will have bad thoughts, and that's when you need to be aware of it! For example, this song isn't doing me any good—blah, blah, blah . . . This is your negativity that is resisting and manifesting itself in the field of your thoughts.

The songs often finish or weave around harmonization.

Senen paramayona: everything harmonizes
Metsashama neteque: everything becomes beautiful
Parama youshamagen: harmony is put in place

A song can also be made up of a series of two or even three songs. For example, the first is for the opening and the alignment of the intoxication or the diet, the second for the cleansing, and the third to give strength. The whole series can last twenty minutes.

So, read the phrases (scattered through the first part of this book) and try to memorize certain key words. Don't learn them to sing them; that's not the point. If you sing during the ceremony, you can chocar (provoke a shock). Is your cockpit ready? The only anti-shock coating is a long diet opened and closed by a maestro. As a caution to apprentices, you have to be careful not to sing certain cleansing songs during an open diet; it's as if lightning strikes the plane on the ground while the spirits are in the process of taking it apart to strengthen it. They don't like that much. Also, don't forget that the damp ground of the diet conducts electricity.

I will return later to the attitude you need to have in receiving a song and will give some advice for inspired singers. The healer's real art is something more complex, but that cannot be approached except from within the experience of the diet.

PREPARING FOR AYAHUASCA

Mind, Ceremony, and Intoxication

Go and see *Avatar* again in 3-D.

Millions of us saw *Avatar* and, in journeying on Pandora, we discovered a world that is not so distant from the aboriginal's world: interconnections among plants, animals, the tree of souls, and so forth.

We rode the dragon, which is close to the archetypal visions offered by the plants. With no difficulty, we also entered into fully experiencing the emotions of the movie character who was asleep in his pod while his adventure was being lived by his avatar. This is just like the experience in a ceremony, where you are seated in the maloca but your mind can be on a distant voyage. What's more, with *Avatar* you're experiencing this adventure in 3-D, projected with depth, within a sensory immersion that is continually all around you in a way that's similar to the visions in a ceremony!

Remember what you felt, immersed in the film. It's the best example you can experience because you become the character and also the screen! So good, okay, I'll stop now. Right. Nobody wants to be pursued by the big black doggie with six feet. You can cross his cousin with ayahuasca. There you go; suddenly it's not as attractive.

I shouldn't have said that, because now you're going to have big expectations. You should know that you might very well not have visions—the medicina may work only in the form of sensations and emotions. You will be disappointed for sure, but that's the way it is.

Visions will always come in the end, but it may take quite awhile. And besides, they are not necessary for the patient.

In preparing yourself, there's nothing more useful than meditation. I'm not about to give you a course on meditation here. I'm not qualified and there are many books devoted to it. I'm just going to briefly extol its benefits. Meditation is a medicine in itself, a practice and an apprenticeship to live one's life well. You will learn to observe the movement of your mind and open your perceptions. It's a way of positioning yourself in yourself, of finding your inner resources without necessarily belonging to a religion. You can use only cognitive practice and choose your own direction in orienting your meditation. You will find it to be a very useful practice when a maelstrom of perceptions assails you during the experience. It will give you some basis for remaining present within the experience.

There are any number of books you can read to understand meditation's usefulness, learn its rudiments, and then begin to practice.

Yoga combines well with the vine.

In both of these practices (yoga and meditation), make use of the techniques, but without a religious focus (like mantras or the visualization of divinities) because those energies are different from the energies of the plants.

Besides, if you don't think you're going to the Amazon, just work with meditation and yoga. There will be fewer fears, but the problem is, unlike with the vine, how do you stay within the experience? For me, the two are really complementary. Of course, I am an ayahuasquero, but I meditate a lot during my trips, and I really appreciate yoga. In the Amazon it's a useful tool. The other way around works too—if you are a great practitioner of yoga or a meditator, ayahuasca will allow you to make progress in your vocation. I often run into yogis over there. The vine allows them to have other encounters and provides them with indications about their art and their practice.

Try to lighten your food consumption. For the week before your departure, don't eat any red meat, use little or no salt on your food, and do the same for sugar. Of course, what's best is none at all, and no alcohol.

■ ■ ■

Be clear about your objectives. Don't have too many expectations. You're doing it—that's a big decision in itself. Now let the journey work on you and . . . do what you can.

⚔ How do I prepare for the first ceremony?

T minus twelve hours until takeoff.

The ceremony will take place at 8:00 or 9:00 p.m.; it has to be after nightfall. Be calm. Try not to have too much uncertainty. I know that I myself have been responsible for creating some of that uncertainty from the visions described in my films or, even worse, from what I related earlier in the notebooks that you have just read. Manage your anxiety. Meditate. Don't read any serial-killer novels—it's just not the right time. (I've seen people do that and I thought it was pretty funny.) Listen to music. Along those lines, you should avoid satanic groups and heavy metal, without necessarily drenching yourself in spiritual music from India, ancient Tibet, or Gregorian chant. For myself, I find a beautiful feminine voice, sensual, with a salsa or jazz background, to be cool and full of joy.

Have a good breakfast and a good midday lunch, fruit if you're hungry. Be light. Don't eat anything more after 5:00 p.m.

Drink a lot—water or herbal teas—up to 7:00 p.m. After that, avoid liquids.

T minus one hour until takeoff.

Go to the maloca to find your spot, if that hasn't already been done. Arrange your stuff: flashlight, small bottle of water to rinse your mouth if necessary, blanket, cushions. All spots are good, don't worry if you are a bit far from the curanderos, but do take the first free spot that is close to them—or right in front of them, which is also very good. Set down your stuff. Stretch out and do a final check. Relax, rest. You can talk quietly; the goal now is to relax in a reclining position.

The maloca is going to fill up. The healers arrive and have some discussion; the time is close. The person who is going to serve the drink may call people by name or may simply say a little louder "ayahuasca."

Go up when it's your turn or if no one else gets up. Sit down opposite the healer. If it's your first time say, *"Primera vez para mí."* Let the healer serve you. Some healers may or may not ícarize the glass—that is, hum a melody, or sing over the full glass. Concentrate as you are offered the glass. Observe a small inner silence, a final tranquil thought. For example, "I drink this for my welfare" or "Medicina, look after me." Or, "Humbly, I am here to discover your world."

It's *T* minus zero . . .

Glug, glug . . . gloup . . .

Ohhhhh? Is that ever bitter!

⚔ How do I prepare for the rising intoxication?

You're off, press your lips together; the taste lingers for a few moments in your mouth. You go back and sit down. You can rinse out your mouth if the taste is really unbearable, but don't forget to spit out the water. In general, the first time the taste is not as unpleasant as people say; the sensation comes with time. Also, it's good not to rinse out your mouth the first time so you can really feel the vine and retain its unique taste. Find a comfortable position. That's very important. Try not to stretch out fully because you might fall asleep. You can do that later when the intoxication becomes strong and when that position seems right for you. The first signs of intoxication arrive between ten and forty-five minutes after you drink—an hour and a half at most.

During this period, try to place yourself in a state of light meditation. Not zazen or a restrictive position even if you are a practitioner. Otherwise you will be using those positions as a refuge when the intoxication becomes strong. I've often seen meditators adopt a perfect lotus position at the beginning only to collapse an hour later. So, be seated with legs stretched out, letting go, relaxed. Don't go looking for visions or effects—wait. Concentrate on the letting go and on your goals, your questions; reformulate them calmly. This is very important for making it through the experience—a letting go that arises out of the concentration.

There are several exercises for that. In order to focus on the body's perception it's not a question of directing your mind to looking for the first effects; instead you need to concentrate on helping the plant move into your body and bringing your attention to your stomach. In order to connect your awareness to your stomach—nothing could be simpler: place your hands on it. Breathe, concentrate on the respiration. Tense the muscles of your legs lightly when breathing in order to become aware of them in your mind, then let them go, relaxing them completely while breathing out. Practice this during the day so you don't let go too deeply and so you don't fall asleep in the evening. Use the rising intoxication to direct your thoughts in a connected way to your goals for healing or for discovery. I repeat: the intoxication is going to take between ten and forty-five minutes to climb, and if this is your first time it could be up to an hour and a half.

⚔ What is ayahuasca intoxication? Why are you afraid? What do you feel? How should you behave?

The First Time

I have gathered many first-time accounts, which are always special stories, as with love. The first time, marvelous or terrifying, is a moment that is intimate and unique because it's your first encounter. (I tell the story of mine in "Bonus Track 1," on page 237.) It can have an absolute rightness such as total confusion or even . . . nothing happening at all.

With time, and often starting with the second or third occasion, things fall into place and you discover the episodes described below.

The "All's Well" Version

The intoxication climbs, and you perceive its mechanical action. By bringing your awareness to it, it filters harmoniously into your body. You feel better and better, more relaxed than ever before; little or no nausea; many very beautiful, incredibly detailed visions. All is well. Reconnecting with yourself and with nature both take place. Knowledge and joy invade you and stay. Keep the contact with the body. Let yourself be cradled by the song and try to remain humble in your joy. That is the right self-esteem.

In this case, it's the following day that will require more work. I'll come back to that later.

And Now, the "That's Not So Great" Version

A numbness, a sleepiness that is light or strong takes hold. Struggle a little, maintain your posture, try to not fall asleep. Stay seated.

Nausea: no matter how strong it is, it usually comes as a surprise. You're expecting visions, and it's the nausea that rises up—a nausea that, little by little, is going to submerge you. The reflex is to resist. We are programmed to want to avoid this unpleasant experience. Whether it shows up during the ceremony or not until the next day, either way it is one of the important elements of the experience. If you have been vigilant with your stomach, you'll be better able to feel the first signs of it coming. You have to get used to it; managing it well is one of the keys to the practice.

Nausea is something we're familiar with in cases of minor poisoning, illness, or overeating, and we know how unpleasant it is. Ayahuasca's nausea is new and unique. It takes over your whole body, it orients your mind, and you're going to react. The reflex is to tense up a bit, to resist. The discomfort, combined with other effects, can generate fear. You may experience a series of thoughts of the type, "Ai ya! I'm sick. The plant is reacting badly in my body! I've been poisoned. I've got to get out of this state. What the hell have I done here? Oh, no! Why did I take it again?" (For people who aren't taking it for the first time of course.)

In short, all these thoughts are full of subsets, subgroups in relation to how you think and to your situation. You're in the dark, in the jungle, people around you may be beginning to groan. Assessment: not good, not good at all.

I'm going to give you a picture of the most difficult experience so that, in case it happens to you, the reading of this chapter may be useful to you. If, on the other hand, all goes well, then . . . have a good flight.

In pilots' school they tell you about all the problems you can run into, but most of the time the plane behaves well. Here, the metal bird is your body and your mind is the pilot.

Now if the motor on the right starts to sputter in the midst of takeoff—pilot, listen up.

Only one attitude to have:

You don't have to try to escape the nausea.

Do not resist. Let it overtake you; let it take your whole body. If you think it's time to vomit, go right ahead! Place your head gently over the pail and wait. Don't try to provoke the throwing up and don't hold it back either. Instead, slip yourself into the discomfort and let it fill you, with the nausea just behind your lips. This is a warrior's act in cognitive art. The nausea will then come out in vomiting or will dissolve. If you resist, you're going to tense up, feel bad, and slow down the process. The nausea will diminish but will last, with its load of dark thoughts and the awakening of all the territories of suffering. It is an important element in the work of the medicine. The nausea is going to position you in a state of great fragility, a state of great sensitivity. This is the right state for visions. You're not in the cinema casually eating popcorn. This fragility is necessary for you to fully experience the journey. How can the flow of life be perceived without sensitivity? How can one encounter spirits? With humility. That's how. The plant necessarily places you in a state of great humility. Be humble, little organic animal, don't resist; it's for your own good. Nausea never killed anybody.

Let go, feel yourself from the inside. If you throw up too soon, nothing's going to happen because the medicina will have left the body too quickly. You have come from a far country for this, so concentrate! Leave your body alone; it knows exactly whether it needs to throw up or not. Don't push it in any direction; let it manage on its own. The nausea will depend on the preparation, which contains at least two plants, ayahuasca and chacruna, cooked together. If it contains more chacruna than ayahuasca, then it will be light and very visionary, which is what is best. If, conversely, it's the ayahuasca that predominates, then the nausea will be strong and the visions weak.

A good healer will prepare a well-balanced ayahuasca with both—nausea and strong visions. Remember this is a medicine; getting operated on isn't a walk in the park, so look at it that way.

So, Nausea.

Here I am, I slip inward.

I let thoughts of fear and doubt clear out.
And I promote other ones.
I'm not poisoned—the medicina is taking care of me.
It's a part of the process.

Open your intoxication:

Medicina, move into me.
Medicina, take care of me.
All is well.
I concentrate myself.

You can recite this repeatedly, like a prayer. And you'll see then that everything gets better quickly. You will be harmonizing the relationship with the vine that is in progress. At the same time, intoxication with ayahuasca isn't just the nausea. Nausea is only the carpet on which the intoxication is set up. The intoxication will unfurl along several axes.

At first you will feel a lessening of your control over your body. Oh my God, I've always controlled my body! I've never taken drugs, what's happening to me? Help! Like Shiva, who spends much time in meditation to control the anger that can destroy everything in its path, I maintain it correctly, even in deep meditation—this control, I must not lose control, if that happens it's the end for . . . me?

Drop the control as you've always known it.

What?

Yes! This bloody control. We Westerners are control freaks. The greatest fear that taking ayahuasca stirs up is that of losing control. And, I'm sorry, but it's true—you're going to have to lose a certain amount of control. When, in the notebooks, I told you about this feeling of being in a car on a desert straightaway road, having the headlights slowly going out while the accelerator is jammed to the floor—that's the type of control I mean—the control of the all-seeing despot of the mind over the body.

Take care—it's not a matter of leaving the body without any control at all; otherwise, in five minutes it might be so very happy that it will want to dance nude, which could upset the ceremony a little. Then control of who, of what?

I'm talking about the control of your body that begins to look like the control of your life. One locks the door of the apartment before going to sleep; in this way we control our lives, and now here we have someone moving into . . . us!

Let's say that in your normal state the mind controls the body as if the mind were a person and the body a dog trained and on a leash. Once under the grip of the ayahuasca, the mind becomes a Lilliputian figure and the body a whale or a tiger that keeps on growing. You have to forget about the leash and use gentleness and concentration to ride this enormous beast that is in the process of waking up—your body. It's a dizzying sensation. The Lilliputian mind needs to gently stroke the animal so it doesn't bolt.

Let's imagine, of course, that at this moment the healer has not begun to sing, and may even have gone out to pee. Let's take the kind of situation where the motor is sputtering badly, the control tower is no longer responding, and the plane has become an intergalactic shuttle leaving Earth space. Houston do you read me? . . . Houston? . . . Aaaaargh! Let go of the control stick right away! Then take it again with the tips of your fingers. Now look at all the dials, gently adjust the fuel supply and the motor kicks in. All is well.

You don't understand?

In fact, you have to give yourself to the body, abandon the domination of the mind over the body, and then take it back gently. Once control has been dropped, the body lets go a bit; you need to watch the thoughts, not hold on to them, and accept each opportunity to drop a piece of this lousy control—so long as it doesn't lead you into an exaggerated situation. For example, you drop the control and the body starts to jiggle: moderate this jiggling and it will move inside the body. Yes, I know, it's the guy who was jiggling as much as he could in *D'autres mondes* who is telling you this . . .

So, do what I did at that stage: do what you can. Conversely, it may also be that you don't feel your body at all. It's no longer responding. Don't panic! Gently touch yourself a little to regain contact with the physical body. It's rare to be totally paralyzed—really calm down; you can do it. If that doesn't work, don't worry, slow down your thoughts, open your perceptions, and regain control of the inside, with the tips of your fingers.

What?

Yes, control of the inside. This is the second Kiss Cool effect of the intoxication again. A new perception of yourself—you feel the fluids of your body and your organs and muscles in their relaxed state. Fear comes on the scene; it's normal, you are in an unknown zone. Usually you feel your muscles in your mind, if you activate them consciously. For example, if you place one of your upper limbs in the air making an arm of steel, you are aware of that arm and not the other arm relaxed at your side. Imagine now if you were to be aware of your whole body. Immediately you will want to get rid of this perception, it's dizzying. It's normal, it's new! Consider it a new relationship between body and mind. Remain connected to your organs—this is the most beautiful gift of your being coming together. Let yourself slide, conscious, into the intoxication, into the vertigo of yourself. Allow a vegetative state to unfurl in which you become the witness of the activity and of the presence of your body, that fabulous organic mechanism. You become tiny, a spectator. Calm. Good. As for the calm, without stopping, try to . . . "Oh, no! It's too strong; I feel like I'm dissolving; I'm going to explode; I see visions that describe my life, the universe, its birth and death; spirits are around me, demons too. Have pity—it's too much—I'm never going to get out of here!"

Bravo! You've come in through the big gateway. You are having *the* peak experience; the plants are working deeply. You're going to come back in great shape. A warrior of love! Congratulations!

"Hey! But he's nuts, this guy; he doesn't understand. No, it's too strong! I'm going to *die* . . . or become *mad* in the best case scenario! I implore you, make it all stop!"

Be calm, it's classic, one of the fundamentals, a great experience, one you'll remember with a twinge in the heart, years later, regretting that you didn't take more advantage of it. You want to come back, are you sure?

For yogis and meditators of all disciplines, this is the moment for the lotus or for your preferred meditation positions—if you can. The refuge position will come, use it to take refuge in the world of ayahuasca, and you will see, it will take place all by itself, if you have a good practice.

"Yessireeeeeee! I swear, I will *never* take ayahuasca again, never again, help me!"

When you arrive at thoughts such as these, remember what follows here. I've run into many people who, the morning after the ceremony, have said to me, "That's it for me" and who, the next evening, or even the same evening, have returned to the maloca. Of course they ask to drink very little, very little . . . then afterward they kick themselves because this time it was a good experience, and they begin to regret that the effect wasn't stronger. And that has happened to me too.

Another great rule about ayahuasca: no two sessions are alike. Monday, you travel through the universe; Tuesday, it's a nightmare; Wednesday, no intoxication, but everything comes together, not according to your modalities—not what you want, not what you hope for, or not what you deduce—but according to the mysterious logic of the plants and the healers. It is also important to never presuppose the experiences that are to come. One day at a time. That's the best way.

The "Hey! Help! I Need Help!" Version

Okay, fine, let's calm down! First of all—what posture are you in?

Positions Connected to Various Strengths of Intoxication

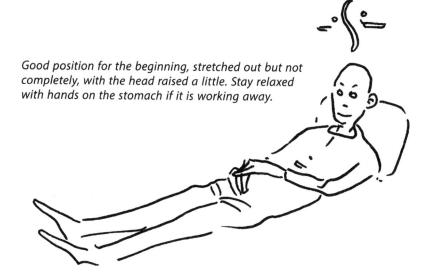

Good position for the beginning, stretched out but not completely, with the head raised a little. Stay relaxed with hands on the stomach if it is working away.

Seated, legs stretched out, relaxed and vigilant. The effect climbs.

I move through, concentrated, seated, and relaxed.

It gets strong; I keep the back really straight. I can pull up my legs but I don't tense my muscles.

I don't collapse if the intoxication is very strong; at least I try not to.

If I feel like I might vomit, I put my pail in front of me, I bend my head, but I don't try to force the throwing up. I concentrate on my guts and I repeat in my head, "Medicina, look after me."

If I have a stomachache and I'm having trouble stabilizing my wandering mind and my stomach, which bulges hard, I stretch out on my stomach so that making contact between the ground and my stomach allows my mind to feel it and to quiet it down. But I don't stay in this position for very long.

I don't let the intoxication take me upward by raising the head or looking up too much. If I do, I'll lose contact with the body and let myself be taken by my thoughts. I'm going to become restless and end up moving, then getting up. When the intoxication is strong, don't try to escape from it regardless of whether it's positive or negative; don't get up; don't cry out in joy or in fear, just concentrate (out of consideration for the others . . . and for your own treatment).

Be careful not to stretch out completely if you're a beginner. A healer can stretch out, even fall asleep, and will be awakened by the strong intoxication. Because it's a familiar territory, a healer can then sit down and start working, but if that happens to you, you have a surprise in store! I remember a friend who fell asleep right after drinking. An hour later he woke up and told himself that he wasn't feeling much this evening, that he was not going to drink, and that he was going to bed. He tried to get up, then remembered . . .

Strong Intoxication

Coming back to our topic of intoxication—you're too uncomfortable, you want out.

Are you sure that it's really going that badly? Really question yourself. Take stock and do the exercises. If the answer is still yes . . . leave the song. Open your eyes! Move your body, very carefully. Ask yourself what's happening in your body and where you are. Delicately touch your body and your stuff beside you. Reposition your thoughts into the room. My flashlight is there. And look at that—this is my leg. This thing trembling against my leg, that's my dear neighbor who's spilled off his mattress a little. My pail is here.

And that, right here—my second leg. I move it gently. Don't knock over the pail. Who is here in the maloca? I look at the others around me, whom I'm finally able to make out in the dark. In short, come back, not in running away, but by repositioning your mind in your body, with both of them in the present and the totality present in the room. Once you've come back, calm yourself and slide once again gently back into the intoxication.

Above all: remember that you *cannot die*! J. C. Callaway, Ph.D., a medical researcher in the department of pharmaceutical chemistry at the University of Kuopio, Finland, has presented findings that a lethal dose of ayahuasca requires ingestion of about two gallons of a beverage of normal strength. Let's imagine that it's an extremely concentrated preparation: the lethal dose will certainly be above, let's say, two quarts. Now remember the small glass that you drank. You already feel better. No? You're not better? If it's still *Star Wars* and Darth Vader's ship is approaching, calm down and say to yourself, "Good, this will give me good memories for my golden years," and slowly try to get up. Just because you have less chance of dying taking ayahuasca than taking aspirin* doesn't mean that you should try to drink three glasses of it. A big psychological crash can happen in the case of a real overdose. Let the healer serve you, that's what's most important. No fear, but no provocation either.

---

*Olivier Chambon, *La Médecine psychédélique* [Psychedelic Medicine] (Paris: Les Arènes, 2009).

You may find yourself in two kinds of situations.

I. You Can Get Up

Get up and move gently, step by step. Stay in contact with your belly all the time you're moving, because moving can bring back the nausea. Go and see the healer, sit in front of him at some distance. If he's in the midst of singing don't interrupt, wait until the end of the song. He will question you, if that doesn't happen, then ask for help.

YOU: *¿Estoy mal, puedes ayudarme, por favor?*
(I'm not doing well, can you help me?)

YOU: *¿Puedes levantar mi mareación?*
(Can you withdraw my intoxication?)

Usually, the healer will sing for you, but it may also be that someone else has a greater need and you will have to wait. If the response is "*Ya?*" "*Was?*" or "*Haaa?*" (which could mean "Who is it?" "What did you say?" or even "Help! A dark spirit is speaking to me!") it means that you're not sitting in front of the healers. Remember that you have to move forward gently and watch closely. At night, when you are mareado, you can very easily address the wrong person.

2. You Can't Get Up

Try again, gently, breathe out, breathe in, come back!

Extreme case: "Sorry, but I can't tell where the ground and the ceiling are. I can't bring order to my body. It's the end; I quickly think of my children, my friends, and my relatives so I can say farewell. It's very beautiful, but I would have liked to live if only to tell them about it! It's happening, that's it, I'm dyyyyyyying!"

Stop!

Hey, stupid nonsense. Remember, I'm saying it over again because we have a tendency, surprising as that may be, to forget it—a lethal dose when ingesting ayahuasca . . . blah, blah, blah. Remember the small glass that you drank.

If you drank three big glasses, it's because you were reckless. You're not dying, but okay, it's too late to get upset about it, nothing to be done except to get through it. Above all, stay in the maloca! That's it. Now, calm down. The only thing that might possibly kill you is your own fear, if you really have a weak heart (but, in that case, as you are told on page 209, there are other solutions). So, if you are not in that kind of situation, don't panic; you're going to live better, but . . . that's for later. Now go ahead. Die!

What? He's nuts!

Let death come, death of the thoughts, of the ego, the big letting go. A symbolic death; let it take you in a big spasm. May your consciousness take root in the body and a psychological death happen. Breathe. Better now?

Yes . . .

So now, since you've reached this point, this is the time to speak of suffering. The healers say, though I will translate it into words of our language, that at each entrance into a new stage of self-knowledge or of an awakening of one's consciousness, the doorway is a death that is presented to you, you must pass through it, and so on. You move forward from one stage to the next. Therefore, if you are a patient without any heavy pathology, the doors are wooden with a classic lock and they appear on the road to healing. If you're on the path of apprenticeship, each room is sealed off with a big double door in stone and it will be difficult to open it, you will hit your head against it. This is the suffering of the teaching.

Each symbolic death leads to psychological suffering, fear, terror, confusion, and inner pain. Losing a dear one is a great suffering, both physical and mental. In a flash you're going to lose this being with whom you have spent all your life. It's hard, even though, just like a best friend or one of your progenitors, sometimes this being really annoys you. You've grown used to and even grown to like this person, this asshole, which is normal: that's you.

It's the moment to say farewell, and to die for a brief moment to yourself, becoming aware that you are at one and the same time *more* than this person and *nothing but* this person. You die, and in the end, it's good, so good, to finally let go, to no longer have any expectation, to breathe for a moment. You find peace and you enter into a new space—yourself, but broader. It's too strong. You tell yourself, watch out, that one's coming back. Who? Er, well . . . yourself. A bigger version, aligned, stronger, but one who can grab your head once again.

Oooooooooooh, no! It's starting up again . . .

So go back into it, die again. Pick up the exercises again. If, all of a sudden, you see a strange spirit leaning over you, speaking in a mysterious and incomprehensible tongue, and he seems very real to you in your world of visions, if he stumbles a little, comes near you and says . . . *"¿Por favor, dónde estan los baños?"* Don't panic. It's your buddy who was seated opposite you, who is in the same state as you, and for him, on top of it all, he urgently has to use the toilet, and he's a little lost.

There are nights like that.

All that to say that such things happen and also to say that you are not alone! There are many surprises in the visible world of this type: a hand on your shoulder that you didn't see coming while you were on your journey, with your eyes closed; a noise beside you; some guy who starts doing yoga on his head (of course, it's the vine that has given him the order to do that, wouldn't you know it!) and stretches up to his full height (it really happened) . . . Anything can send you into a tailspin.

Now, I don't advise you to take the vine in France. There, in the place of toilettas-man, it may be a spirit with a red armband who says to you, "Police! Please get up and move into the paddy wagon." Even if the man is considerate, you have a very good chance of making a catastrophic scenario for yourself in your dear little head, something resembling the ending of *Apocalypse Now.*

So, good, I'm stopping here because I've really gone over all of it. Don't worry about the toilets; you always get there, or almost always. And in Peru, beneath the trees of the forest, you're not risking running into spirits with red armbands. You'll get used to the movement of pail-sharing companions. To reassure you about that, I'll tell you about a ceremony that was really fuerte, not that long ago, where, well settled into my intoxication, immersed in my visions, carried away by the song, I stumble and put out my hand to catch myself on my neighbor's shoulder, except that my hand passes through him. Surprised, I take a look at him, just eight inches away from me. He turns around: it's a spirit, very beautiful. He looks at me; I read a gentle reproach in his face. He is seated beside me and is listening to the songs. Clearly I'm bothering him. Lifting my arm, I say excuse me (out loud) and I straighten up. He turns back, I go off again on my journey smiling inwardly, "That's huge. I've just experienced a shamanic joke, what a great intoxication!" Then I leave these thoughts behind and continue the ceremony. If you had this vision on your first time, you might cry out in surprise or terror. This congenial little episode could then, as a result, plunge all the other participants into dark thoughts, "He's getting tortured by demons, my god, the poor guy." Very quickly each person cogitates and jumps to the obvious conclusion: "When they've finished with him, they'll come and get me . . . Fuck, fuck, fuck! There's only one way out of here, I've gotta make a run for it through the forest."

Logical.

So if, on top of it all, after toilettas-man is trying to speak, someone cries out or shouts, don't panic, don't imagine all that you could be thinking; instead tell yourself, "As for him, he's cashing in on a good treatment; it's okay, bear up my friend, you'll be better tomorrow." Or better still, "Hey, it's likely an encounter with a kindly spirit but one that came too soon for my bucket companion . . . Let's go, I'm concentrating and looking after myself."

We'll laugh about it the next day, because stormy nights paradoxically leave us with the best memories. "Do you remember when the Austrian began shouting, 'I'm being cruuuuuucified by a snake'? Whoo! He really cashed in last night."

"Hang on, there was Patrick who showed up in front of me, I couldn't understand a thing he said! I thought he was a spirit, ha ha ha!"

We're really laughing—now! We weren't as quick to talk about it last night. We weren't showing off as much . . . Ah, well, that's how it goes. You find that a bit amusing, you imagine that the next day is much more collected. And you're right, it is! With joy and sharing there's nothing better than laughing at one's own expense. Frankly, it's healthy to cast off the anxiety of the night in gales of laughter. Like the fireman who carried a screaming woman in her nightie down his ladder and saved her—it wasn't funny, he had to really pay attention, calling on his inner resources of self-control all the way down the dangerous descent of the ladder. Fear was there. However, the next day everyone at the firehouse laughed as he recounted the wrigglings of the good lady in his arms, himself most of all. We put things in perspective; it relaxes and attaches joy or derision to the memory so as to reduce its dramatic dimension. Besides, at the end of the ceremony, a good laugh with the healers can be priceless.

If you feel like holding on to your emotions and studying them, and you don't much want to laugh, go off by yourself! That's what you do before or after sharing.

So, good, let's get back to the intoxication. After the nausea and the control, we have the thoughts.

Thoughts

I've already spoken of this. There are lots of diverse and varied theories in the notebooks. After reading all that stuff, you should know that you have to pay attention to the thread and cultivate particular thoughts. When you take off in a panic, the thinking process can tell you thousands of things that are simply wrong. You're going to have thoughts that you've never had before. Don't let them run off with you. Whether they are beautiful or horrible, don't trust them. They seem to be negotiable truths, a trick of the mind. We have a tendency to let ourselves be taken in by beautiful thoughts, but then the consciousness is nothing but thought. We leave behind the sensation of the body, thoughts speed up, and you need only a small energetic shock to find yourself in horrible thoughts. So—focus on presence. Come back to the body. And start repeating in your head two or three refrains like this:

Medicina, look after me.
I center myself in my intoxication.
I quietly concentrate myself.
Medicina, enter into my body.
I connect myself to my heart.
I do it now.

(If I start to be afraid, I say:)
I drive out the bad thoughts.
I reject the bad thoughts.
I reject the bad energies.
I reject the bad visions.

(Then, come back:)
I connect myself to my heart.
I do it nicely . . .
I am a melodious path.
(Then I repeat from the beginning.)

This creates a kind of actualization of the present—a mix of self-description, "My intoxication is strong, I let it take me," and intention, "Medicina, look after me." You can refer to the songs in the appendix, not to learn them so you can sing them but to be acquainted with them in order to be able to get certain parts of your mind moving.

I think I've told you the main things. What's left is the chapter on visions. I'll come back to it later, because it's too big a subject to cover now.

I've presented you with perhaps the worst portrayal of the adventure, but, in a way, it's also what happens if the experience is strong. Now, let's look at the opposite.

⚔ My body hurts and there are no visions, what does that mean?

Be resourceful. Tell yourself that the medicina is working. Concentrate on the areas that hurt, often these relate to bad memories, unhealthy lifestyle, trauma, or even just a weakness lodged in an organ or muscle. Disappear into it. Tell yourself that you're in treatment. Don't panic, it will pass. Definitely don't say things like, "I'm sick, the vine is reacting badly in me, I'm poisoned." Sometimes, over several days, this medicine is going to be rebalancing your body. Afterward, visions and good sensations will come. The motors and the cockpit need to be repaired first before you can take off.

⚆ If nothing happens, what do I do?

Nothing is happening. No intoxication, no visions. Around you people are groaning, reacting, vomiting, but for you—nothing. They're all on the journey and you're still on the dock. "You know, I just knew it, I'd be the one left out . . . (sniffles)." It's forty-five minutes now, maybe an hour since you drank. Not a thing. Get up. Still nothing?

You're stumbling a bit but that's it. Study the situation. Often we think nothing is happening because we're not very aware of our perceptions and our consciousness is locked up by a mental demiurge that never lets go. Go and see the healer. If you have trouble walking, it means you are in a state of intoxication; gauge your state. Wait until the healer has finished singing, sit down, then explain your situation.

For example:

YOU: *No siento el effecto.*
(I don't feel anything. There are no effects.)

YOU: *Siento un poco pero muy poco.*
(I feel, but very little.)

YOU: *¿Puedo tomar más?*
(I can take again?)

The healer serves you; you drink and return to your place. This time, concentrate strongly as at the beginning. No panic, this often happens. Sometimes it takes two or three ceremonies for the effect to finally open. I'll always remember the annoyed face of a boy who had no effect for a week, then, all of a sudden, in one ceremony everything opened when he was on the point of giving up.

If there is no effect, take advantage of the songs, concentrate on them, the medicina is working on you no matter what takes place. So, patience. If you really feel nothing, then certainly go back and take some more, but not too soon—not before an hour and a half. Don't tell yourself, "Perhaps tomorrow." Go for it.

VISIONS

Advice for Encounters with
Scary Serpents and Talking Plants

The Indians say that there are two types of visions, visions from the imagination and real visions. The person experiencing them can tell the difference. I would say also that there are visions from your past, meaning visions of people who are close to you and, we could say, visions of your own world. These are the three main categories for the patient.

Visions from Imagination

In my own case, I haven't had this happen much. I had two strong visions of this type in ten years. They occurred at the beginning of the journey, and I allowed them to dissolve. In the first one, I saw the National Assembly (the lower house of the bicameral Parliament of France), but instead of deputies (assembly members) there were toasters. It was a vision that was extemely clear and very realistic. I was surprised; it lasted a few seconds, then I let it go. (I should say that I am not an ardent follower of the debates of the above-mentioned assembly.) The other time, I had the vision of a pizza man making a delivery in an apartment; I still remember his face. And that's it. Often these visions happen at the beginning of the ceremony or during someone's first time. It's a clearing out of the mental part. There can also be mixtures. For example, at the end of the shooting of *99 Francs* in Venezuela, I made a side trip to Iquitos, and during the first ceremony I had a vision of a small boat with Indians in traditional costume moving down the river (a vision of the universe of Shipibo myth). However, in the back of this pirogue was Jean Dujardin, not in the role of Octave but instead with his blond wig in the role of Brice de Nice. He was smiling at me and seemed to be asking if the surf was up.* I had just spent a few months with him; I smiled, the vision faded.

Vision of Your Own World

This is like a rebuild of your hard drive—memory and tasks. For example, you see the face of someone you haven't seen for years. That might simply suggest contacting him again; his expression and your feeling at the moment of the vision can give you some indication. If he seems sad or angry, there is a latent conflict that should be resolved on your return. Conversely, the vision of someone with whom you are not on good terms may look at you in a kindly way, and this can indicate the force that connects you to this person and make you feel like seeing them again. Interpretation is up to you. Watch out for mistakes. Be cautious.

You can see forgotten locations and scenes from your life. Clearly, anything that is not linked to the very recent past, and which therefore cannot be a mental imprint from your data or from last week, is pointing out something to you. Don't begin to study the question during the ceremony; do it the next day or later on in the night. Go on with your journey.

The vision of your own death can come to you. Don't be frightened if this happens; it's not likely prescience but a doorway in your journey.

Pure Vision

Understand that by *pure* I refer to the vision of the world of spirits, of cosmovision, and of mythology. First and foremost, you need to connect these visions to an emotional and energetic state and categorize the type of attitude to adopt when this vision is before you.

There are two major categories: inner visions and outer visions. They correspond to two different states of energy and intoxication.

---

*Jean Dujardin played the role of Octave Parango in *99 Francs*. He had previously played a surfer in the title role of the film *Brice de Nice*.

Inner Visions

Inner visions are those I described for the most part in *D'autres mondes*. These can be further subdivided into two categories—the good ones and the bad ones.

In general, at the beginning, it's motifs: you will discover motifs in 3-D that you might have seen on fabric prints. Each plant has its own motif. It's the energy of the plant penetrating you. With a strong intoxication you seem to be floating inside yourself, and the song will organize the motifs.

Let's look at animal forms. I'm going to take the example of the serpent. This is only an example, because some of you won't see any serpents. In my case, I see lots of them; in fact, my ayahuasquero name is Inin Rônin, which means "perfume of the serpent."

What I'm describing about serpents can be applied to all animal forms and even to abstract worlds. I should mention that there are healers who don't see serpents, and when I do ceremonies with them, I don't see serpents either because I am taken into the healer's world since their force is stronger than mine. Serpents, generally anacondas or boas, can be realistic and light brown, bright green, or multicolored with a pure white belly. They can be jewels or take the form of dragons—which is the highest form of treatment. Hang on because you're going to vibrate and your fear can rise up. If there are very few of them and if they are little and cute with big gecko-like eyes, it's because you're working at a low level at the beginning of the treatment. If they are cobras, black and aggressive, then concentrate, the energies are not gentle; don't grab them, let them slide away. If there are a lot of them and they are intertwined with each other, concentrate on the song, which should untangle them. Afterward they will build mandala shapes and will move slowly. Sometimes there will be a real sea of serpents. The slower their movement the better it is. It's not a question of looking at the vision but of merging with it while keeping an intentional correctness, a presence, and relaxation in the body. I should say that I've heard Shipibo healers from a community sing, *"Rônin hospitalo quepenqen,"* which means "I am opening the serpent hospital," a cute cultural mixture. The serpents can inhabit cathedrals of organic forms.

What you need to be mindful of is that, regardless of the manifestation, if there is a slow tempo, an organization, and a unity, you're doing well. The plant is transmitting its strength to you. If there is confusion, anarchy, a mix of archetypes of all kinds, you are being treated and cleansed. Don't panic, just get through it and let the plant act. The song will harmonize your visionary worlds.

Any of the jungle fauna can appear, or the visions can remain purely abstract, or, yet again, archetypes can emerge from your own or some other culture. The plant manifests its presence by making use of a language that is, in essence, fairly easy to interpret and is sometimes linked to language coming from your own worlds or from cultural or genetic implants.

Let's go back to the example of the animals.

There are animals we admire for their strength, those who frighten us with their ugliness, and so on. Birds such as blue parrots are airy energies, while spiders and beetles are heavy energies, but if the spiders are well organized, all is well, the cleansing takes place calmly. The jaguar is synonymous with strength, but if he jumps on you in the vision, it's going to be terrifying. The plant is going to test you; you have to master your fear whatever the vision might be.

You can find yourself in tunnels made of motifs or animal forms that change with the progress of the song. You may move down into organic or psychological cares where the forms are dark and mingled, or you may move toward organization and color.

Anthropomorphic Visions

It's always difficult to speak of the world of spirits as a reality—the cultural leap is gigantic. I like Romuald Leterrier's concept best of all: the visions of spirits are the linguistic bridge between plants and men. Which is to say that we don't necessarily see them in their own forms; it's simply that they manifest that way because we are humans, in the same way that a plant imitates perfectly the posterior of a female bumblebee so that the male will fertilize her and thus pollinate the plant. Perhaps jaguars crunching ayahuasca see the spirits of the plants in the form of a beautiful female jaguar and the powerful demons as human hunters?

Each teaching plant has its spirit and its world. I'm not going to list them, but I will speak of the recurrent ways in which we can see the world of spirits in an inner vision. In general they are pictures that can have some depth or they can be flat. And they are in movement. The world of spirits moves slowly. Spirits appear to you. They can present themselves or present their worlds (towns, hospitals, nature), or they can take you on a journey to the stars. You may be able to watch one scene after another as in a cinema; in this case, the spirits are not looking at or paying attention to you. You can see them in human form, animal form, or a mixture. Note especially that the same spirit can manifest in various forms. A spirit can be a kind of totem slowly beating feather-covered wings. Or yet again you can be in the presence of helmeted samurai or the *chaiconis* (the plates of armor are feathers or motifs). Or you can see the spirits of plants from your diet or ones that the curandero calls.

In general, the corresponding state is very gentle. During the encounter you feel light, vibrant, airy. Your breathing takes place in little puffs, and the air seems perfumed. The ending of the encounter will set in motion a transmission of knowledge or a treatment. If the encounter is deep, the continuation of the journey will be more turbulent!

Remember, the further you move up, the further you will come back down! If it's not during the same journey, it will happen the following day and the following year.

Mythic Worlds

The world of the spirits can connect you to the world of myth. You can also be part of various scenes or meet individual spirits. For example, you could be present at the encounter of the first Shipibo with the world of the spirits that was brought about the first time ayahuasca was taken. Or you could see the chaiconis, the spirit of a community that moved as a whole into the invisible world because the children had mixed a plant into the drink that the whole community drank.

The Human World of Spiritual Visions

If plants have their world and their spirits, so do humans. Spiritual medicine of human and celestial origin exists in the invisible worlds. This is a very sensitive topic, one that makes the atheist immediately pounce, or stirs up the person who is religious. So I'm going to try to be careful.

It's logical that humans have their spiritual worlds; after all, even though they've not been on the planet nearly as long as the plants, they have a significant intelligence and power of sensitivity.

Let's pay a little homage to the human.

I would like to really limit my reflections on the subject of this section.

In fact, it is possible, during an ayahuasca ceremony, to find oneself in relationship with energies that are connected to the worlds of the religions. In some way, prepare yourself so that these energies can move toward you. Remember that prayer nourishes a spiritual space. Place yourself firmly in your heart and remain vigilant.

I've often been told accounts of individuals who were visited by a saint, by the Virgin Mary, by Christ, or by angels. (Take care, even if it's very good therapeutic energy, it can shake you up psychologically as well as energetically.) Just as plants have various spiritual worlds—a world of medicine, a world of power, a dark world (which is why diets are important to link you only to the medicine world of a teaching plant)—the spiritual worlds of humans have two sides: the world of medicine and compassion, and the world of power and sorcery. You need only look at human history to realize that the two sides are manifested through religions and through mankind as a whole.

If you are an ayahuasquero and you go into French cathedrals such as the one in Reims, or Notre Dame in Paris, or others, you will be disturbed by the resemblance to certain visions of the world of medicine of the plants, which I described earlier as living cathedrals with arches breathing in movement. Are the cathedrals medicine vessels built by the ancients?

There have been great healers in history whose devotion and acts of relieving human suffering have been immense. On the other hand, it is sad to sometimes see religions diverted from their initial paths, the message of love transformed into an object of spiritual and political power. Religions and their intransigent dogmas have been among the greatest sources of suffering for humanity.

You get my point; I am not religious, even if I have a great respect for the work of religious folk who work for harmony, peace, and balance. In short, if you have a religious vision, that doesn't mean you have to convert.

Nonterrestrial Spiritual Worlds

After the religions come the extraterrestrials. You're frowning? Okay, once again, apologies for losing the little bit of credibility I might still have with some readers. In spite of that I have to continue. During the ceremonies it can be that you will find yourself in relationship with visions that seem extraterrestrial. I remind you that if you are in the presence of high technology in your visions, it could be because of your own language (the plant speaks to you that way because you are a technology freak, or a science-fiction devotee), or because of certain spirits in the worlds of the medicina who have technology, or because of spirits or beings from other dimensions or coming from nonterrestrial spaces—thus, extraterrestrials. Let's talk about it that way, as visions that might be extraterrestrial. And, once again, remember that some of them are healers and teachers, but others are less well intentioned.

In concluding and in giving my opinion on the subject, if I think of these visions today, so real and so incredible, it's because I'm writing this paragraph; otherwise, they are never present when I take ayahuasca, nor in my life, nor in my everyday discussions or thoughts. I have personally had very few contacts of this type, and when I have it's always been with Kestenbetsa. In the book *Visions: regards sur le chamanisme**he speaks for example of the "regulators," beings who don't have, or no longer have, a home world and who travel through the cosmos to balance planetary forces. For me, this is a beautiful, poetic reality.

Be forewarned then, for you too can brush up lightly against the energy of the great creator-regulator of the whole system of reality beyond time, space, matter, and energy. Watch that you don't grasp at your thought and thus lose your footing.

---

*Jan Kounen, Guillermo Arévalo, Corinne Arnould, and Jean-Patrick Costa, *Visions: regards sur le chamanisme* [Visions: perspectives on shamanism] (Paris: Éditions Télémaque, 2005) (out of print).

Outer Visions

Visions external to you belong to the world of the healer and the apprentice, but if you have them, that doesn't mean you are one! It just means you can see it. In general, they happen with a very strong intoxication. At the beginning you think that you're going to die; fear of a new, unknown state appears with the vibration of your body under the skin. There can be a high-pitched, whistling sound in the mind that becomes very strongly concentrated, driving thought out of consciousness and driving out the perception of your organs—as if you were becoming translucent, as if you were being passed through a slow scanner that leaves you naked. There you are, the nausea just behind the lips, and your vision moves all of a sudden to the outside, while the state is maintained. You need to remain calm in this state, which of course takes years and requires long diets.

Forms, thoughts, and energies emerge from other people, dark or luminous. They arrive and are suspended in the maloca.

The maloca can become a temple that is covered by motifs. The healer seems to be on a seat, face and body covered in motifs.

If the healer is doing a treatment, one or several medicine spirits position themselves alongside. Motifs can descend from the mouth of the spirit onto the top of the healer's skull; the song of the curandero can be seen as a vision. For example, a great, colored serpent comes out of the healer's mouth and begins to cleanse the body of the patient. Or the motifs come and place themselves on the shoulders of the patient, or yet again the patient is in a sphere in which birds are flying around. Or, more frightening, the song of the healer sends out terrifying bumblebees and big flies that buzz around the patient. The most terrible is seeing the death mask or demonic forms emerge from the patient and circle around until the healer is able to drive them away. Everything depends on the healer's work and, of course, on the patient. If I'm telling you all this it's because if it happens to you, you can quite quickly fall into a hole. We are really very ill prepared for this type of experience. So move through it and don't think about it too much the next day.

Ah! I almost forgot the big songs for the group. You can also see, for example, the roof of the maloca dancing in the form of slow waves made up of bats harmoniously nestling together and moving with the song. In the end, they move aside, making room for great luminous modules, a kind of module of white energy that descends from the sky to form a dome. In esoteric language, we say that it's the opening of the low astral in order to bring down the high astral. In terms of the medicina, we say that it's the call to protection space before treating the patients. Understand that it's difficult for me to define that with our words and our knowledge.

⚡ As soon as I have a vision, it disappears right away. Why?

In general, a vision disappears because it has been grabbed by a thought, this happens often at the beginning. The process is simple. You have a strong vision. Your mind reacts. Thought jumps in, "Hey! Wow! I'm having a vision!" Your body tenses instinctively. The vision disappears. It seems that, except with a strong intoxication, either you're thinking or you're having visions. What's needed then is to be in a meditative state and to try not to seize your vision with the thought right away. You need to concentrate on breathing, a quiet state of perceiving the body as a whole, thus limiting the hold that thought has on the overall consciousness of the self. Stay on your slow automatic description of the event.

⚡ I see a serpent that wants to swallow me. Help! What should I do?

All is well! Let it happen. Healers say that if a serpent shows up and if your mouth really opens, it's the spirit of ayahuasca that wants to enter into you. You will feel it descend and coil up in your stomach. (I can share with you that this happened to me on my third ceremony with Guillermo.) If the serpent swallows you, a variation is that it's a possible journey: the serpent becomes the vehicle, you enter its stomach, and visions start to unfold.

⚡ I see incredible things. What should I do with that?

The hardest thing: don't try to theorize, you'll just tire yourself out. Conceptualizing all of life's experiences is our apprenticeship mode, so it's normal that this kind of thought will rush to the surface. Thoughts about the trees that surround you, nature, yourself, life—in short, thoughts directed in the morning toward the material world. Try to be in the felt sense. Only emotions and sensations remain connected to the experience. If this is really important to you, take brief notes before going to bed or on waking up—a memo that will serve as a link for you to each experience. After several ceremonies memories of the first ones can begin to fade; simple notes will allow you to think about it again much later, when you are back in your own world.

⚖ The plant seems to be speaking to me. Should I listen?

Yes, but be careful, it is sometimes difficult to be discerning. For example, if the plant says to you, "You must live here with us," don't make any decision; let a few months go by in order to reflect about these messages. If the plant says to you, "You are turning into a great healer, you need to learn," be careful also, because sometimes your ego is going to transform a message that should have been, "Your relationship with the plants is good, you can advance more deeply in this medicine." In this case too you have lots of time to think about it. Always remember that these are *plants of power* and that they have their own intentions. The objective is to come to agreement in a relationship that balances the two parts for the good of the whole.

You need to know that it is a good and positive thing to work for the vegetable kingdom in exchange. Cultivate, plant, protect, and communicate. And that can be done with ayahuasca's cousins—radishes and tomatoes. You can think of several such types of activity. You need to beware of prophetic or pseudoreligious desires; on the other hand, it is good to work with an NGO (nongovernmental organization), a community, or to spearhead an initiative, even in our world, to slow down the massacre of the Earth by modern agriculture. In short, nothing esoteric, just practical things! Remember also that it's the indigenous world that maintains a connection to this knowledge and that our culture tears that connection down a little more every day. See what you can do if the desire is there. Otherwise, you came for a treatment, you paid for it, and therefore the exchange is complete. No problem; that may be enough for you.

Sometimes, with a very strong intoxication, you experience an account of what you have done as an individual for the Earth and for the ecosystem. These accounts are given to you for yourself.

⚔ A very beautiful spirit wants to enter into me. Call for help?

Be careful, it's not because he's beautiful that you need to invite him. Stay neutral and don't call upon the spirit but upon the medicina. Do that in a concentrated way and not precipitously. Ask him inwardly why he has come. Be wary of suggestions of making a pact. "I can give you power, strength, and such things." In such a case, you are certainly with a cunning spirit in the pejorative sense of that term. Respond calmly, "I am not interested. You can return home. I am here for the medicina."

SONGS

Receiving the Ícaros

⚞ What should I do when receiving a song?

The very first song is to open the healer's intoxication, and then comes a first series of songs for the group. These are opening songs. In general, they begin with humming, whistling a peaceful melody. Then words come. They are sung in the healer's language. (In Peru, mixed blood healers sing in Quechua and Spanish, and other ethnic groups sing in their own languages.) Concentrate on the song; I've already spoken to you about that. The songs unfold an emotional journey. The singer activates the visions; this is the healer's strength coming out of the strict diets of the curandero. A healer's voice carries the vibration of the world he is entering into. At the beginning, the world of visions is opened, the healer's own visions are harmonized, and the general energy is positioned. *"Rama kano abano."* Now, I open the world of visions. Afterward, the singing will be in an individual way. If there are a lot of people, you won't always have a turn. When a song finishes, the healer calls someone. During an individual song, continue to connect in the same way as with a group song, unless . . . you're the one being called. With a bit of luck, it'll be a day when the healer makes the rounds and comes and sits down in front of you. If you can, try to be sitting. It's good to have a distance of about one foot between your legs and the healer's. You may be asked a question. If you don't understand, tell yourself there's a good chance that you've been asked how you are doing. Reply briefly—bueno, malo, sin visions, fuerte, and so on. Afterward, the song will begin.

Sit very straight to receive the song.

At the end of the song, lower your head, the curandero takes your head in his hands and blows his breath out onto you.

Then you hold your hands out toward him at the level of his hands. He may moisten them with floral water or simply clasp them in his own.

He draws your hands toward his mouth, let him guide you. He blows on them, sometimes several times. Wait until he has let go of your hands before withdrawing them.

He will ask how you're doing; then you try to return to your place and, surprise, you manage it much more easily than you thought you would!

Concentrate. Open yourself fully and dissolve into the song. The healer will be seeing visions emerge from you, and the song will change based on what is seen. Stay very concentrated. When the song is over, bend your head forward; the healer is going to take your head in his hands, blow his breath out onto it, and then let it go. Then hold out your two hands toward him, palms down; he is going to sprinkle them with flower water, then close them together, and move them toward his mouth.

The healer is going to blow on them (instead of flower water, tobacco might be used, or nothing but just blowing on them). That's it. It's over. Remember to say gracias, or *irake* ("thank you" in Shipibo).

If the curandero doesn't make the rounds, you will hear your name. Quietly, taking your time, come back (see above) and go to the healer. Be careful not to sit too far away. And check that you have a bucket handy. Sometimes the song can make you vomit, but you will have time to feel the movement; you don't need to have the bucket between your legs, unless the liquid is already just behind your lips before you sit down.

> Whoa! The song is coming out of the depths of my body, it's rising up . . . Jesus, Mary, Joseph . . . I'm going to sing, the plant tells me to, what do I do?

Usually, singing a song is only for those who really want to learn and are therefore on a diet. But if you are alone with the healer and it's not the first time, let's say not even one of the first ten times that you have taken ayahuasca, go ahead—sing! Position in your mind the intention and thought of the song and let it rise up from the depths of your body, passing by way of the heart in order to pick up a little shot of humility and . . . emerge from your mouth. Position your voice under that of the healer; sing softly, almost for yourself alone. The song comes from the mind, but its sound box is the stomach. Stay connected to your emotions, sing from those emotions, be humble, aware, and concentrated.

Stop as soon as you lose your concentration. Be sure to have a good

intoxication for singing. If you have a singer's talent (a good voice, well positioned), that's an inconvenience at the beginning because you're naturally going to concentrate to sing well, but it's not a matter of making a pretty song; it's not *Star Academy* or *American Idol*. It's a matter of making a song that is right and concentrated, a song that gives wing to your sensitivity in the moment. You have to know what you're doing; it's much harder.

In the event there are other patients with the healer—shut up! The other patients are going to hear your song and that can disturb their healing and their journeys. They are in a very sensitive state.

In fact, why are you there? To listen. You're not giving a concert; song is the healer's tool. Are you going to pick up the surgeon's scalpel in the middle of an operation? You can always sing in your head; that works too and doesn't affect the others. So go ahead and sing your head off in your own head if you want to. But, better still . . . listen.

AFTER THE CEREMONY

Determining If This Medicine Is Right for You

✍ When and how does the ceremony end?

The night proceeds, you come back quietly, a few hours have passed. Try not to think too much about all that you've seen. I know, sometimes that's hard.

Keep an eye on your channels of elimination. At a given moment you'll have the impression that everything is moving to the exit. If you feel that it's air that wants to be released as quickly as possible, don't trust that feeling and remember the saying, "The height of self-confidence is farting when you've got diarrhea." So be careful, because there's a pretty good chance that what's moving to the exit is in liquid form. The opposite is also possible. You are in a sensitive state, so you think you have to run to the toilet, which, of course, you have had the foresight to locate; you have memorized the night path and taken the time to grab your flashlight, as described in the chapter "Preparing for Ayahuasca," the chapter about what exits from the oral cavity; center yourself and judge the urgency, for each trip takes an effort. Try to go at the right moment. And fine, don't wait too long either; remember that within the intoxication it's easy to make an error in judgment. During the night you have died a virtual death three times, and you have traversed the universe—it would be pretty dumb to end the evening laying waste to your underwear.

⚔ And if it's over but it isn't over for me?

You go to bed, you're on the point of falling asleep and . . . everything comes back. In fact, it's not over! Don't panic. Yes, you are alone, but it will necessarily not be as strong. Do the exercises again. Settle into the intoxication. Turn on good thoughts. Stay centered; you will fall asleep. If you don't manage to fall asleep, avoid reading and mental activity. Have an apple or a banana (be careful, for some people it brings back the intoxication), look at the stars, listen to the forest (don't wander too far away). Breathe outside in peace and calm—then back to bed.

⚔ What do I do the next day?

I'm going to do this in two parts. It's easier.

Either it went well or it went badly.

1. Paradise

It went well! Total ecstasy. You have only one desire—to be back in the maloca the following night. Now, be careful, regulate your good mood, relax your brain stem, don't impose any scenarios on the coming night such as, "I'm going back, it's going to be great!" Avoid that for sure. Save the energy that you think you have in infinite quantities. In short, relax . . . And above all, no prophetic or messianic thoughts; stay humble, don't tell yourself that you're "special." All you've done is enter a new and different world.

2. Hell

It went badly—frightful nausea, no visions or only terrifying images, fear, terror, pain. You have only one desire: never again to return to the maloca! Try to relax your mind. Talk about it with others who, with ecstasy beaming from their eyes, will relate their cosmic adventures to you. Share your doubts and your moods. Don't tell yourself, "There you go: for me—horror; for them—happiness." Starting tomorrow, the roles could be reversed, ecstasy for you, and for them down and out. Remember, that's how things are with the plant—one day way up, one day way down, then to the right, and then to the left. That doesn't make you feel any better? I understand. Don't mull it over too much alone; go and speak to the healer. And that leads us to the next question.

✘ How do I know if I should take the vine again this evening or not?

Remember to ask yourself this question about once again taking the vine at the end of the ceremony, at the very end. That's when you first need to take stock. If your feeling is "I'm finally okay, now," then you can continue the next day. If you're not sure, ask the question again early in the morning. This is because if you ask this question two hours before the ceremony is beginning, when the jungle has plunged into darkness, there's a strong chance of deciding no, "Not tonight, I don't feel so good." Not feeling good before a ceremony is normal. The part in you that wants to be in control doesn't want to go back there; the mental part hangs on to control for dear life. It will trot out all kinds of arguments that you—that is, your inner control freak—will find very persuasive. You're queasy, almost nauseous? That's normal; your body is getting ready. The body knows what it is in for. This process will only get stronger with time, going so far as to provoke intoxication, nausea, and visions even before you've taken the drink.

Several times I had a strange thing happen. At a time when I had not taken ayahuasca for months, one hour before the ceremony, the vine rose up toward my mouth, either in liquid form or as a burp perfumed with ayahuasca! How is that possible? I have no idea. Intriguing. The body keeps the memory of it.

So, take it again, or not take it again? Your decision must be freed from fear. That's why you need to remember what your thoughts were about this at the end of the previous ceremony. What was your state of mind at that moment? You were afraid during the night, but you were fine, serene, at the end of the ceremony. Establish calm in yourself, remember what you experienced, and from that place of peace, decide to take it again this evening, tomorrow, or the day after tomorrow. If you say "never," fear is guiding your decision or you're not cut out for this medicine. In general, it's your fear that murmurs, "You're not cut out for that! You are too afraid now, imagine having even more fear!" Besides, there's no need to go to Peru, you can tell yourself that after just reading these lines—too afraid, too much fear. One point to remember is that you're in the grip of fear; we all are, more or less. Go ahead, have courage! The goal is to take care of oneself and to balance oneself.

For those who have spent an awful night, you can still go back to the maloca but not take ayahuasca; listen to the songs, and sleep there. Doing that every night is not recommended, especially not in the first few times. Don't let yourself be influenced by your fear nor by the others.

Anecdote: A woman traumatized by a strong experience, comes back three days later to drink. The healer offers her a small glass; she brandishes . . . a small spoon (I laughed a lot).

> ⬟ **I've read part 1, "Inner Journey Notebooks," and other books, looked at films, heard the accounts of friends, and I can tell you, this medicine is for me!**

Very well. No comment. However, sometimes after this statement, I've heard this one: "I want to learn—that is my goal!" I don't mean to offend people who say this, but many would find such an idea ridiculous. However, to my great surprise, people often made a point of telling me this—too many people do not take the time to respond to it. Don't project anything and don't leave with the idea of learning; first go and discover. In spite of what you have read or seen, wait until you have . . . drunk, and not just once, before rethinking all that. You're going for healing and for discovery. Once you have at least a dozen strong experiences under your belt, your path will begin to take shape. It always takes the route that is right for the patient, and it can stay that way; it's calmer—a calm that is completely relative.

Are you are out of step with the social model being proffered, alienated from studies or from family? Ayahuasca is *not* the solution to your problems. It has to be a path for resolving the pieces and putting them back together, calming tensions, but *never* a place of flight or escape.

■ ■ ■

You have to go in order to come back with new tools for anchoring yourself once you're back among us. Don't forget . . . *you have to come back.*

The first thing to ask the healer is to help you manage problems in adapting to the Western jungle, for help in reestablishing a balance. For the indigenous peoples, illness is a lack of balance between you and the world. Reestablish this balance in yourself first and then, afterward, you can once again find your place in society or reestablish dialogue and peace in your family; that change begins with work on oneself. Put a bit of harmony back in your inner universe. Often we want to change the world before we have begun to listen to it. Putting yourself in listening mode, understanding the world's simple music hidden beneath a complex melody—it's work. Act, yes, but then?

The aim is to live happy and calm, and to create beautiful things wherever you are, right? For example: in the subway, with the flu coming on, with everyone glaring at you, and with your little daughter who's screaming that she doesn't want to go to school. Or on the other hand, while on the most beautiful of the planet's beaches, dancing at sunset, or laughing with your little daughter so happy in your arms.

That's the final aim—being just fine everywhere. Utopia, certainly, I give you that, but not completely. Your little daughter, in the end, is right. (This virtual little daughter can take the form of a certain quality of desire in you.) You are an adult, the aim is not to reach this state, it's the road. The aim is to be *on* the road. Keep listening to your inner daughter, the guys too; not the little boy, no, no, the little daughter. Be careful, she is capricious. She wants everything, right away; she lets herself be carried away by her emotions; she thinks she has understood everything. So be vigilant with her, you have to guide her. For in fact she is your most precious treasure.

> ⚔ **Isn't it hard doing ceremonies with people who come from different countries and speak different languages? Wouldn't it be better to see your traditional doctor alone, like when you go to a doctor in France or the United States?**

Capricious little daughters, I get it! "I want a shaman all to myself."

Okay, now, those who want the experience with a personal curandero, one-on-one, can go dive into the jungle to find one. But, in the first place, it's really not necessary. I advise you to drop fantasies that are based on various and diverse models that are common among us.

I've seen French people arrive in Espíritu de Anaconda and be disappointed: they had been told about an Indian community, and they discover a treatment center for Westerners, a relaxed shaman in shirt and shorts. I've seen them leave again on the spot to look for someone with feathers on his head. It's dumb; it's a long trip to take based on an empty stereotype.

I've known a broad range of experiences, from being alone in the forest with three experienced curanderos to guide me to the time when I arrived late and the only place remaining in a maloca full of an important group of first timers was right at the back, near the door leading to the can. It's not like the subway and the beach: the two places have the same value. Clearly these are two different experiences, and I prefer being alone, but I have actually discovered that with a noisy group I can work on something else, something that is also important, and I see that my journey can still be strong, carried by the energy of the group, a profound journey in the world of this medicine.

Today, when I enter the maloca, I say to myself, "Hey, there is no one here, terrific, it's going to be my party" or "Hey, the maloca is full, terrific, it's going to be our party."

> ⚔ **I followed a diet, took ayahuasca, and I want to learn; what should I do?**

Something you should know is that there are several paths in the apprenticeship that lead in two directions.

The first is to learn how to become familiar with the medicina. This is with the aim of working on oneself, for one's own self-knowledge, in order to discover indigenous cosmology as well as traditional concepts and to do it traditionally; that is, from the heart of the experience—long diets. All this so that you can toughen up the thought processes and acquire tools for a new existence—the path that I was speaking about earlier.

The second is to learn to become a healer within traditional Shipibo medicine. I give the floor to Guillermo, who once defined his job as follows: "The healer has fully entered the visions, he has a sick child in front of him, he sees the illness, and he treats it with his song and with his knowledge; that's what he needs to know how to do." I would add: he does that six evenings a week, and he has to know not only how to care for the person but also how not to take on the negative energy that he pulls out of the person. No doubt it's this second stage that requires the most knowledge. The apprenticeship is accompanied by a lot of suffering and a lot of sacrifices. So, before plunging into this work, you really need to know why you're doing it and what you're willing to give up to get there.

> ✍ **I've read part 1, "Inner Journey Notebooks," and other books, looked at films, heard the accounts of friends, and I can tell you, this medicine is *not* for me!**

You could also add to that, "I understand that it's interesting and that it's a beautiful adventure. I know myself well, and it doesn't seem that all that stuff is good for me."

That's great if you're fine, relaxed, happy in life, and in peace. All is well. I hope that the notebooks have taken you on a journey and amused you for a while. I understand completely. We each have our own thing. If, on the other hand, what you're telling yourself is basically, "It's not for me because I'm too afraid; I could never do it!" That's something else.

It's the unknown that scares people stiff, and the greatest fear is . . . fear itself.

So don't throw out the baby with the bathwater, don't break the bathtub, and don't set fire to the bathroom. It's a normal impulse, even a healthy one. Fear protects us. Well-placed fear is a protection. Without fear, there would be no prudence. Otherwise, you would put yourself in harm's way and risk having a shorter life.

It's normal to have fear in this adventure, because your imagination is boundless. We enter into the unknown and you know unconsciously that you are descending to an encounter with yourself. Moreover, you are reading a book just now that sometimes describes terrifying things. You accept experiencing big emotions secondhand. In a novel or a film you die with the hero, you save the world, you traverse the universe— but happily it is not you, and if it's too strong, you can close the book or leave the movie theater.

With ayahuasca, you can't leave the theater. With the vine, the hero of the film is you. But, as in the cinema, you're not going to die for real either. And, as in the cinema, the putting yourself in danger is virtual. Certainly there are contraindications where the experience can turn out to be really dangerous for you. But they are rare, or nonexistent, if you are in good physical and mental health, or in any case are not suffering from a serious illness. (I give details later on.)

Amazonian medicine offers a strong experience. It resonates with some people and not others. Don't go unless you think it's for you and that you have need of it. Don't let yourself be influenced by anyone, including me!

⚔ The ceremony just finished, and I had the impression that the healer was coming on to me. Am I delirious? Am I imagining things?

You have very little chance of being delirious this time! This is definitely, along with the "reality of the spirits," another cultural gulf that separates us from the indigenous world. Let me explain: We have the tendency to see the healer as a kind of monk, being one who works with the spiritual world. In actuality, you need to think of the healer as a therapist, but not a shrink.

Consider then, if your therapist or your counselor were to entice you to a café after a consultation, how would you take that? This is an exaggeration, of course, and would likely raise concerns due to our Western considerations of professionalism, but deep down, within our social mores it would not be a scandal. In the end, if you feel that amorous vibes are coming from your healer, the first question to ask is, "From my own point of view, do I find this person attractive?"

Now from the indigenous point of view: At the beginning of the twentieth century all men were polygamous, they could have up to three wives. But, as an exception to this, a healer could have up to twenty. Today, the missionaries have been through and everyone is now monogamous. Healers, however, have remained very open to amorous jousting.

Ayahuasca is also an aphrodisiac, not during the ceremony but afterward. It has a tendency to clean out the libido and develop sensuality and sexual desire, giving rise to the difficulty of maintaining one's diet. So, when over there, if some creature turns you on, it can seem natural to you to propose that you stretch out on the moss and get rid of those stupid bits of fabric that hide our bodies! So . . . be vigilant.

But also be aware, a good healer on a diet is capable of having amorous relations without breaking the patient's diet. Yikes? No, it's very simple, you just need to know about it. There's no manipulation, there is just desire. You can always politely accept or refuse a gesture or suggestion that you find misplaced.

So, ladies, be relaxed but forewarned. And guys, be vigilant about what those "neurons" between your legs are telling you.

CHOOSING A HEALER

Healer Recommendations and the Ethics of Paying for Treatment

⚔ How to choose the place and the healer?

Travel and scout around in South American countries where it's not illegal—Peru, Ecuador, Brazil. Preferably, you should choose indigenous or mixed-blood healers who are over thirty. If you decide to choose a Westerner, make sure to find one who is trained with diets in the traditional way, who is over thirty-five, or has at least five years of practice. That's the minimum length of training and age necessary to achieve balance in the healer's own internal forces. Often you make a choice based on a personal recommendation. A friend speaks to you about a healer: take a close look—how is your friend on his return. Is he happy, more collected, well settled into his life? The best press for healers is not the tales they have to tell but the healed and balanced patients, or the stable apprentices. If your friend has very strange things to tell you, don't get frightened but do observe him. If he plunges into a messianic delirium of the kind: "I am a warrior of the light!"—be careful; this isn't the effect of the medicina, it's an old egoistic demon disguised as an angel of redemption who has taken advantage of the situation to come to life. Or, another reaction you might see is, "Come, it's all happening down there; we've understood nothing, and the Indians know everything." (By the way, that comment came from me on the third day after my first return.) If so, wait to see if he softens, which is what happened to me, then reconsider his case. If the guy stays in a prophetic and messianic loop, it means that the treatment failed for him. He missed a step; he is a prisoner of an in-between reality. Or he has not followed the instructions of his healer after his return. He will extract himself from that if he runs off to get a good treatment in the Amazon, or if he puts himself in the hands of a good therapist (magnetizer, reflexologist, shaman working with a drum, or the like).

Beware of people who paint the indigenous peoples as diabolic, who tell you that they engage in black magic. Painting a healer in that light is, in itself, an act of black magic. Words are a form of magic, aren't they? Sorcery is using powers to manipulate. It means, instead of healing, making someone sick or taking away their strength.

What's sad is that, essentially, it's easy to become a sorcerer and difficult to become a healer, just as it's easier to learn how to hit someone than it is to learn how to heal the wounds.

> ✍ **Your shaman has become a star, he makes you pay. That's pretty far from the spirit of the indigenous way, isn't it?**

If you see the Amazonian doctor as a sort of hermit monk who is dedicated to humanity and gives away treatments, then, yes, the indigenous healer that you will meet is far from that. The curanderos of the Shipibo communities who practice traditional medicine generally have some other activity, such as fishing for example. They do very few ceremonies, perhaps once a week, and when they treat someone, they receive something in return, which could be in the form of a meal, a chicken, fabric—not money but barter, because when it comes to money in these communities there just isn't any.

Healers coming from the traditional world who have opened themselves to the Western world, and who have no other work except being a healer, are going to ask for money in exchange. It's reasonable, because they are doctors—not traditional doctors, of course, but doctors nonetheless—and that's how you need to look at it. Personally, I find it normal to pay my doctor; he's going to see me, make a diagnosis, and give me a treatment. If it's effective I'll go back, otherwise I'll go and see another therapist.

I'd like to speak for a moment about Guillermo Arévalo. After *D'autres mondes* and *Blueberry,* many people went to see him, and after that his practice grew by word of mouth. Thanks to the money he collected, he built a center that is quite a pleasant spot. When I met him, the ceremonies took place in a little hut behind his house, and the patients were mainly Shipibo and métis (mixed blood); he would make a little money when a white person came to see him. Today, Guillermo still offers treatments to the local population. It often happens that foreigners who have come for treatment or for learning share a ceremony with an Indian. Except that now the roles are reversed: the Indian must feel a little out of place among all the Westerners.

So, come to your own conclusions, consider your budget, of course, but have some discernment. Don't think right away, "That's a lot of money for an Indian," but instead think, "How much does that amount to in relation to my need for treatment?"

You should know that in 2011 the center adopted a new orientation and changed its name; it became Anaconda Cósmica. Its activity is no longer directed at personal development or discovery but solely at the treatment of disease.

The center has stopped devoting itself to the dissemination of Shipibo knowledge, which means that Guillermo is no longer taking new apprentices. In the past few years, teaching has required a lot of energy. Currently he wants to open the first clinic of indigenous medicine and concentrate all his work on that for the years to come. At sixty-three, he has spoken for several years about taking retirement so as to enter into the third part of his life (the first, learning; the second, sharing and working; the third, becoming engaged in his personal spiritual path).

Anaconda Cósmica accepts severe pathologies (physical, mental, and spiritual). Supplementary treatments are offered to reinforce the treatment, such as flower baths (to clear out negative energies), steam baths using teaching plants, application of plants to the body, and the use of nebulizers (powder in the nostrils).

Ricardo Amaringo, a very good curandero who was Guillermo's student and worked with him for seventeen years, is working on his own treatment and apprenticeship center, Ronin Saini (Echo of the Anaconda).

TREATMENTS AND CONTRAINDICATIONS

Receiving Plant Healing Safely

⚔ What are the illnesses and diseases that these plants can treat?

These plants can help you gain physical and mental strength, reduce mood fluctuations, and get your spirits back to a good and stable place, which means treating depressions. In general, diets of teaching plants prescribed according to the pathology are very effective for all forms of gastritis, bodily tension, insomnia, hormonal problems, hemorrhoids, and high blood pressure. They can also aid in treatment pre- and post-chemotherapy for cancer. (Be careful: it's not a replacement for our medicine, but instead can provide a complementary treatment.) Other conditions that can benefit from plant healing include muscular dystrophy (offering a possibility of stabilizing the condition—I know of three examples: in one there was no effect and the other two stabilized for six years without getting worse) and autoimmune diseases.

I am not a doctor; these are examples that were reported over the years by patients on diets.

Individuals suffering from serious illnesses *absolutely must* bring their medications with them in order to treat crises (epilepsy, for example), and they need to find a local clinic or hospital as a fallback in case of emergency.

⚔ I have a weak heart. Is ayahuasca inadvisable?

Sorry, ayahuasca is not for you! If you have a really weak heart—don't do it. For example, if you've been warned to not sprint two hundred yards because you might suffer a heart attack, better to forget about it; the plant is not really capable of provoking tachycardia, but your emotions certainly can. You can go to consult a curandero and follow diets without taking ayahuasca. You can attend ceremonies and experience the relationship with the world of plants in dreams. That in itself is a real and powerful experience.

✍ I'm in treatment, is it compatible with ayahuasca?

Any treatment that acts on mood, morale, or sleep—in short anything that affects the psyche—is not allowed. (This includes *all* psychotropic medications.) Combined with ayahuasca they can provoke a harsh shock. Antidepressants, Prozac, sleeping pills, any of these chemical straightjackets are not part of the journey. Those treatments need to be stopped at least two weeks before departure. Do it progressively and above all absolutely with the help of your prescribing physician.

Aspirin or antibiotics, in principle, are not a problem. However, the healer must be informed of any pathology or any medication. A curandero living in a traditional community may not be able to answer your questions. Seek out a good translator who can help you describe your illness and explain exactly how your treatment works.

✍ I'm losing blood, is that a problem?

Ayahuasca is a vasodilator. If you are losing blood, be careful, because the amount of blood loss can increase. If the loss is significant, come with a specific diagnosis to convey to the healer so that the right treatment with a diet can be found for you, before you're able to take the vine. For women, let the healer know before the ceremony if you are menstruating. For other plants, consult the healer.

✍ I'm asthmatic, is it possible for me?

Asthmatics can use Ventolin or their usual treatment at any time. Have some beside you during the ceremony if strong emotions have the effect of setting off your crises. There are no contraindications to using it during the ceremony if you need to, but do not exceed the prescribed dosage.

✍ I'm diabetic, is that a contraindication?

If possible, e-mail your chosen healer about it before your departure. Explain what type of diabetes you have and engage in a consultation to determine whether the healer can help you and whether you can travel to the Amazon. Above all, while you're there, be very vigilant. Do your blood testing more often than usual, probably twice as often. The treatments and the food can cause your blood sugar levels to plummet. I know of one case of a diabetic person who had a crisis after an insulin injection. No one knew why he was in a state of crisis. Luckily, a physician was present and made a quick diagnosis so it ended well. Do speak with and bring your healer up to speed on the evolution of your illness. Always consider calling on a translator in case of linguistic difficulties.

✍ I'm hooked, or a heavy user; can I go?

Tobacco

If you're thinking of giving up smoking, this isn't the place to do it. In my case I even started again there. If you've just stopped, good luck. Tobacco is part of the ceremonies; it's a diet plant that has therapeutic power. Of course, we're not talking about American cigarettes but a brown tobacco, mapacho. Try to use cigarettes without additives.

Cannabis

If you smoke cannabis, try to reduce your consumption well in advance of your departure, and certainly don't smoke it while you're there. Even as a simple consumer, you risk big problems with the police, much more serious than in France and many parts of the United States. In addition, marijuana doesn't go well with ayahuasca. It's time to stop. And be careful, take it easy on your return or you could have some disagreeable surprises. Taking any strong psychoactive substance can take you back to the modus operandi of the vine. In short, you will find yourself back under the effects of ayahuasca.

Alcohol

If you're hooked on alcohol, your illness can be treated with traditional Amazonian medicine. Of course, you need to stop first. Engage in maximum cutting back before you leave and drink no alcohol once you get there. Absolutely nothing, otherwise—ka-boom! You can solve the problem with the vine, and you will discover that it's not so difficult. Here too, be careful on your return. You can very quickly fall back. Don't ever believe that the jungle treatment is a miracle and an inalienable right; we'll come back to that.

Heroin

This is an even more serious subject. Diets and ayahuasca can detox you. There is a high rate of success, but it takes several months. It can be the goal of your journey. According to various accounts, it seems that getting through the experience can be hard during the ceremonies. There is also a terrible danger of relapse on your return, because then there's every chance of taking an overdose. The treatment will make your body much more sensitive. Death can be waiting at the end of your next encounter. *Be careful!*

⚔ Can I take other psychotropic substances there?

No! Nothing other than what you are offered, whether it comes from the chemistry or from the alchemy of the plants. Nothing! There must be *absolutely* no other psychotropic substance interfering with the process.

On top of that, let me repeat, be careful! On your return you will be more sensitive, and taking a substance that modifies your consciousness can send you back into the universe you encountered during the ceremonies. So be careful and let some time go by.

It is also highly inadvisable to jump from one plant to another. The most blatant example is the relationship between iboga and ayahuasca. If you have encountered one of these two traditions, leave a gap of six months before moving toward the other one. An interval must also exist between the taking of peyote, or the San Pedro cactus, and ayahuasca so that you don't mix the messages; but the period of time can be shorter—at least a few weeks in the case of diets lasting more than two weeks.

PRACTICAL PREPARATIONS

What to Bring and When and Where to Go

⚹ How do I prepare for the trip?

Inner Preparation

First of all, assess your objectives and your life as it is now. Make a kind of recapitulation of your situation—health, work, love, behavior. Try to calibrate the weaknesses and strengths in your life, without judgment, without lying to yourself. For example, if you live as a couple and you are leaving for this trip alone, take a close look at this situation. Where do you stand in relation to what you want, your goals, your plans, what do you really share? You need to realize that if your life as a couple is not going well, without really going badly either, and if you are living together because in the end you don't want to be alone, the trip is going to expose your relationship, and, upon your return, seeing each other again may end in your separation. Ayahuasca will show you the reality of your relationships, and you will update your situation. So, take stock before leaving. In general, with couples, a distance between you in the spiritual domain and in desire can create a break.

Preparing yourself also means getting in shape, working on body and mind.

Material Preparation

Buy *Lonely Planet* or *Le guide du routard* (France's equivalent travel guidebook); they have all the info. Points I don't cover below you'll find in the *Lonely Planet*.

Brief notes . . .

The Season
The best season is the one that corresponds to summer in our hemisphere: less rain, fewer mosquitoes, less humidity. Let's say June to September. If you can manage that—it's more pleasant.

Clothing
Pack garments that are lightweight and dry quickly; clothing with long sleeves and long pants (to protect from mosquitoes); sandals, flip-flops, and hiking shoes; a sun hat; and sunglasses.

Equipment
Take two kinds of flashlights. The first is a small one with low light so you don't dazzle people in the maloca, for example, the little hand-crank ones. Take several as you will misplace one at some point, and you will also have spares so you can provide one to someone else once you're there, which can be very helpful. The second kind to bring is a more powerful light—for moving around outside the maloca, or if you lose your passport at night in the forest. A powerful forehead model is ideal. Also, take one or two good lighters, because the local ones can stop working very quickly. Travel light so you have room to bring back Amazonian fabrics (*kénés*).

Medications
There are no recorded cases of malaria in the regions in question (Pucallpa, Iquitos, the upper Ucayali River), so no need to take those little pills that cause nausea. It's up to you though. In July 2009 I visited several clinics and no case of malaria was noted except for those workers who were deep in the forest. I don't guarantee anything for you and do look into it yourself, but consult local organizations. In France everybody will load you down with medications as if you were going into a region swarming with infection. It is likely the same in the United States. Consult local blogs. Make your choices. I can simply tell you that in ten years I never caught anything.

Bring along a little first aid kit that contains Aspivenin (a small vacuum device that removes venom from an insect bite), soothing creams for mosquito bites, and also an insect repellant. You should also consider my secret weapon—saro (*Cinnamosma fragrans,* which you can easily order on the Internet), an essential oil from Madagascar with strong antibacterial properties. Have a sore throat? Use one drop on the tongue; do the same thing for a digestive problem. Mosquito bites or scratches from your wanderings in the jungle don't dry up? Apply saro and they're gone. Also, when diluted in water it treats your insides. In short, inside or outside, it works.

I take a homeopathic kit with me, which is also how I look after myself in France. Put together your own kit, without paranoia. You know yourself; it's not helpful to expect the worst. There is an American clinic in Iquitos.

Staying Healthy

You have to drink! (You won't be very thirsty in the Amazon because the humidity is so high.) But, be careful about water and fruit. I saw one case of hemorrhagic fever, and I especially see cases of tourista (traveler's diarrhea), which are always due to a lack of vigilance. Drink bottled water, and that is only if you are in diet mode, otherwise it's soft drinks. Be careful with fresh fruit juice, ice creams or sorbets, and anything that might contain water that has not been boiled. That's my only recommendation.

For those who are going to Espíritu, the water is filtered so you can eat and drink what you're served without any concern.

Plane Ticket

It's best to buy your ticket on the Internet (last minute or the equivalent) all the way to Iquitos. For maximum safety, only check your bag to Lima; pick it up there and recheck it on the domestic flight.

Once at Lima

Take an official taxi and pay attention to the fare. It's better to look for a taxi in the domestic arrivals area. Fares to each district of the city are posted.

If you're spending a few days in Lima, don't miss the Museo Oro del Perú and go right to the basement. Also, for dinner I like Toto's in the Barranco district, the most pleasant quarter. It's not expensive, has local flavor, and even though the quarter has changed a lot in ten years, it has kept its charm, unlike Miraflores.

You can reserve your hotel, guest house, or youth hostel by e-mail. Peruvians are warm and welcoming. There is little chance of mix-ups, less than in Paris in any case.

The weather is rarely fine (Lima is often cloudy and damp from May to November) and is rather cool.

Try to avoid arriving in Pucallpa or Iquitos at night. It's always more agreeable to discover these places during the day.

Arriving in Pucallpa
Be careful in Pucallpa: this city, an important river port, has become dangerous. You will meet very few tourists. Be cautious. In general, it's just some place that you pass through on your way upstream to the aboriginal communities.

Arriving in Iquitos
More cool. The various centers for the medicina are in the surrounding jungle. The city is less dangerous than Paris, but be careful in the Belen market. There are areas where you shouldn't wander around with a camera in your hand.

You'll find lots of information about these cities in the guidebooks.

Leaving
When heading back to the West, don't forget to set aside money for the Airport Departure Tax* (at least $40 for each airport).

Arriving Home
Keep a close eye on urges once you're home. Bad habits can come back quickly—in all areas. In order to maintain the effect of the Amazonian medicine, you need to maintain a certain healthy lifestyle. Pay attention to your nutrition and mind. This is the work of integration.

If you are continuing your diet outside of the Amazon region, do not bathe in sea water. It's too salty. In any case, consult your healer, because

---

*Since January 2011 this tax has been added to the ticket price. On occasion though, a travel agent may not add it in when booking the flight, so it is better to be prepared.

certain plants will tolerate an immersion of the body but not the head. My thanks to Dr. Aziz Kharzai for this information, which they often forget to tell you since in the Amazon region there is only fresh water.

Be discreet about your trip—don't talk about it too much. Few people will be able to understand and you risk isolating yourself. There's nothing to hide, but you also don't have to become an apostle of the plants. Be content with answering if you're asked questions, while monitoring the limit of what the person is able to hear. If the person overreacts (the eyes will tell you a lot), change the subject. It is important to maintain good relations with family and friends.

For those of you who've had an undeniable and deep experience, don't rush into anything; take the time to see what's happening, what is coming back. Integration takes months. It is important for you to find your place in *our* jungle; and that's what you need to concentrate on.

If you're missing the action-filled nights in the maloca, you can always go back in six months or more. Concentrate on the balance that is hard to find and yet essential—having one foot in each world.

The vine is the art of finding an equilibrium in all domains: emotional, family, professional, social, and spiritual. In other words, the Amazonian medicine is effective if it calms you and helps you find your place in our society.

Remember also that, once home, you need to do everything on a day-by-day basis. The plants show you your imbalances; and now it's up to you to do the work. The aim is not to put feathers on your head but to once again activate the ones you have always carried in your heart.

JAN KOUNEN
JUNE 2010

He who learns too quickly
he who works too quickly
shortens his life.
When calm is there,
when patience is there,
with a certain slowness also taking part
life extends out.

KESTENBETSA

GLOSSARY OF PLANTS

Each plant has its own world and its own energy. Certain plants have a spirit world; these are the teaching plants that the healer works with.

Medicinal plants treat psychological and physiological diseases. Teaching plants also treat spiritual illnesses and are used in apprenticeship training. The plants have different worlds—schematically speaking, the world of light and the world of darkness. Medicine is found in the world of light. The different plants have variable connections with these worlds and are in various states of balance with them. Certain plants, for example, have a dark work of significant proportion and a lesser, but very powerful, medicinal world.

Traditionally it was the Shipibo women who possessed the knowledge of medicinal plants and transmitted it from mother to daughter. They are active healers; however, the majority of curanderos are men. In fact, it is rare that women are able to follow long apprenticeship diets, because most of them have to look after their children. Often they enter fully into the medicinal world somewhat later.

Aire sacha Kósmika (a teaching plant)

This plant fosters a connection with Nature and her elements, as well as the Earth and the universe. It allows you to distinguish the dark world of false light from the true light. It is mainly a teaching plant.

Ajo sacha (a teaching and medicinal plant)

Medicinal usage: This plant clears addictions and cleanses the blood. It is also used in the treatment of psychological illnesses.

Teaching usage: The plant is used to open and purify the thinking mind and the body; it fosters the work of personal evolution.

Ayahuasca (a teaching and medicinal plant)

This is the basic plant of traditional medicine and is a doorway leading to all the other plants. It is rarely used in diets for healing.

Medicinal usage: It opens the vision during therapeutic diets.

Teaching usage: It is the principal tool of healers, with the strength coming from diets using other plants. It's the local celebrity without whose good graces nothing is possible. You begin dieting with it naturally during the teaching. Feminine, the madre has her own medicinal world. This is a generous plant, with whom, however, you don't engage in boasting or else you might receive a good maternal spanking. (I speak from personal experience, and I take this opportunity to thank her for setting me on the right path by slapping me a little, when necessary.)

Ayahuma (a teaching plant)

This plant, which looks like a skull, is used in teaching mainly to acquire protection when practicing healing. It contains the two energies, positive and negative, in equal proportions.

It is a toxic plant. The dosage must be very precise and scrupulously respected. Ayahuma can be very dangerous.

Azusena

This is not a plant for diets. Used only to induce vomiting, it is used to cleanse the body at the beginning of a diet (combined with ojé). Taking it is never a picnic; it's done during the daytime and makes you nauseous for a few hours.

Boawasca (a medicinal plant)

Medicinal usage: This plant is used for serious physical problems, for a cleansing of the organs, and a general physiological rebalancing. Boawasca is not a teaching plant.

Bobinsana (a teaching and medicinal plant)

Medicinal usage: This plant lives on riverbanks and is used to treat rheumatism and arthritis.

Teaching usage: This plant teaches the techniques of healing and the art of a warrior, in a general way.

Camalonga (a teaching and medicinal plant)

Medicinal usage: This plant treats the nervous system. It removes inner blackness and darkness. The plant contains two energies, positive and negative, in equal measure.

Teaching usage: In apprenticeship it is useful in opening visions leading to medicinal treatment. It's a very fragile, sensitive plant. When it is taken alone, its energy easily fades away, so it is never taken alone in a diet. Whereas, if it is combined with another plant during a diet, the two mix together and in this way the camalonga is less volatile.

Chay (a teaching and medicinal plant)

Medicinal usage: This plant is used for the extraction of tumors and abscesses, and for the setting of fractures.

Teaching usage: It is useful for coming into contact with the worlds of water, air, and earth.

Coca (a teaching and medicinal plant)

Medicinal usage: Used for all types of infection, clarification for the thinking mind, and shortage of physical or mental energy.

Teaching usage: This plant opens a connection to the astral world and to the world of spirits. It clarifies conceptual thought and is used during surgical operations conducted by spirits.

Marosa (a teaching and medicinal plant)

Medicinal usage: This plant is useful for promoting female fertility; it opens the thinking mind and the heart and relieves heartache. Its leaves can be used in a bath to awaken love.

Teaching usage: Connected to the world of water and to the serpent yacuruna, this plant opens the world of love like a mother, and it opens the thinking mind, consciousness, and the heart. It develops the feminine element in song.

Ojé (a teaching and medicinal plant)

Medicinal usage: This plant is useful for the treatment of addictions. It's often combined with tobacco and azusena, the vomit-inducing plant, for detoxification.

Teaching usage: This plant teaches how to cure addictions.

Piñon blanco (a teaching and medicinal plant)

Medicinal usage: This plant has many medical properties and is used for numerous illnesses, physical as well as psychological. It is effective in treating problems of fertility in women.

Teaching usage: It fosters an opening toward the world of light. This is a plant that contains very little darkness. Certain healers even say that it has no dark world; therefore it is used to open love and peace for those who need that.

Piñon colorado (a teaching and medicinal plant)

Medicinal usage: This plant treats external as well as internal infections.

Teaching usage: It maintains a fragile balance between the world of light and the world of darkness. The dieter must choose and must be very vigilant. This plant therefore is more difficult to use for teaching than piñon blanco.

Tobacco (a teaching and medicinal plant)

Medicinal usage: This plant allows for a deep clearing of various addictions and is used for protection.

Teaching usage: In apprenticeship training this plant is a strong spirit.

Toé (datura/*Brugmansia*) (a teaching, medicinal, and psychoactive plant)

Medicinal usage: This plant fosters rapid repair of bones in the case of fractures and treats pain and abscesses.

Teaching usage: This very powerful plant is considered by the Indians to be the root of all plants. It is able to reveal the secrets of nature. It enters into conflict with the ego. As a very difficult plant having a significant dark world, it can turn against the dieter without one being aware of it. Demanding, it is the most difficult plant to use in one's diet. In cases where the diet is not respected, a psychological crash can result.

This plant can damage eyesight and be lethal if the dose ingested is too large. Do not begin a diet of toé unless a healer *in whom you have complete confidence* recommends it to you for your healing or for your apprenticeship.

A SMALL SHIPIBO LEXICON

The Shipibo people number about sixty thousand and dwell in more than two hundred communities along the Ucayali River. Smaller communities also exist in the cities of Iquitos and Madre de Dios. The largest concentration of traditional healers is to be found in the communities along the upper reaches of the river, above the Pucallpa lagoon.

The communities are of variable size, from as few as fifty people in the smallest to more than two thousand inhabitants in the largest ones—such as Kako and Paoyan (along the lower Ucayali River). The Shipibo traditionally engage in fishing and agriculture. Today their economy also benefits from their handicrafts, which are devoted largely to representations of the visionary worlds of medicinal and teaching plants.

The Shipibo are animists. They weave relationships with nature spirits; those spirits have above them Ibo Riosqui: God, the Creator, the Dean of the Universe.

The Shipibo have specific relationships with the spirits of the forest and plants, but the use of ayahuasca came from their encounters with the Inca. This feature is based on their myths in which the Inca are often referred to.

Here are a few words and expressions in Shipibo that will help you show your hosts that you have an interest in their language and their culture. If you go to the communities, you will very likely encounter Shipibo who speak very little Spanish.

Rather than alphabetical order, I have used a grouping by theme:

daily conversation, sensations and feelings, the natural world, and parts of the body. Sometimes the name of an organ can be enough to explain to the curandero where the problem is.

The entry that begins this lexicon, "Help me: *Ea akinwe*," is clearly a nod to the anecdotes in the notebooks.

Note that *j* is pronounced like a *k*. A word that reappears often, *ajon*, therefore is pronounced *akon*. (Don't worry, when you make an effort to pronounce Shipibo words, everyone will be right there to help you.)

This small lexicon was drawn up with the collaboration of Panshin Copé (James Arévalo) and Sani (Ricardo Amaringo).

Daily Conversation

Help me: *Ea akinwe*
Good morning: *Akonjamakiri*
Hello: *Jawekeskarinmia*
Good afternoon: *Akonjantan*
Good evening: *Akonjame*
Thank you: *Irake*
Thank you very much: *Ichabires irake*
Thank you very much for receiving us: *Ichabires irake noamaton biakopi*

Sensations and Feelings

It's beautiful: *Metsa*
It's good: *Jakon metsa*
It's bright: *Kikin pene*
It's dark: *Kikin yame*
It's colorful: *Joshintani*
It's hot (weather): *Kikin shana*
The sun beats down hard: *Bari shana*
The weather is nice: *Nete akon*
I feel good: *Earajakon iki*
I feel bad: *Eara jakon ma iki*

Faith: *Jakon kuchi shinan*
Love: *Noi*
Humor: *Husanya*
Happy: *Jacon shinan canora*
Joyful: *Osan*
Joy: *Raro*
Good health: *Jakon*
Sad: *Unis*
Illness: *Isinkanai*
Pain: *Isin*
Fear: *Jake*
It's spicy: *Kikin moka*
It's mild: *Kikin bata*
It's strong: *Kikin kushi*
It's bitter: *Kikin moka*
It's very strong: *Kikin bires kushi*
What's above: *Buchiki*
What's below: *Naman*
Soft: *Wacho*
Hard: *Churish*
Rigid: *Chankata*
Cold: *Matsi*
Hot: *Shana*

The Natural World

Rain: *Ui*

Sun: *Bari*

River: *Ian*

Forest: *Ni*

Trees: *Jiwibo*

Plants: *Roabo*

Edible plants: *Yubinbo*

Medicinal plants: *Jiwi raobo*

Insects: *Nabonbo*

Spider: *Shinakosho*

Mosquitoes: *Naka*

Wasps: *Vinabo*

Animals: *Yuinabo*

Monkey: *Shino*

Jaguar: *Ino*

Dog: *Uchiti*

Cat: *Misho*

Anteater: *Shawe*

Crocodile: *Cape*

Serpent: *Rono*

Boa: *Ronon ewa*

Ananconda: *Ronin*

Birds: *Isabo*

Parrot: *Bawa*

Hummingbird: *Pino*

Woman: *Ainbo*

Man: *Joni*

Intelligent woman: *Shinanya ainbo*

Intelligent man: *Shinanya joni*

Demons: *Yudhimbo*

Death: *Mawati*

Life: *Jati nete*

The spirits of the forest: *Jihue unibo* or *yoshin*

Spirits: *Unibon*

Parts of the Body

Body: *Yora*

Eyes: *Bero*

Ears: *Pabiki*

Mouth: *Kesha*

Teeth: *Ketan*

Skin: *Bishi*

Tongue: *Jana*

Head: *Mapo*

Hands: *Meken*

Feet: *Tae*

Arms: *Poyan*

Legs: *Witash*

Fingers: *Metoti*

Buttocks: *Chisho*

Genitals: *Poi*

Heart: *Kinan*

Veins: *Pono*

Skeleton: *Joni shao*

Skull: *Mapo shao*

Bones: *Shao*

Muscles: *Yora kushi*

Lungs: *Bonshan*

Belly: *Puro*

Stomach: *Poro*

Intestines: *Boshi*

Blood: *Jimi*

Urine: *Jison*

Feces: *Jointi*

Vomit: *Pokobo*

Note: In Shipibo the word *magic* does not exist.

FOUR OF KESTENBETSA'S ÍCAROS

Ícaro Number 1: Spiritual Feeling

Kepenyobanon rama kepenyobanon;
  I am going to open it, now I am going to open it;
shinan kepenyobanon (repeat two times).
  I will open consciousness.

Kepenyontana (repeat two times)
  By opening
shinan akon makeya makemakebainki
  with good thoughts, I am the melodious path
nete jakon kanoman (repeat two times).
  with the beautiful light of the universe.

Kanon shamameara (repeat two times)
  From the fine depth of knowledge
soi chano beai;
  I bring back a beautiful young girl;
chono beai, soi chono beai.
  I bring back a beautiful woman, I bring back a beautiful
    young woman.
Kanomabeiranshon
  In bringing her back

nete metsaayona;
   I will embellish the light;
metsaayonbanori (repeat two times)
   I will make her beautiful
Jakon parata.
   She will be well balanced.

Kanon jakon parata.
   The energies are well balanced.

Paratatoninbi chono joyomatana je je je;
   With the energy, I place the beautiful women;
chono joyomatana, mestamayontana.
   in placing the beautiful women, I make them beautiful.
Akin shamanra, jakon akin shamanra;
   I do it delicately, I set myself to do it;
nete metsaayona, metsaayonbanori.
   I embellish the universe of light, I embellish it very
      much.

Kanon abanon, rama kanon abanon.
   I am going to open the visions, now I am going to open
      the visions.

Nete nachiakiri (repeat two times)
   From the depths of the universe
nokon joi ronona, ronronaitoninra.
   my words resound, how they resound.
Nete soi ayona, paro soi ayona
   I embellish the universe, I illuminate the river
soiya toninra, soiyatoninra je.
   with the echo of my voice.

Noma akakaira je
   The multitude of beautiful women
senen parabetana je;
   come and arrange themselves in an ordered fashion;

jawen tae rebonbi je
    with their pretty feet
mai kano abea je (repeat two times).
    they come to give power to the earth.
Kanon abeiranshon je (repeat three times)
    At the moment that it is given energy
nete senemayona je.
    the universe becomes harmonized.
Joi senemayona je;
    I make it the gift of my songs;
rama kayara je (repeat two times).
    I do it now.

Ícaro Number 2: The Strength of Feeling

Rama kanon abanon (repeat three times),
    Now, I am going to open the visions,
nete tori joyoni, torin ewa joyoni,
    visions of towers of light, tall towers,
shinan tori joyoni.
    the tall tower of consciousness.

Weninabainshonra, nichinabainai
    I raise it up, I raise it up and I balance it
nichiankebainshonra (repeat three times).
    by letting it move through.

Shinan tori weninai,
    I raise up the great force of consciousness,
joi tori weninai,
    I raise up the great force of the word,
nete tori weninai.
    I raise up the great force of the universe.

Jakon akin weninshon
    By raising it up with great care
weninabainshonra (repeat two times)
    by raising it up

jakon akin shamanra (repeat three times),
   as much as possible,
shinanbora ponteai;
   I align the thoughts;
jakon akin ponteai (repeat two times),
   I align them as much as possible,
bensho akin ponteai (repeat two times)
   I align them as I care for them and heal them
ponteinabainshonra (repeat four times)
   by aligning them
nete kanon seneman.
   in the energy of the universe.
Joyonibo shawebo (repeat three times)
   The men of the universe are there
joi biananakin (repeat two times)
   they exchange in conversation
tepiboki joyoni,
   about the knowledge that is there,
eonshaman joyoni.
   the knowledge that is placed above me.

Ronin kanonbaini
   The energy of the anaconda
bainikan seneman
   follows the path
joi kanonmaboai (repeat four times)
   of the energy songs
kanonmayontanara (repeat four times).
   by providing the power of the songs.

Enki kanon abanon
   Now I open the visions
rama kanon abanon (repeat three times)
   now, I open the visions
jakon akin shamanra, shinanbibobibokin
   with wonder, I obtain thinking

joi bibobibokin
   I record the words
nete metsaaboai (repeat two times);
   I harmonize the light;
metsaabotanai (repeat two times)
   they become more and more beautiful
tanaibotankinra.
   in all this beauty they proceed slowly.

Rama caya cayara (repeat two times),
   Now, now,
metsa isa keota,
   the beautiful bird sings,
noi isa keota,
   the bird of love sings,
raro isa keota, jakoninra keota
   the bird of felicity sings, he sings melodiously
nete shaman keota.
   right to the infinite reaches of the universe.

Keotiki joyota, jototatonbikaya
   In all this beauty there sing
shaweboya chonobo biananamaboai (repeat two times)
   men and women all the while loving each other, each
      one, each one
biananamaboai,
   immersed in love,
senen kanon kakinra (repeat two times)
   they travel the path as one
kanon kanon kakinra, shawanboya chonobo,
   united energetically, the men and the women travel
      the path;
senen raromaboai (repeat two times).
   they are delighted each one in the same just
      measure.

Raroraromabokin (repeat three times)
   I take them along with love
jakon akin shamanra (repeat three times)
   as best I can
nokon joi kanonra;
   with my powerful speaking;
senen paramayona (repeat five times)
   all is harmonized
jakoniki kanoa,
   union is positioned,
kanon iki senena.
   I position the energetic union.

Senenato bikaya
   Where that ends
kori joa ronota (repeat two times)
   he touches it with his flower of gold
seneniki ronota
   from which shines forth the energy
senen parabaina (repeat two times).
   where they are united in the same just measure.

Ícaro Number 3: Spiritual Love

Rama kayakayara (repeat two times),
   Now, I am doing it now,
nokon joi kanoa, kanoatoninra,
   the uniting, with my words, with their echo,
metsatibi metsani
   more beautiful, so beautiful
nete shaman joyoni
   at the infinite reaches of the universe
joyoni nomabo (repeat two times)
   out there, there are beautiful women
shinan biananama (repeat two times),
   united by a single thought,

manaira beai.
> they come to observe.

Biananamaira
> In being united

senen parabetankin, senen prabetankin.
> they approach, they approach, together and balanced.

Nete joe kanpana, metsa ronromayona
> With his gentle nature of light, I will make him resonate melodiously

nokon chishka joninra (repeat two times);
> with all my being;

jawen noma betanbi, senen parakiranshon
> he is coming near his dove (his wife)

jawen meken rebonbi (repeat two times)
> at the tip of his hand

josho shoto reninshon
> in setting down the white dove

nete raromayona (repeat two times)
> in brightening life

raromayontana
> in brightening it up

metsapishamanra, metsatishamanra.
> he embellishes himself, he embellishes himself.

Nete nachiankiri
> From the depths of the universe

metsabetanai (repeat two times),
> they come while embellishing themselves,

nete sheka kanora
> the aroma of the universe

jawen inin kanoa (repeat two times)
> which he envelops with his perfume

kanoatoninra.
> from the presence of the energy.

Oka reshin kaini
  They multiply, the little birds
kaini okabo
  the little birds which are multiplying
metsa shebirinana
  with their beautiful lips
shebirinabetani
  their shining lips
joi biananana
  linking their voices,
biananantana, nete raroaira
  unifying their voices, making the world joyful
metsatira parata
  with a beautiful presence
parayonbaina
  in the uniting
nete senenatonra, nete senenatonra;
  up to the infinite universe, up to the infinite universe;
kanon paramatana
  uniting the deep secret wisdom
joi rebomayona
  my final words
ja resibikaya.
  those words.

Shaweboya chonobo
  The men and the women
ja kanon makenon,
  I tell them again,
makenon ishonra
  so that they can repeat it
shawe nishon akama
  even though they are not important men
enra kanon mayonke, je je je.
  I have united the energy. I have united it.

Ícaro Number 4: Song of Rejoicing

Jemameash je
  From the village
nokon jemameara je,
  from my home,
senen kanonkiranshon je (repeat three times)
  coming with my energy
min joi bitana je (repeat two times)
  receiving your word
ramaronki makeai je;
  now, I sing;
makemakebainkin je (repeat two times)
  I sing while following the path
san shobo nachia je (repeat two times)
  from the melodious house
nachiankonia je
  from its depths
enki iaketana je (repeat two times).
  I was out there.

Ronin poromeabi je (repeat two times)
  From the entrails of the anaconda
jawen inin bitana je
  obtaining its perfume
enki mia akinon je (repeat two times).
  I will help you.

Nokon inin biweri je (repeat two times)
  Receive my perfume
iki ira ikai je (repeat three times)
  it's what they're in the midst of saying
rabirabikinpari je (repeat two times)
  being between the two of them
nokon noma betanbi je (repeat two times).
  close to my spouse.

Paro nachiakiri je
> Toward the course of the river

nokon ronin kawati je
> my bridge is the anaconda

namayontana je.
> who moves gently.

Eara kai kai je (repeat two times)
> I take my leave

kakonkiranshon je,
> with my deep secret wisdom,

senen kanonkiranshon je
> with my secret wisdom balanced

kai karibanoshon je;
> I take myself there;

enra mia akinai je (repeat two times)
> I will help you

inin joa kanonra je (repeat two times)
> with the power of the perfumed flower

enra toemayonke je (repeat three times)
> I have made it flower

akin aribatana je (repeat two times).
> so that you say it this way.

Nokon joa maiti je
> My crown of flowers

maiyontana je (repeat two times)
> placing it on your head

en kayakayara je
> myself

min meken rebonbi je
> right to the tips of your fingers

enra kanonmayonke je (repeat two times)
> I do it in this moment

nokon ani kanon je
> with my great power (the power of the ayahuasca)

nokon kori kanonra je (repeat two times)
    with my secret wisdom of gold
rebomayontana je (repeat two times);
    I will do it;
kanon abanon je
    with my deep wisdom, I do it
enki kanon abanon je
    I transmit to you my deep wisdom
metsa birimayona je (repeat two times);
    which is beautiful and I will make it shine;
biribirimatana je (repeat two times)
    in making it shine
nokon tae rebonbi je (repeat two times)
    with the tips of my toes
eara kaikaribai je.
    I come back to it.

Mai ronin ayona je (repeat three times).
    I have made a beautiful earth.

Kairibi kai je (repeat two times).
    He takes his leave, he takes his leave.

Nokon niwe bitana je (repeat two times)
    In bringing together my deep secret wisdom
ea kabatanon je (repeat two times).
    I take my leave.

■ ■ ■

These ícaros were translated from Shipibo to Spanish by Laida Mori and Guillermo Arévalo, then from Spanish into French by Rama Leclerc and Jan Kounen.*

---

*They were then translated from French into English by Jack Cain.

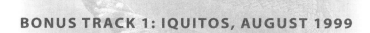

MY FIRST CEREMONY
WITH GUILLERMO

Don't read this right away, but don't forget to read it either.*

When I first met Guillermo, I initially thought he didn't work with ayahuasca but with other, stronger plants of the same family. I hesitated; I had come for ayahuasca. The next day, after giving it some thought, I went back to see him to ask him if I could participate in a first session. Guillermo asked me why. I replied that I want "to see," to discover. He suggested I come that same evening, and he asked me about my job; I told him that I'm a student.

That evening I discover him in the company of other shamans, my childhood friend Frederic Sanchez del Rio (musician, translator, and mystic adventurer), along with a few Indian patients who had come for treatment. I had no personal need for treatment—I was just curious. This was all taking place at Guillermo's home, in the jungle behind his house, in a little cabin that is called the maloca.

You are not acquainted with those sitting around you. You also don't know the nature of the plants, and when you don't know something you feel a certain apprehension. I sit down in the midst of others who are there. There is no particular ceremonial paraphernalia. Guillermo is not

---

*The description of this first encounter was first published in *Visions: regards sur le chamanisme,* the book I wrote with Guillermo Arévalo, Corinne Arnould, and Jean-Patrick Costa.

dressed up and has no special accessories; there is only pure tobacco to smoke—mapacho—and a cheap cologne called Agua Florida. We are sitting on a dirt floor, and the room is lit by a neon fixture on the ceiling. Each person drinks in turn. At the moment Guillermo is preparing to serve me, just before filling the glass, he pauses, looks at me, and again asks the question, staring deeply into my eyes:

"Why are you doing this?" Surprised, because all the others had drunk without him asking them anything, I hesitate; then I reply, determinedly, "I want to know."

Guillermo then fills a big glass with a brown liquid. I swallow this very bitter mixture, and the light is turned out.

I do not immediately feel nauseous. A certain amount of time passes during which many very dark forms appear. It feels like being glued to the wall of an aquarium; I can make out something like spiders stuck in front of my eyes. It quickly occurs to me that I am seeing my own fear and that's how it is manifesting. So I try to breathe, to relax. I'm afraid. Under the effect of the plant, the spiders are becoming more and more visible, their outlines more and more distinct. That lasts a long time, in silence; in spite of all this I have the impression that I am kept at a distance, as if I'm protected from the spiders by a glass wall. Around me everything is very dark, and at the same time I perceive the silhouettes of my companions, three or four yards away. I experience only a growing intoxication. It's as if I was holding myself at the edge of a cliff, my back to the void, and on the point of swaying. The body tenses because the mind refuses to let go . . . It's dizzying, as if everything organic in you is becoming undone little by little, like some part is trying to take control but the mind refuses. It's the climbing intoxication, the fear of the unknown, the fear of being afraid. You try to remain seated, in meditation, but it's less and less possible. The Westerners get restless—the Indians remain motionless. The intoxication is irresistible. My first thought in encountering the unknown that is in the process of presenting itself is: "I knew it; I should never have drunk it! What an idiot! What a mess I've gotten myself into . . ."

It's difficult, especially for a Westerner, to accept that a link is in the process of being formed between oneself and a sacred plant. You want to get up, but you can't. You want there to be light, and there's darkness. The mind rejects the experience.

The thinking then becomes incoherent; you become an observer of your own inner monologue, your own voice resounds, then several voices.

I manage nevertheless to unglue myself from the fearful, black thoughts. I let them go. They come back. The spiders are still there. I encounter my fears. I hear nothing and don't sense any odor. The dark visions become more precise, taking the form of insects with a realism that the imagination alone could never produce. Suddenly, although the session had begun quite some time before, Guillermo begins to sing.

Instantly all the visions are transformed—forms spring up and are transformed following the inflexion of his voice. It's an act of magic.

As for me, an atheist Westerner, I find myself flung into a totally unexpected, unknown territory, into a magic universe in action. I'm plunged into worlds of light with indescribable architectures, real living cathedrals. With the song I feel a form of ecstasy; I am no longer afraid. "I am finally home."

As if I had been expecting this moment forever, everything makes sense. It's a total upset, the awakening of new thoughts, unsuspected thoughts, in the deepest recesses of oneself.

At this very instant, I am convinced that I am an integral component of these visions. Immediately the voice and song of the shaman are inflected to take on a much more serious tone, as if he had just intercepted my thought. And I find myself immediately flung into the midst of dark and tangled little serpents, and the voice of the curandero resounds in me saying, "No, no, you, you are here!" Fear grabs me: I'm dealing with someone who can read my thoughts.

It's terrifying—thoughts are usually inviolable territory. Happily, I am immediately aware of Guillermo's great kindness. There isn't the slightest aggressiveness in his intervention. Next, his song invites me: "Latch on now, follow me."

I didn't anticipate what I saw; there's no way you could anticipate it. What was shown to me that first night cannot be told. On the edge of madness, I swung between terror and humility as I found myself facing the power and the vast knowledge of that man.

In the small hours of the morning, I noticed that I could no longer communicate with Guillermo, although I believed I had conversed with him the whole night long telepathically.

During the session I had the impression of understanding perfectly both the Shipibo language and his songs. It was as if the visual language that the songs invoked in me was transformed into words in my own language and into emotions. (A year later, I had the confirmation of this intuition: I had the songs translated. In black and white I read what I had heard.)

I could not leave it at that. I had to go back and see Guillermo. I phoned him. He was open to seeing me again. I come back then the following evening. The process picks up where it left off. We drink ayahuasca. A few minutes go by, and I discover that the other people around me are also shamans. I am then taken into a universe that is even more indescribable. It is now not only the apparitions of animals but also of human presences, from the worlds of light, from the cities of light. The visions unfold and weave together in an indescribable way. These are the first signs of what the Indians call the spirit world.

The first session was centered around the growing relationship between Guillermo and me; this second one was opening up other worlds, new dimensions linked to shamanic culture. The first evening he was presenting himself to me. This time, he is showing me that this knowledge is shared among other men and that it has an origin: their culture, their people—a very advanced civilization in the land of the spirit.

Regardless of what the particular vision may be, what is important at this stage and what very quickly became fundamental for me is the process that accompanies the vision. Guillermo communicates with me without having recourse to words—that is, solely using sensations and images. From the second session on, he is putting in place the structures for a sharing of knowledge. I don't know if he wants to test my sincerity and the reliability of my approach or if this is the way he always proceeds.

He apparently wants to know if I'm there just to try out an experience, as strong as that might be, or to really be initiated into a culture, into a unique way of perceiving the world and reality. This particular evening I once again experience some very strong moments—so strong they unbalance me.

On this day also, I cannot leave it at that, even though I am supposed to leave again the next day. In the end I put off my departure. I feel a little like Richard Dreyfuss in *Close Encounters of the Third Kind*: up against a phenomenon that's impossible to convey. I am lost because suddenly the totality of my psychological reality, everything that I have known for thirty-five years, everything that I had been taught was solid and tangible, all of this melts away in two nights. All of it is gone, brought back to zero. It's dizzying.

This is how I came to decide to take part in a third ceremony. I show up without saying anything.

It's not exactly what you might call a silent prayer, but I try, without words (in any case I don't speak Spanish), to make Guillermo understand that if what happened last night happens again, I will either die or become insane. My friend Fred is also very shaken; he hasn't put as many holes in the foundation of his reason, but the two of us look at each other in silence. What can you do when reality becomes as crazy as the weirdest fiction?

Glug, glug. Away we go, no choice, I cannot stay between two worlds.

The session is very gentle this time. A feeling of well-being inhabits me, as if I am stretched out on the shores of a majestic river, while I remain in the center of the room. I have a few visions, very luminous. It's as if Guillermo was explaining the nature and aim of his work to me and was making it clear that the sessions that I was experiencing were special because his usual role was healing people, not initiating them.

Something strange takes place: I have an irresistible desire to get up. The well-being has given me a new strength. I crouch in the center of the maloca, and slowly, in a spasm, I enact the symbolic gesture of cutting off my head.

In our culture, this action is essentially negative and frighteningly violent. In this specific context, it takes on the meaning of a purely symbolic offering (even though, in the moment, it's a rather upsetting gesture). You feel a form of death and physical pain, but at the same time a sensation of great freedom is at work. I'm on the ground. I make the gesture of slitting my throat, not decapitating myself. I then have the impression of seeing my blood spreading out, then a light that is very strong and white. I am very relaxed. A silhouette in human form appears in the center of the room.

The third session ends.

In the small hours of the morning I go to see Guillermo to thank him for having guided me toward this new birth and the feeling of a deep peace.

I confess to him that I am not a student but a film director, and I assure him that I am going to help his community.

These three nights had lasted more than a thousand years. I seemed to have known this man forever. I had never sought a spiritual master or guide, but I was instead a believer in "no god, no master." Nevertheless I had found one; he was nothing like the image of a colorful fictional personage, but he opened the door for me.

Gracias maestro, the journey is only just beginning . . .

MY FINAL CEREMONIES WITH GUILLERMO

THIRD FROM LAST CEREMONY

Since my arrival about ten days earlier, no ceremony has been really special, it's been a work of cleansing. Guillermo, who has not given me any treatment, tells me that he's going to begin to align me (*areglar*). Having followed a strict, four-month diet, the closing of the diet is going to begin tonight.

Shock. Right from the beginning, I find myself in a distinct vision of unbearable darkness. My skin is burning, my body is pressurized, but just the same I enter into the visions. I concentrate, preparing myself to intone a last-ditch ícaro. Guillermo is singing, and everything is released. I am delivered, rising up (it's a sensation) and encountering luminous spirits who, very close to me, touch me. Then the elevator immediately goes down again. I find myself once again in the maloca, surrounded by yoshins who come up to me and shake me. It's like something out of Dante and certainly new to the usual progression. Very quickly I go back up again and find Guillermo surrounded by light; I receive grace, then I leave again for hell—in short, a yo-yo like never before.

It is once again the strongest ceremony I've ever lived through. I joke about it when I am able, in the morning (between two spasms), and I recall Guillermo saying to me the day before, "I'm going to begin your alignment." Okay, so that was the beginning.

244 Bonus Track 2

SECOND FROM LAST CEREMONY

The Shipibo participants leave this evening. Antonio Vasques, his wife, and their two sons arrive to take part in the ceremony. They all have good reputations as healers. There are about thirty of us in all—a few students, about fifteen patients, and six healers (including Guillermo and Ricardo), which is going to take us far and heralds the new organization of the center.*

I am still a little intoxicated from the day before, and I confidently drink a regular dose of a very black ayahuasca. The day before had been hard, but there had been such light for a long stretch that I'm expecting a luminous continuation . . . Oh, imbecile that I am—as you can guess if you have carefully read my book.

And on the spot, I undergo what is without a doubt the worst ceremony of my life.

A thing that cannot be named.

I don't manage to open my intoxication. Therefore, there are few visions. With the songs as a scalpel, my body begins trembling in attempting to resist thoughts that roll out a terrifying reality. I'm not going to go on about this nightmare, perfectly suited to a megaproduction of Gotham City, but I'm going to give you a brief summary (it lasted a full five hours—an eternity psychologically).

From the first steps, I've been on the wrong path.

I've understood nothing.

In the course of time, I've become a *brujo*.

I'm someone who makes evil.

I'm going to kill everyone this evening with a single thought.

So it would be better for me to die.

I'm making Guillermo suffer.

(Just look at how many of these contain *I!*)

I am a monster.

All these healers have come this evening to make a last ditch effort to get me back on the right path.

But it's impossible because I am cursed by God.

*See the description of the center's change from Espíritu de Anaconda to Anaconda Cósmica on page 207.

Cursed by the spirits of the medicina.

(Notice the puffing up of my importance or power.)

And this is the last judgment.

Poor me! I swear to you, I'm trembling, teeth clenched, wanting to scream, not "It's true I'm a good person," but "My God, how is it that I did not see this sooner!"

I don't manage to pray.

The slightest of my faults, the slightest little sin becomes a demonic act that activates its truth on the terrible destiny of my life.

I look for love by trying to visualize my companion, my children. Impossible.

After a few hours, the intoxication lessens but I remain tense. If I don't get out of this state before the intoxication disappears, I'm done for; I'll be in this world for the rest of my life.

I think that what I experienced there was the equivalent of a big fit of insanity. I went beyond the boundary and entertained thoughts that this was something to be disgusted about for the rest of one's life—that any person of sound mind, even ten years later, could drink just one single drop of this concoction.

So there you have it, you who might have thought that this experience was attractive; you ought to blanch, and say to yourself, "Yikes! This stuff is not for me. Now that's clear. The story doesn't sound very sweet at all!"

Be reassured, this isn't the kind of thing that can happen to you. This is the closing of an apprenticeship diet, an experience that the typical patient would never encounter.

Okay, in the end, I did resist, I did not obey the inner voice that ordered me to cry for help and run away—in short, throw in the towel.

Toward the end of the night, Guillermo came to sing at my side; not too close—about six feet away. I really only become aware of this at the end. I feel calmed, and then I hear his voice *"Fuerte carapate* cósmica."* He laughs tenderly, and I laugh too.

---

*Remember that my name in Shipibo means "centipede" (carapate).

I stretch out. In a state of great relaxation, I laugh quietly. Delirious!

A few minutes before I was dead; my life was nothing but a horrible failure. I ended up accepting it. I no longer had hope, no longer a future—nothing at all. And here I am cool and relaxed.

The curanderos are speaking among themselves in Shipibo, in the otherwise silent maloca. Their voices take me back years into the past, to the time when I listened only to the music of the language, and when, feeling shaken like a prune tree being harvested, I was the foreigner—someone well liked and someone they were observing going through his discoveries, with good will and with impeccability. So near, so far. Now, at the end of the ceremony I often go to speak in Spanish with Ricardo, Guillermo, and the students, and we all have a good laugh.

This time, from the Shipibo come laughter. From the others, there is silence.

I remember my admiration for these conscious madmen who joked and laughed after a ceremony to which it seemed that all the little guys from Mordor had invited themselves and who were then kindly escorted back to their home.

I also told myself that, in the end, I had behaved well—in silence, not disturbing my neighbor.

I fall asleep peacefully (it's true!) with sweet thoughts finally for Anne, for my children, and for the others, the curanderos.

The next day I am intoxicated the whole day.

I run into Ricardo for a short conversation.

RICARDO: It was hard for you yesterday.

JAN: Yes, I've never had such a hard ceremony, but now I'm okay. I wasn't able to open my mareación.

RICARDO: When it's like that, you need to sing.

He spits on the ground and moves away without looking at me. And then, on the spot, just when I was doing fine, I am taken by a new terror. Of course you have to sing! But it's not possible!

I enter gently into the songs. Too gently certainly, but you must understand: ten years ago, unconscious young idiot, I sang my heart out with the melodies during my fourth ceremony, as if I was one of them, sure of myself and of my place. And I took the hit of a big scud of negative energy, a really big one, and that calmed me down for years. It's only been a year now that I have been singing. In the maloca with Guillermo I am very discreet. I am too intimidated, and also there has to be a minimum of respect . . .

Nonsense.

You are afraid to sing when the intoxication is too strong or when the visions are too dark!

Er, well, yes, but what could I have sung yesterday? The song, *"Non, non, je ne regrette rien"* (No, I regret nothing)? "La Cucaracha"?

Yesterday, you did well in keeping your trap shut, but this evening, my boy . . .

Ai, ai! I understand. Quick, have to change that. Right away. A part of me is leading me astray and telling me: "You will never be able to!" The other part says, "You do have faith don't you? Yes or no?" Now is when the question really gets asked, as if for the first time. "Do you have faith in love as a force that is greater than fear? Yes or no?"

The day is gray, and I'm at the bottom of a pit. I spend the afternoon concentrating on the topic at hand: singing for myself. I'm so intoxicated that I'm having visions. I move back and forth from the darkness and the light, between love and fear, between confidence and doubt.

Finally a bare fact rises up.

Faith doesn't question itself. It's an act.

The act of faith that this evening I can take the regular dose of that black bomb—with utter confidence in the medicina, and in Guillermo. I will have done what I can. And if nobody sings and my intoxication is strong, well then, sing! You're a big boy now.

For sure you cannot experience anything worse than yesterday's ceremony, right?

That makes me hesitate for a moment.

I haven't made it yet.

LAST CEREMONY

When evening comes I move into the maloca, stumbling. Yes, I am still intoxicated. My intoxication of the day before has not opened and it is still there, reinforced by the songs sung during the day.

I stretch out. I have faith. I calm myself. I chase away doubts and I wait. I connect myself to love. It works. Confidence returns. A miracle?

It's my turn to drink. I go to see Ricardo and sit down in front of him. He studies me and, with a gentle look, says, *"Poco?"* (a little?)

¿Poco? Coming from the one who usually laughs at me when I ask for poco! But he sees that I am strung out and that it makes sense.

I don't reply, and I get up (very slowly) to go and sit down in front of Guillermo, who is resting. He opens one eye.

JAN: Guillermo, I am still very intoxicated from yesterday. I can take poco, but I can also take the normal dose, what do you think?

GUILLERMO: Normal would be good.

The die is cast.

I slide toward Ricardo and declare calmly, "Normal."

He shrugs his shoulders (I force myself not to assign meaning to his gesture).

He serves me properly; I get up and move to sit in front of Guillermo again so that he can ícarize my glass. Calmly, I drink and stretch out.

A few minutes later, the light goes out.

Black.

The intoxication starts off with visions. Right in the middle between darkness and light, the worlds of the medicina open as never before, and it continues to climb.

I sit up really straight.

Silence.

I'm going to wait for someone to sing. Still silence, and it continues to climb.

I've got to do it or I'm going to lose it completely.

I breathe out and establish my connection—a good feeling. And from this sensitive place, I sing strongly. The intoxication increases with the song. I have the impression of melding song and visions. I hold it for a moment, and then I lose my concentration. A dark veil drops over me.

I return to where I was the day before.

But this time I don't just let it be. I concentrate and I do not grasp at the dark thoughts that spring up, even though my mareación ends up under a cloak of blackness.

I don't move. Ricardo begins to sing an ícaro to align himself and then he calls me.

He does a healing for me, a very strong ícaro that aligns me completely.

I go back to my place.

Guillermo sings. I listen. The visions come back. I enter into the dance, into a song in response. Guillermo's song sustains me. I have the impression that the songs are blending. It's a sensation of unequaled harmony. I must stay concentrated on the intention of the song to maintain the connection to the world of the medicina; while at the same time I have to keep track of the information that I'm receiving in return through my song.

It's a little like the opposite of the previous night. There is so much good. But I have to remain concentrated. I spoke in the very beginning of this book of the great reach of Amazonian medicine: these last two ceremonies are for me the strongest examples of that.

One evening you are the worst person; the next evening you are the best.

You are neither one nor the other. You mustn't latch on to either of these thoughts.

The preceding dreadful ceremony was something I had to go through. It's a question of flinging the apprentice into the deepest nightmare. Proceeding in this way will foster an understanding afterward that the "unquestionable" and fearful truth that springs up in the mind during the ceremony is only a mental construct resulting from contact with the yoshins, the bad spirits, or the bad energies, which will seek out the slightest psychological fissure to rough you up. This way the apprentice will become more vigilant.

We are sometimes connected to dark energies, sometimes to luminous energies. We mustn't grasp (appropriate to ourselves) either one or the other.

You have to keep a good feeling in the heart.

I sang the whole night through with Ricardo and Guillermo. Alone too. At the end, Guillermo turned toward me and told me with a great gentleness how much he had appreciated my songs. This brotherly moment is a fresh and lively memory. A first loop closes harmoniously. It had been opened the evening of my first meeting with him, right from his first song, when I knew in an instant that my life was going to change, that this man was going to lead me into a long adventure.

November 22, 2010

A BIG THANK-YOU

To Kestenbetsa, Panshin Beka, Anne Paris, Panshin Biri, Sonia Chuquimbalqui, Ricardo Amaringo, James Arévalo, François Demange, Aziz Kharzai, Rama Leclerc, Romuald Leterrier, Paolo Jesus, Alexandre Liedo, Bastien Gerday, Jean Giraud, Alejandro Jodorowsky, Jeremy Narby, Marc Caro, Gaspar Noé, Vincent Ravalec, Alan Shoemaker, Frederic Sanchez del Rio, Michel Barthélémy, Stéphane Watelet, Ariel Zeitoun and Thomas Langmann, Romain Rotjman and Brigitte Maccioni, Capucine Henri, Tigrane Hadengue and Michka Seeliger, and Laurence.

To all the curanderos who treated me, all of Guillermo's apprentices, the dieters, the Anaconda team, and the Espíritu cooks.

To all those who sustained me.

Books of Related Interest

The Psychotropic Mind
The World according to Ayahuasca, Iboga, and Shamanism
by Jeremy Narby, Jan Kounen, and Vincent Ravalec

The Psychedelic Explorer's Guide
Safe, Therapeutic, and Sacred Journeys
by James Fadiman, Ph.D.

The Ayahuasca Visions of Pablo Amaringo
by Howard G. Charing, Peter Cloudsley, and Pablo Amaringo

Ayahuasca Medicine
The Shamanic World of Amazonian Sacred Plant Healing
by Alan Shoemaker

The Ayahuasca Experience
A Sourcebook on the Sacred Vine of Spirits
Edited by Ralph Metzner

DMT: The Spirit Molecule
A Doctor's Revolutionary Research into the Biology of
Near-Death and Mystical Experiences
by Rick Strassman, M.D.

Plant Spirit Shamanism
Traditional Techniques for Healing the Soul
by Ross Heaven and Howard G. Charing
Foreword by Pablo Amaringo

Black Smoke
Healing and Ayahuasca Shamanism in the Amazon
by Margaret De Wys

INNER TRADITIONS • BEAR & COMPANY
P.O. Box 388
Rochester, VT 05767
1-800-246-8648
www.InnerTraditions.com

Or contact your local bookseller